The Complete Guide to Open Scholarship

The Complete Guide to Open Scholarship

Victoria Martin

LIBRARIES UNLIMITED®

An Imprint of ABC-CLIO, LLC

Santa Barbara, California • Denver, Colorado

Library of Congress Cataloging-in-Publication Data

Names: Martin, Victoria, author.
Title: The complete guide to open scholarship / Victoria Martin.
Description: Santa Barbara, California : ABC-CLIO, [2022] | Includes
  bibliographical references and index.
Identifiers: LCCN 2021055785 (print) | LCCN 2021055786 (ebook) |
  ISBN 9781440872808 (paperback) | ISBN 9781440872815 (ebook)
Subjects: LCSH: Open scholarship.
Classification: LCC AZ101 .M38 2022 (print) | LCC AZ101 (ebook) |
  DDC 001.2—dc23/eng/20220118
LC record available at https://lccn.loc.gov/2021055785
LC ebook record available at https://lccn.loc.gov/2021055786

ISBN: 978-1-4408-7280-8 (paperback)
       978-1-4408-7281-5 (ebook)

26 25 24 23 22   1 2 3 4 5

This book is also available as an eBook.

Libraries Unlimited
An Imprint of ABC-CLIO, LLC

ABC-CLIO, LLC
147 Castilian Drive
Santa Barbara, California 93117
www.abc-clio.com

This book is printed on acid-free paper (∞)

Manufactured in the United States of America

Figures in chapter 3 are reprinted from Creative Commons for Educators and Librarians, Creative Commons (https://www.creativecommons.org), https://certificates.creativecommons.org/about/certificate-resources-cc-by, licensed under a Creative Commons Attribution 4.0 International license (https://creativecommons.org/licenses/by/4.0), published by the American Library Association (http://www.ala.org/).

Figure in chapter 5 is reprinted from Cable Green, "Open Education: The Moral, Business & Policy Case for OER." Updated Keynote Slides, November 2014. https://www.slideshare.net/cgreen/updated-keynote-slides-october-2014. Licensed under a Creative Commons Attribution 4.0 International license (https://creativecommons.org/licenses/by/4.0).

That ideas should freely spread from one to another over the globe, for the moral and mutual instruction of man, and improvement of his condition, seems to have been peculiarly and benevolently designed by nature, when she made them, like fire, expansible over all space, without lessening their density in any point, and the air in which we breathe, move, and have our physical being, incapable of confinement or exclusive appropriation. Inventions then cannot, in nature, be a subject of property.

—Thomas Jefferson, Letter to Isaac McPherson (August 13, 1813)

Contents

Preface

Openness as a new approach to knowledge production and knowledge distribution is gaining a foothold in nearly all phases of the research life cycle—starting from the beginning where an idea is born and onward to the end where final research results are disseminated. Openness can accelerate scientific progress, facilitate wider and more diverse scholarly collaborations, and enable a more balanced approach to copyright management. At the same time, open scholarship (and the concepts underpinning it) is still a vague idea for many scholars and for others in the academic community. Even the meaning of the term "open" continues to be debated, making it challenging to provide a clear definition of openness in scholarship. As Daniels and Thistlethwaite (2016, 75) posit, "[o]pen scholarship, and the debate about it, bears the certainty of messy understandings, confusion, conflict, misappropriation, and tangential focus." On the one hand, this debate speaks to the complexity and multidimensionality of open scholarship. On the other hand, the inconclusiveness about what openness in scholarship really entails and how it fits into the traditional practice of research and scholarly communication is one of the impediments to a greater adoption of open practices in the academic community.

This book seeks to bring clarity to the key concepts, rationales, and concerns associated with openness in scholarship, even though it does not offer a single, crisp definition of open scholarship. To the contrary, this book uses the term "open scholarship" as an umbrella term for a variety of open approaches to knowledge creation and knowledge distribution, and it points toward the diversity, and sometimes ambiguity, of the current discourse on openness. It provides the reader with a brief conceptual foundation for open scholarship: how it has come about, where it is today, and what its outlook for the future may be. By doing that, this book strives to enhance the reader's understanding of the benefits of open scholarship, as well as the potential issues associated with it that still require close attention. It aspires to help scholars (and librarians who work with them) make a conscious choice between open scholarship and the more traditional scholarly practices, while taking advantage of openness (where it makes sense) as a means of increasing the effectiveness, visibility, and impact of their work. This book also strives to fill the gap in the library science literature on openness, which has primarily focused on how to lower price and access barriers to research and less so on other aspects and consequences of openness. By providing a broader survey of the topic, this book will hopefully contribute in a positive way to the discourse on openness in scholarship that still deserves more study than it has yet received.

To accomplish its goals, this book draws upon the scholarly literature and the author's own experiences as an academic librarian and a research writer to do the following:

- Define and explain key terms and concepts associated with open scholarship
- Provide an overview of the most prominent models and initiatives that fall under the praxis of openness
- Describe how these models complement and overlap with traditional research approaches
- Highlight the benefits and challenges of each model
- Present material in a fair-minded manner, without endorsing any particular initiative over any other and without opposing any particular causes

This book can serve as a useful reference source for anyone who is interested in open scholarship—from academic scholars to the general reader. However, the primary audience for this book is academic and research librarians for whom the enhanced understanding of open scholarship can help them engage in meaningful discussions on the topic with faculty and students and help educate them about the benefits and challenges of conducting research "in the open." This book can also serve as a valuable complement to the author's previous works on innovative research models: *Demystifying eResearch: A Primer for Librarians* (Santa Barbara: Libraries Unlimited, 2014) and *Transdisciplinarity Revealed: What Librarians Need to Know* (Santa Barbara: Libraries Unlimited, 2017).

Similar to the author's previous works, the focus of this book is more conceptual than pragmatic. Technical descriptions of tools related to open scholarship and instructions on how to use them are beyond the scope of this book.

For the most up-to-date developments in the dynamic, ever-changing field of open scholarship, the readers are encouraged to consult suggested online resources included at the end of each chapter. Additionally, the annual conference held by the Open Access Scholarly Publishing Association (OASPA), the Latest News section on the Scholarly Publishing and Academic Resources Coalition's (SPARC) website, and the online Scholarly Communication Discussion Group of the Association of College & Research Libraries (ACRL) are all good sources of information to keep up to date on current trends and events in open scholarship.

The book is divided into chapters, which are further divided into subchapters to make the specific content more readily accessible. Each chapter introduces a new topic, explains the topic's key concepts and terminology, highlights important events and initiatives, and refers readers to additional sources they might need to help them form their own position on the topic. The material in each chapter can stand on its own with minimal context from other chapters. The readers can take in the entire book at once, pick a chapter of interest, or skip around. However, readers without the background knowledge of open scholarship are advised to read this book in a linear fashion, chapter by chapter.

While most acronyms and terms in this book are familiar to readers with a background in library science, other acronyms and terms may be new for readers outside the library profession or due to the terms' specificity to open scholarship. For the reader's convenience, the book includes a list of acronyms and a glossary, as well as a detailed subject index and a list of references.

Acknowledgments

No single-authored monograph is entirely an individual effort. I am deeply indebted to all of the authors cited in this book whose insights into the vision of openness in research and education have been an important source of inspiration to me and who will, hopefully, also become an inspiration to the readers of this book and help stimulate a continued discussion on the topic.

I am also grateful to the following people whose administrative and editorial assistance, comments on various portions of the draft manuscript, and guidance during the production process helped me shepherd my book through its development, starting from an abstract idea and bringing it all the way through to the finished work:

- Barbara Ittner, former senior acquisitions editor at Libraries Unlimited and the editor of my two previous books, for being my enthusiastic reference and supporter
- Jessica Gribble, senior acquisitions editor at Libraries Unlimited, for helping shape my book idea into a successful book proposal and for guiding me diligently through the writing process
- Emma Bailey, project editor at Libraries Unlimited, for offering helpful suggestions regarding the book's layout
- Saville Bloxham, editorial assistant at ABC-CLIO, for reviewing the first draft of my manuscript
- Richard Stallman, leader of the Free Software Movement, for providing invaluable comments on Chapter 2 to ensure that I properly describe the concept of free software
- Lisa McCoy, copyeditor, for conducting a comprehensive, rigorous review of the final manuscript

- Nicole Azze, senior production editor at ABC-CLIO, and Rashmi Malhotra at Westchester Publishing Services, for managing the production of the book

As always, a special thank you goes to my husband James for being my loyal and thoughtful first reader whose time, effort, and dedication I will always treasure.

Acronyms

APC	article processing charge
API	application programming interface
BIC	Broader Impact Criterion
BMC	BioMed Central
BOAI	Budapest Open Access Initiative
CC	Creative Commons
COPE	Committee on Publication Ethics
CS	citizen science
DFCW	Definition of Free Cultural Works
DMP	data management plan
DOAJ	Directory of Open Access Journals
DOI	digital object identifier
FAIR	findable, accessible, interoperable, and reusable
FSF	Free Software Foundation
GNU	"GNU's Not Unix!"
GNU GFDL	GNU Free Documentation License
GNU GPL	GNU General Public License
IFLA	International Federation of Library Associations and Institutions
IR	institutional repository
ISNI	International Standard Name Identifier
MERLOT	Multimedia Educational Resource for Learning and Online Teaching

MOOC	massive online open courses
OA	open access
OAD	Open Access Directory
OAI	Open Archives Initiative
OASPA	Open Access Scholarly Publishers Association
OCW	OpenCourseWare
OD	open data
OEC	Open Education Consortium
OECD	Organisation for Economic Co-operation and Development
OER	open educational resources
OKF	Open Knowledge Foundation
OpenDOAR	Open Directory of Open Access Repositories
OPL	Open Publication License
OPR	open peer review
ORCID	Open Researcher and Contributor ID
OSD	Open Source Definition
OSI	Open Source Initiative
PDM	Public Domain Mark
PLoS	Public Library of Science
PMC	PubMed Central
ROARMAP	Registry of Open Access Repository Mandates and Policies
RoMEO	Rights MEtadata for Open archiving
SHERPA	Securing a Hybrid Environment for Research Preservation and Access
SPARC	Scholarly Publishing and Academic Resources Coalition
TD	transdisciplinarity
TOP	Transparency and Openness Promotion

One Term, Many Meanings

Interpreting Openness in Scholarship

> Open scholarship does not necessarily lead a steady march toward one truth or vision.
>
> —Daniels and Thistlethwaite (2016, 75)

Open scholarship (or open science[1] as it is sometimes called) is a term that most researchers have heard of but they are not entirely sure what it means. Open scholarship is both a concept and a practice, and the assumptions about it vary depending on the context in which openness is discussed. Even the word "open" is a vaguely defined term. As Morozov (2013) states, "[f]ew words in the English language pack as much ambiguity and sexiness as 'open' [...]. Open could [...] mean virtually anything." In a similar fashion, Watters (2014) writes that the word "open" can mean many things depending on who is using the word. She argues that while such "multivalence" can be a strength, it can also be a weakness "when the term becomes so widely applied that it is rendered meaningless." Weller (2014, 28) echoes this sentiment by saying that a multitude of interpretations of the word "openness" is "both its blessing and curse," as it is "broad enough to be adopted widely, but also loose enough that anyone can claim it, so it becomes meaningless."[2]

Openness in scholarship has been interpreted in many ways, including the following interpretations.

Openness as Transparency

Openness as transparency (as the opposite of secrecy) refers to a new way of conducting research that entails "freedom of access by all interested persons to the underlying data, to the processes, and to the final results of research" (Stanford University, n.d.). The ideal of transparency does not imply, however, that anyone should be able to access *any* information without restrictions. Rather, it implies that there should be "no *unwarranted* impediments to the widest possible circulation of the ideas and information" (Willinsky 2006, 146; emphasis added). Temporary secrecy may be required for reasons of national security or private industry research, or it may be governed by certain norms of scientific inquiry—for example, when scholars need to safeguard the privacy of research participants. The desire to protect ongoing research or to achieve recognition for being the first to report research findings may also lead to temporary secrecy. Long-term secrecy, however, is universally regarded as a barrier to the advancement of knowledge because it impedes the flow and exchange of information, and it can result in duplication of research efforts and thus decrease the effectiveness of research.

Openness as a Scientific Norm

The idea of openness as transparency is closely related to Robert Merton's norms comprising the ethos of open science (Merton 1973). These norms include "communism,"[3] universalism, disinterestedness, originality, and skepticism (often abbreviated as CUDOS). Among these norms, the norm of "communism" is particularly relevant to the idea of openness. "Secrecy," Merton states, "is the antithesis of this norm; full and open communication its enactment" (Ibid., 274). The norm of "communism" prescribes that research findings always result from social collaboration and, therefore, they belong to the scientific community. Merton argues that "[t]he communal character of science is [...] reflected in the recognition by scientists of their dependence upon a cultural heritage to which they lay no differential claims. Newton's remark—'If I have seen further, it is by standing on the shoulders of giants'—expresses at once a sense of indebtedness to the common heritage and a recognition of the essentially cooperative and selectively cumulative quality of scientific achievement" (Ibid., 274–275).

Openness as an Ethical Obligation

Merton's norm of skepticism, too, suggests openness. This norm prescribes that scientists have an obligation to open their work to the scrutiny of their peers through peer review and replication of experimental findings so that they can reach a consensus of opinion regarding facts and theories, and that is only possible within the framework of open communication of research results (Merton 1973). Scientists also have an ethical obligation to produce knowledge that is socially valuable. This view has a strong ideological basis rooted in the pursuit of the democratization of knowledge reinforced by recent developments in research funders' policies. These policies have introduced the societal impact criterion in the evaluation of grant proposals that requires researchers to prove the societal return on investment of publicly funded research. For example, all research proposals submitted to the National Science Foundation (NSF) must include a "broader impact" statement describing how the proposed research would benefit society. These developments are further contributing to the openness in scholarship by urging researchers to seek effective venues for openly sharing their research findings with other scholars and with the public.

Openness as Freedom of Inquiry

Openness as freedom of inquiry has its historical roots in the social justice movements that led to passage of the Freedom of Information Act (1967)[4] and the Electronic Freedom of Information Act Amendments (1996).[5] These documents enforced the public's rights to have access to official information held by the government and public bodies in order to ensure that "government decision-making at all levels is transparent, public records are open to public scrutiny, and individuals have rights of access to such information" (Peters and Britez 2006, xvii), unless there are *reasonable* grounds for withholding such information from the public domain.

Openness as Freedom from Cost

The term "open" is often used synonymously with the term "free" as in "free of charge." According to Downes (2007, 32), "the concept of 'open' entails, it seems, at a minimum, no cost to the consumer or user of the resource." However, true openness is a matter of freedom, not price. Project Gutenberg clarifies the difference between free of charge and freedom in this fashion: "Free of charge means that you don't have to pay for the book you received. Freedom denotes that you may do as you like with the book you received" (Project Gutenberg, n.d.). Richard Stallman states it even more succinctly when explaining the meaning of free software: "To understand the concept, you should think of 'free' as in 'free speech', not as in 'free beer'" (GNU Operating System, n.d.).

Openness as an Author's Right

The concept of openness in scholarship is closely connected with the authors' rights movement. In traditional publishing, the transfer of copyright from the authors to the publishers for getting works published through their publishing channels is still a common practice. When transferring copyright of a work to the publisher, authors actually transfer the entire bundle of their exclusive author rights, namely the rights for reproduction, distribution, public performance and display, and creation of derivative works.[6] The goal of the authors' rights movement (and one of the goals of open scholarship) is to return control of scholarly and creative works from the publishers back to the authors. One way to accomplish this goal is to use a free legal tool developed by the Scholarly Publishing and Academic Resources Coalition (SPARC) called the Addendum to Publication Agreement.[7] If accepted by the publisher, the addendum enables authors to retain individual copyrights, including the right to self-archive[8] their works in a disciplinary or institutional repository. Retaining the right to self-archive is becoming increasingly important to researchers whose works fall under research funders' public access mandates that require grant recipients to share the results of their research with the public.

Openness as a User's Right

Some of the foundational definitions of openness require that information should not only be freely accessible but also be allowed to be freely used and reused. Openness as a user's right was originally advocated by the leader of the Free Software Movement, Richard Stallman, whose goal was to "[spread] freedom and cooperation" in order to "make our society better" (Stallman 2006, 75). According to Stallman, a software program is free if the program's user has the four essential freedoms:

1. The freedom to run the program in any way, for any purpose
2. The freedom to change the program to suit the user's needs
3. The freedom to redistribute copies of the program to help others
4. The freedom to distribute copies of the improved version of the program to give others a chance to benefit from the changes (Ibid., 133)

The Open Knowledge Foundation (OKF) has adopted a similar definition of "open knowledge:" "Knowledge is open if anyone is free to access, use, modify, and share it — subject, at most, to measures that preserve provenance and openness" (Open Knowledge Foundation, n.d.). For works not in the public domain, openness as a user's right depends on the will of the copyright holders, who must consent to the use and reuse of their works. This goal can be easily accomplished by applying an open content license[9] to a copyrighted work. As Kreutzer (2011, 135) asserts, open content licenses help prevent the interests of authors and the interests of users "from being neglected in the system of one-sided privileges for rights holders that modern copyright law has become."

Openness as a Mindset

Openness has also been envisioned as a particular mindset associated with such qualities as imaginativeness, intellectual humility, and the receptiveness to new ideas. Some of these ideas are enshrined in *The Charter of Transdisciplinarity,* which defines openness as "an acceptance of the unknown, the unexpected and the unforeseeable" (Freitas, Nicolescu, and Morin 1994). Similarly, Wiley (March 1, 2013) states that "[o]penness facilitates the unexpected." Although Wiley does not elaborate on the meaning of his statement, he might refer to openness as intellectual flexibility that enables people to change their perspective based on new insights from others and imagine new ways of being in the world. Openness as a mindset is also related to the question of ethics, the goal of which is to support a culture based on open communication and trust, both in professional and personal relationships.

Openness as a Technological Advancement

Lastly, openness has been described as a phenomenon that is simply taking advantage of digital and networked technologies. Veletsianos and Kimmons (2012, 173) posit that one of the assumptions about open scholarship is that it is often treated as "an emergent scholarly phenomenon that is co-evolutionary with technological advancements in the larger culture." Burton (2009) describes an "open scholar" as "not simply someone who agrees to allow free access and reuse of his or her traditional scholarly articles and books [but someone] who makes their intellectual projects and processes *digitally* visible and who invites and encourages ongoing criticism of their work and secondary uses of any or all parts of it—at any stage of its development" (emphasis added).

Weller (2011, 136) argues that digital scholarship is "really a shorthand for the intersection of three elements: digital, networked, and open, [although it is] really the open aspect that brings about change in the scholarly communication practice." Regazzi (2015, 163) simply asserts that the very existence of open access is due to one factor—Internet technology.

Akin to a variety of interpretations of openness as a concept, the interpretations of openness as a practice vary depending on the goals of initiatives that fall under the praxis of open scholarship. Although most, if not all, of these initiatives have descended conceptually from the ethical ideas of the Free Software Movement[10] pioneered by Richard Stallman in the 1980s and share a similar motivation, which can be described as their intention to lower or remove restrictions to use and reuse of various types of resources, these initiatives have not yet formed a coherent and coordinated open scholarship movement. Fecher and Friesike (2014) group all open initiatives into five distinct schools of thought based on their goals: 1) the infrastructure school, which creates openly available tools, services, and platforms for researchers; 2) the public school, which aims to make knowledge openly accessible to all citizens; 3) the measurement school, which develops an alternative set of metrics for measuring research impact; 4) the democratic school, which aims to make knowledge freely available for everyone; and 5) the pragmatic school, which promotes collaborative research as a way to make the process of knowledge creation more efficient and goal-oriented.

On the one hand, a multitude of interpretations of openness in scholarship speaks to its evolving nature and potential for growth. On the other hand, the lack of consensus about the conceptual meaning of open scholarship often leads to confusion that may prevent open scholarship from reaching its full potential in academia. At the same time, as Tarantino (2019, 66–67) notes, the lack of consensus on openness "may be an inescapable feature of dealing with 'open' initiatives which are by their nature diffuse and often fractious."

Acknowledgment

Portions of this chapter (with minor additions and modifications) are reprinted with permission from Martin, Victoria. 2020. "The Concept of Openness in Scholarship." In *Open Praxis, Open Access: Digital Scholarship in Action*, edited by Dana Haugh and Darren Chase, 3–18. Chicago: ALA Editions.

Notes

1. The term "open scholarship" is often used interchangeably with the term "open science." However, the concept of open scholarship is broader. It is not limited to scholarship in the sciences, but rather encompasses any discipline, including the humanities.

2. Weller further cautions not to define openness as a unified approach, but rather use it as an umbrella term for a multitude of open approaches to knowledge creation and distribution, as well as for various motivations that people have for adopting open approaches.

3. The quotes around the term "communism" are in the original in order to distinguish this norm from communism as a sociopolitical ideology.

4. "What Is the Freedom of Information Act (FOIA)?" Available at: https://www.foia.gov/about.html.

5. "The Freedom of Information Act Update: The Freedom of Information Act, 5 U.S.C. sect. 552, As Amended By Public Law No. 104-231, 110 Stat. 3048. Office of Information and Privacy, U.S. Department of Justice." Available at: https://www.justice.gov/oip/blog/foia-update-freedom-information-act-5-usc-sect-552-amended-public-law-no-104-231-110-stat.

6. "Copyright Law of the United States. Title 17." Available at: https://www.copyright.gov/title17.

7. A copy of the Addendum to Publication Agreement can be downloaded at: https://sparcopen.org/wp-content/uploads/2016/01/Access-Reuse_Addendum.pdf.

8. Self-archiving, also known as "green open access," refers to the practice of making a copy of a work openly available in an institutional or a disciplinary repository. Self-archiving is discussed in Chapter 4.

9. Open content licenses are discussed in Chapter 3.

10. The Free Software Movement is discussed in Chapter 2.

Suggested Readings

Peters, Michael A., and Peter Roberts. *Virtues of Openness: Education, Science, and Scholarship in the Digital Age.* New York: Routledge, 2016.

Veletsianos, George, and Royce Kimmons. "Assumptions and Challenges of Open Scholarship." *International Review of Research in Open and Distributed Learning* 13, no. 4 (2012): 166–189.

Suggested Resource

Open Knowledge Foundation
https://okfn.org
A global, nonprofit organization founded in 2004 with the goal to promote the idea of "an open world, where all non-personal information is open, free for everyone to use, build on and share." Promotes openness through teaching, training, advocacy, research, and policy advice. Maintains the "Open Definition," which outlines the principles defining openness in relation to content and data.

CHAPTER TWO

The Free Software Movement and the Open Source Initiative

Unlocking the Source Code

Creativity can be a social contribution, but only in so far as society is free to use the results.

—Richard Stallman (1985)

Good programmers know what to write. Great ones know what to rewrite (and reuse).

—Eric Raymond (2001, 24)

In the proprietary software industry, source code—the basic medium providing a computer's operating system with instructions on producing a software application—is hidden from public view due to the licensing terms, and the software itself is distributed in compiled form. Users can run the program but cannot look "under the hood" to see the source code that the program is built on or make any modifications to that code. While specific license terms may vary, users of proprietary software are typically constrained to a certain number of installations on a limited number of computers. Vendors use this "closed" code approach to make profit by having exclusive control over their products. In addition, vendors use a lock-in strategy to guard off competitors. In vendor lock-in, customers depend on a particular vendor for services and products and are unable to switch to a different vendor without substantial expense, either in monetary terms or in terms of time and effort.

Free software and open source software (sometimes inappropriately referred to as FOSS, meaning "Free and Open Source Software," or as FLOSS, meaning "Free/Libre and Open Source Software")[1] enable rather than restrict the users' ability to see a software program's source code. While advocating for fundamentally different philosophical values, the developers of free software and the producers of open source software have created an alternative to the proprietary approach to the use, licensing, and distribution of software by allowing anyone to see the program's source code, modify it, and distribute modified versions under an open license.

Since the beginning of the Free Software Movement in the 1980s and the launch of the Open Source Initiative in the 1990s, their principles and practices have found wide application not just in the sphere of software development but in scholarly research as well, especially in those research areas that rely on free software and open source software as a way to "ease the pain" of reproducing research findings (Perkel 2018). Researchers increasingly use software to compile, analyze, and share data; uncover patterns; and draw conclusions that are then published in peer-reviewed articles. Yet simply providing a written description of the software used to generate the published research findings does not ensure reproducibility of those findings by other researchers. This can be due, among other things, to the unavoidable ambiguity that happens when describing software in natural language in a journal article (Ince, Hatton, and Graham-Cumming 2012) or due to undetected errors contained by the software program (Soergel 2015). This can also be due to failure to generate the same results when using a different software version or when software is run on different hardware (Perkel 2018). Researchers need to have access to the actual source code behind the software in order to analyze published research findings at a deeper computational level, and this includes verifying underlying data, analyzing workflow information, reviewing various versions and releases of the research project, and replicating the computing environment. The geophysicist Jon Claerbout, a leader in the field of scientific reproducibility, encapsulates this idea as follows: "An article about computational science in a scientific publication is **not** the scholarship itself, it is merely **advertising** of the scholarship. The actual scholarship is the complete software development environment and the complete set of instructions which generated the figures" (quoted in Buckheit and Donoho 1995, 59; emphasis in original).

Having access to the source code becomes especially important for researchers nowadays when an increasing number of scholarly journals require that source code and data used to generate research findings be made openly available along with the published article (Herndon and O'Reilly 2016; Jacoby, Lafferty-Hess, and Christian 2017; Shamir et al. 2013; Stodden, Guo, and Ma 2013). Integrating source code with published research enables others to reproduce research findings by running the same software on data generated by the research study (Sandve et al. 2013). That, in turn, strengthens the quality, transparency, and reliability of research and accelerates the speed at which new discoveries are made.

Although the terms "free software" and "open source software" are often used interchangeably,[2] these terms (and the concepts they represent) are not identical. Moreover, they refer to the two separate "political camps" of software developers that are similar in practice but fundamentally different in principle. Free software can be seen as a sociopolitical movement, which advocates the sharing of software source code as a moral obligation, while open source software is better described as a pragmatic argument, according to which the sharing of software source code simply produces better software. As Richard Stallman, the leader of the Free Software Movement, explains, the two groups "disagree on the basic principles, but agree more or less on the practical recommendations" (2002, 55).

The Free Software Movement

The Free Software Movement predates the Open Source Initiative by over a decade. It was pioneered in the 1980s by Richard Stallman, who was at that time a researcher at the Massachusetts Institute of Technology (MIT) Artificial Intelligence Lab, which is regarded as one of the birthplaces of the hacker subculture.[3] Stallman considered the growing trend toward the commercialization of software as an ethical problem that required software programmers to "feel in conflict with other programmers in general rather than feel as comrades" (Stallman 1985). In 1983, he announced his intention to create a new Unix-compatible software operating system[4] and make it freely available to anyone who wanted to use it.[5] Stallman christened his new system GNU (a recursive acronym for "GNU's Not Unix!") as a way to differentiate GNU from Unix, a historically proprietary software, and named the project for developing the GNU system—the GNU Project.[6] By 1991, the GNU Project team had completed the entire GNU operating system with the exception of the kernel program. It was in this context that a Finnish American software developer Linus Torvalds, in collaboration with an international community of software programmers, took advantage of the GNU code and developed the Linux "kernel," which became the core of the GNU/Linux operating system and one of the most prominent examples of free software (Lessig 2002).

In initiating the GNU Project, Stallman strived to address the "injustice of proprietary software" that "doesn't respect users' freedom and community" (GNU Operating System, n.d.). He described his position as "pragmatic idealism" (Ibid.) and explained his reasons for developing a freely available implementation of Unix as follows:

> I consider that the golden rule requires that if I like a program I must share it with other people who like it. Software sellers want to divide the users and conquer them, making each user agree not to share with others. I refuse to break solidarity with other users in this way. I cannot in good conscience sign a nondisclosure agreement or a software license agreement. . . . So that I can continue to use computers without dishonor, I have decided to put together a sufficient body of free software so that I will be able to get along without any software that is not free.
>
> (2006, 28)

To accomplish his goal, Stallman strived "to eliminate the artificial obstacles to cooperation" (Ibid., 106) imposed by the owners of proprietary software that he considered a contradiction to what he called the four essential freedoms of a software user. In his essay *Why Software Should Be Free*, Stallman stated that "programmers have the duty to encourage others to share, redistribute, study, and improve the software we write: in other words, to write 'free' software" (Ibid., 97). However, Stallman made a clear distinction between "free" as in "free speech" and "free" as in "zero price." According to Stallman, the word "free" in free software refers to liberty, not price.[7] As he clarifies it, "[t]o understand the concept [of free software], you should think of 'free' as in 'free speech, not as in 'free beer'" (Ibid., 35).

In his definition of free software, Stallman articulated his vision of the four essential freedoms of a software user as follows:

> A program is free software if the program's users have the four essential freedoms:
>
> •   The freedom to run the program as you wish, for any purpose (freedom 0).
> •   The freedom to study how the program works, and change it so it does your computing as you wish (freedom 1). [...] .
> •   The freedom to redistribute copies so you can help others (freedom 2).

- The freedom to distribute copies of your modified versions to others (freedom 3). (GNU Operating System, n.d.)[8]

Stallman's definition of free software has a strong altruistic dimension, as it emphasizes the rights of the user as a creative co-producer rather than as a passive consumer of the existing software (as had been prevalent in the proprietary software industry at that time). His idea of the four freedoms was influenced by the liberalist political tradition, especially in the philosophy of Thomas Hobbes, John Locke, and John Stuart Mill, as well as in the philosophy of freedom granted to U.S. citizens (Vainio and Vadén 2012). Stallman had also been inspired by sociopolitical movements that sought to end oppression, such as that of Mahatma Gandhi[9] (Free Software Foundation of India 2004), and by people who fought for liberty, justice, and equality, such as Martin Luther King Jr., Nelson Mandela (Ibid.), and more recently Bhimrao Ambedkar who launched a movement for full equality for Dalits in India.[10]

There is more than one way of making a software program free.[11] As long as a program is licensed in a way that it provides all four of the essential freedoms summarized in Stallman's definition, it qualifies as free and can be used either commercially or noncommercially. Licenses permitting only noncommercial use, modification, or redistribution of the source code are not considered to be free. As Stallman affirms, "[p]utting some of the freedoms off limits to some users […] renders the program nonfree" (GNU Operating System, n.d.). Extended or modified versions of a free software program, however, may not always be free. This situation can happen when a license permits others to create and distribute nonfree versions of an originally free program.

To ensure that the four essential freedoms are preserved in all copies of all versions of a program, Stallman created a licensing concept that he nicknamed "copyleft."[12] He defined copyleft as "the rule that when redistributing the program, you cannot add restrictions to deny other people the central freedoms" (GNU Operating System, n. d.). In that sense, copyleft "turns around" the copyright, rather than abandons it, in order to give users true freedom. As Stallman clarifies this concept, "[t]he 'left' in 'copyleft' is not a reference to the verb 'to leave'—only to the direction which is the mirror image of 'right'" (GNU Operating System, n.d.).[13]

The practical implementation of Stallman's copyleft concept is a copyleft license. In a nutshell, the copyleft license requires that all modified or extended versions of a program be free and released under the same copyleft license as the original work. Releasing a program under a copyleft license is not the same as placing it into the public domain where it may be used by anyone without any restrictions whatsoever.[14] Copyleft licensing does not undermine the rights of software developers who can share their work with others under generous license terms while reserving certain copyrights for themselves. Nor does it prohibit licensors from selling software or charging other users for the distribution of the software. As Stallman (2006, 97) explains it, the price for a copy of free software "may be zero, or small, or (rarely) quite large." However, a copyleft license does prohibit licensors from forbidding the users to share or modify free software, restricting its further redistribution or demanding a license fee, royalty, or other charge for the transfer of the right to use it. Stallman (1985) specifically notes that "everyone will be permitted to modify and redistribute GNU, but no distributor will be allowed to restrict its further redistribution. That is to say, proprietary modifications will not be allowed."

Although the origins of the idea of free licensing can be traced back to 1939 when an American singer-songwriter Woody Guthrie released his lyrics under a free copyright notice (Grassmuck 2011), the momentous breakthrough of this idea occurred in 1985 when Stallman authored the first copyleft license—the GNU Emacs General Public License—which was applied specifically to a free software text editor called GNU Emacs. Four years later, in 1989, Stallman created a new single copyleft license—the GNU General Public License (GPL)[15]— which could be applied to any software program. Source code added to a GPL-licensed program, even if it combines separate modules, becomes part of a larger program that must be released as a whole unit under the GNU GPL.

Copyright law is the critical legal premise of the GPL. As the preamble to the GPL, version 3, states, "[d]evelopers that use the GNU GPL protect your rights with two steps: (1) assert copyright on the software, and (2) offer you this License giving you legal permission to copy, distribute and/or modify it" (GNU General Public License 2007). According to the GPL terms, software developers are required to release the source code, grant others the rights to modify and distribute the entire code, and, if software is based on or derived from a work licensed under the GPL, release the derivative work under the same license terms. By far, the GPL is the most widely used copyleft license approach. The GPL is also the license that utilizes the strongest copyleft provision because it requires that any new derivation of the software should be released under the same protections.[16] Some within the proprietary software industry have derogatively labeled the GPL's copyleft provisions as a "virus" and called the GPL a "viral license" because it "contaminates" each derivative work and is being "transmitted" from project to project.[17] In response to these attacks,

Stallman said that the comparison of the GPL to a virus was "very harsh" and that the comparison to a spider plant was "more accurate" because the spider plant "goes to another place if you actively take a cutting" (quoted in Williams 2011, 23).

The GPL has inspired other copyleft licensing models, including the Free Art License developed by the Copyleft Attitude movement in France for licensing artistic works and the Creative Commons Attribution-ShareAlike license developed by the nonprofit organization Creative Commons for licensing creative works beyond software.[18] All copyleft licenses satisfy the general conditions of free software but may vary in specific rights granted to users by authors.[19]

In 2000, the Free Software Foundation released a GPL copyleft counterpart for textual materials—the GNU Free Documentation License (GFDL)[20]—intended primarily for user manuals and technical documentation accompanying free software.[21] The GFDL is based on the same philosophical principles as the GPL. It grants any user the freedom to copy, redistribute, and modify the GFDL-licensed work, either commercially or noncommercially, and requires that derivative works must be released under the same license as the original work.

Some critics consider the GFDL "a cumbersome" license and "technically confusing for the lay reader" (Liang 2004). Others criticize it for being "fundamentally incompatible with any free software license" (Srivastava 2006). Wikipedia and other projects of the Wikimedia Foundation initially adopted the GFDL for their content but subsequently switched to a dual-licensing approach using the Creative Commons licenses for their texts and images and the GFDL for other content.[22]

The Open Source Initiative

Not all members of the free software community agreed with Stallman's goals and tactics. Some argued that his ardent advocacy for users' freedom was discouraging potential business collaborators and stifling the development of certain kinds of software, including Linux (Perens 1999), and posited that "the pragmatic, business-case grounds [were] a [more] valuable way to engage with potential software users and developers" (Open Source Initiative, n.d.). They advocated for allowing the integration of free and proprietary software as a means to produce better software, "not for ethical reasons but for competitive, market-driven reasons" (Perens 1999, 73), a practice that Stallman and other free software "purists" rejected. In the course of these arguments, a "non-Stallman" initiative emerged as an offshoot of the Free

Software Movement and was subsequently labeled "The Open Source Initiative."

The Open Source Initiative was led, in large part, by two software developers—Bruce Perens, the leader of the Debian Project developing operating systems based on the Linux kernel, and Eric Raymond, an independent software developer and author of the influential essay, and later a book, *The Cathedral and the Bazaar*. Raymond (1999) explained the reasons for the disagreement with Stallman as follows: "[. . .] the real axis of discord between those who speak of 'open source' and 'free software' is not over principles. It's over tactics and rhetoric. The open source movement is largely composed not of people who reject Stallman's ideals, but rather of people who reject his *rhetoric*."[23] According to Stallman, however, the open source "camp" rejected the very heart of his free software concept. In his essay *Why Open Source Misses the Point of Free Software*, he writes: "The terms 'free software' and 'open source' stand for almost the same range of programs. However, they say deeply different things about those programs, based on different values. The free software movement campaigns for freedom for the users of computing; it is a movement for freedom and justice. By contrast, the open source idea values mainly practical advantage and does not campaign for principles. This is why we do not agree with open source, and do not use that term" (GNU Operating System, n.d.).

The term "open source" was coined by Christine Peterson, an executive director at Foresight Institute, and was consequently adopted by the conferees at the First Freeware Summit held in 1998 in Palo Alto, California (later referred to as the first "Open Source Summit") (Peterson 2018). The term was adopted as part of a concerted effort to differentiate open source software from "the philosophically- and politically-focused label 'free software'" and to describe open source as "a development method for software that harnesses the power of distributed peer review and transparency of process" (Open Source Initiative, n.d.). Shortly after the first Open Source Summit, Perens and Raymond cofounded a nonprofit corporation—the Open Source Initiative (OSI)—dedicated to promoting the advantages of open source software development. According to the OSI, the promise of open source is to ensure "better quality, higher reliability, more flexibility, lower cost, and an end to predatory vendor lock-in" (Ibid.).

To fulfill that promise, Perens created The Debian Free Software Guidelines (originally developed in 1997),[24] in which he included the "No

Discrimination Against Fields of Endeavor" provision permitting the use of free software in business or genetic research.[25] The Debian Free Software Guidelines have become the basis for the Open Source Definition,[26] which delineates 10 requirements for an open source license (versus 4 requirements for free software).

In brief, an open source license guarantees the same set of four essential freedoms to users, namely, the freedom to run the program and the freedoms to use, modify, and redistribute the software source code, both commercially and noncommercially, to suit the needs of individual software developers or the needs of companies or entire communities. Some open source licenses are copyleft licenses. They grant anyone the rights to use, modify, and redistribute a program's source code, or any program derived from it, but only if derived versions of the program are released under the same distribution terms as the original work. Non-copyleft (or "permissive") open source licenses grant users the same rights but allow the source code to also be used as part of programs distributed under other licenses, including proprietary, "closed source" licenses (Open Source Initiative, n.d.).

Some software developers choose to release their software components under two or more licenses simultaneously—an open source license and a proprietary license—in order to bridge the gap between their commercial and noncommercial needs. This licensing approach is called dual licensing, or, if the software is released under more than two different licenses, multilicensing. An open source license can be also applied to nonsoftware works, especially when these works can be edited and versioned as source code. Examples of such nonsoftware works include datasets, videos, software documentation, fonts, and mixed projects that include a combination of software and other content.[27]

Any new license labeled as an open source license must go through the OSI's license review process to ensure that the new license conforms to the Open Source Definition.[28] OSI maintains a list of approved open source licenses organized by category and alphabetically.[29] The most widely used open source licenses are the GNU General Public License (GPL) designed by the Free Software Foundation, the X11 license[30] produced at MIT (and thus sometimes misleadingly called the MIT license),[31] and the Apache 2.0 license[32] developed by the Apache Software Foundation. These licenses allow anyone to use the software for any purpose, modify it, and redistribute its modified versions under the terms of the license.[33]

Advantages and Challenges of Free Software and Open Source Software

The development of free software and open source software is a community-driven dynamic production process where the boundaries between creators, users, and testers are blurred. This process presents powerful advantages compared to proprietary software, including the following benefits:

- *Flexibility*

  Without proprietary software restrictions, users are free to modify the software program and develop the program's new features to suit their individual needs or the needs of their customers or companies.

- *Strong community culture*

  Software developers at any skill level have access to a vast and ever-growing source of information where they can tap the knowledge of other programmers and coders, learn new skills, contribute new ideas, and receive rapid feedback from other developers.

- *Protection against third-party attackers*

  The open exchange of information among software developers, who continuously study, inspect, and review the source code, helps detect and remove software bugs easier and earlier in the cycle than is possible in a proprietary environment. As Raymond (2001, 19) summarized it in his famous saying, "Given enough eyeballs, all bugs are shallow."[34]

- *Defense against malicious functionalities*

  Free software enables the users to identify and remove malicious functionalities implemented in some proprietary software programs that were designed to censor users, spy on them or control them in other ways.[35]

- *Faster development cycle*

  Not having to ask original authors' permissions to modify software helps cut down on the time it takes to implement new software features, remove unnecessary components, create security enhancements, and distribute new releases.

- *Freedom from vendor lock-ins*

  Because users do not depend upon a particular vendor for technical support and upgrades, they are free to switch between different platforms, vendors, and software packages.

- *Cost optimization*

  These predominantly free software solutions lead to significant cost savings during the life cycle of a software program, including savings on licensing, technical support, maintenance, and upgrades.

Free software and open source software programs also have limitations compared to proprietary software, mostly due to the fact that they have been developed and maintained by volunteer programmers who create and modify software in their spare time. The limitations include:

- *Code forking*

   Code forking—the situation where a programmer takes a copy of source code and develops an entirely new program—can create multiple derivatives of the same basic software. Although the right to "fork" is an essential freedom granted by free software and open source software, the existence of multiple versions of the same program can lead to confusion for some users and potential compatibility issues between software versions.

- *Coordination issues*

   Given that any free software and open source software community can involve a virtually unlimited number of developers, who are free to join or leave the community at any time, it can be challenging to plan, coordinate, and complete projects on time.

- *Quality assurance*

   Most free software and open source communities consist of volunteers whose competence, time commitments, and levels of involvement vary considerably. The variable nature of these factors can make the software quality assurance challenging.

- *Difficulty of use*

   Some free software and open source software applications are not sufficiently intuitive or lack user-friendly interfaces. Others may be difficult to set up and use. This presents challenges to some users, especially nonprofessional users, who may need to rely on help of professional software developers, and that may incur additional costs.

- *Hardware compatibility issues*

   Open source software may not run on proprietary platforms and that means that users have to rely on specialized drivers to run open source software that can only be purchased from the equipment manufacturer.

- *License incompatibilities*

   License incompatibilities can result when combining two or more software programs licensed under diverging copyleft licenses requiring that each derivative work be licensed under the same provisions as the original work. Obeying one of these licenses would result in infringing on the others.

There is a significant crossover between the ideals of freedom, collaboration, transparency, and cross-pollination of ideas that guide the Free

Software Movement and the Open Source Initiative and the ideals of open scholarship that challenges "closed" methods of knowledge production and distribution. Most (if not all) open scholarship initiatives of today have their originating point in the Free Software Movement and the Open Source Initiative. In particular, there are striking parallels between them and the open content licensing model (discussed in Chapter 3) in how they emphasize the idea of building upon the works of others and modify the traditional copyright law to grant some rights to the public. The Open Access movement (discussed in Chapter 4) also parallels the Free Software Movement in how it challenges commercial publishing as an exclusive method of knowledge distribution and promotes the idea of knowledge as a public good and as the means to achieve a more socially just and equitable society.

While there is a distinct correlation between the aims and aspirations of the Free Software Movement and the Open Source Initiative and open scholarship as a whole, there are also key differences in how they define and implement openness. This is partly due to the fact that the former exist predominantly within a smaller community of software developers where openness has been defined and implemented rather rigorously and precisely, while the latter exists within a more diffuse, inherently diverse, and highly fragmented research environment where an understanding of openness is less unified and more ambiguous (Tennant et al. 2020).

Notes

1. Richard Stallman, pioneer of the Free Software Movement, and his peers at the Free Software Foundation urge people to reject the term FOSS because it "fails to explain that 'free' refers to *freedom* […] and also makes 'free software' less visible than 'open source,' since it presents 'open source' prominently but splits 'free software' apart" (GNU Operating System. "FOSS and FLOSS." https://www.gnu.org/philosophy/floss-and-foss.html). The term FLOSS, on the other hand, while technically correct, makes the names of the two fundamentally different "political camps" sound "equally prominent" and because of that some people may think the two are more similar in philosophy than they actually are (Ibid.).

2. "Freeware" and "shareware" are the other terms that are often used interchangeably in the software development industry.

3. In his book *Hackers: Heroes of the Computer Revolution*, Steven Levy (1984) describes hackers working on early computers in higher education institutions, most notably at MIT, as highly skilled computer enthusiasts who mistrusted authority and looked down on bureaucracy, lack of skills, and secrecy. Levy summarized the rules of the hacker ethics as follows:

1. "Access to computers—and anything which might teach you something about the way the world works—should be unlimited and total. Always yield to the hands-on imperative!

2. All information should be free.

3. Mistrust authority—promote decentralization.

4. Hackers should be judged by their hacking, not bogus criteria such as degrees, age, race, or position.

5. You can create art and beauty on a computer.

6. Computers can change your life for the better" (40–45).

4. Because Unix was a popular operating system at that time, Stallman intended to design a system that would be compatible with Unix so that it would be easier for Unix users to migrate to his new operating system.

5. Stallman's initial announcement about his intention to create a new software operating system is available at: https://www.gnu.org/gnu/initial-announcement.html.

6. The GNU project was launched in 1983. Since 1985, it has been supported by the nonprofit Free Software Foundation (FSF) (https://www.fsf.org), which promotes the ideals of free software.

7. To avoid the ambiguity of the English term "free" regarding either freedom or pricing, free software is sometimes called "libre software" to emphasize "liberty," not price. Relatedly, the term "free software" should not be confused with the term "freeware," which refers to software distributed at no cost to the end user but without making the source code available.

8. Stallman's initial definition of free software included only three freedoms numbered 1, 2 and 3. Freedom 0 (zero) was added in the 1990s when Stallman realized that the most basic of freedoms—the freedom to run the program—should be "mentioned explicitly." Instead of renumbering the freedoms, he made it freedom 0 because it "was clearly more basic than the other three, so it properly should precede them" (GNU Operating System, "What is Free Software." https://www.gnu.org/philosophy/free-sw.en.html).

9. According to Stallman, the Free Software Movement "has much in common with Gandhi's [movement]" because "Gandhi sought to end the rule of the British over India, and [the Free Software Movement seeks] to end the rule of the software developers over cyberspace" (Free Software Foundation of India 2004).

10. Richard Stallman. Email message to author, November 5, 2021.

11. For a description of various categories of software and how they relate to each other, see "Categories of Free and Nonfree Software" at https://www.gnu.org/philosophy/categories.html. For examples of specific free software licenses, see "Various Licenses and Comments about Them" at https://www.gnu.org/licenses/license-list.html.

12. The word "copyleft" itself could have been coined by a programmer and an artist Don Hopkins. As Hopkins was mailing a manual for the 68000 microprocessor that he borrowed from Stallman, he, as a token of appreciation, decorated the envelope with several stickers, including the sticker "Copyleft" accompanied by a backward "C." This sticker inspired Stallman to use the word "copyleft" for his free software license (https://www.gnu.org/graphics/copyleft-sticker.en.html).

13. Dusollier (2007) speculates that the term "copyleft" "results from a play on words where copy*left* stands in a stark contrast with copy*right*," although "[i]n a more strict sense," the term implies the "viral nature" of the license by which the "anti-exclusion effect propagates" through the tree of derivative works derived from the original openly-licensed work (1397–98).

14. While Stallman argued that making the source code freely available to anyone is critical for the advancement of computer science, he cautioned against placing the source code into the public domain where others would have an opportunity to redistribute a program without the source code and that would restrict the freedom of users to modify it and thus make the program non-free.

15. The GNU General Public License, version 3 (https://www.gnu.org /licenses/gpl-3.0.en.html).

16. For comparisons of various copyleft licenses, see "GNU Operating System/Various Licenses and Comments about Them" at: http://www.gnu.org /licenses/license-list.html.

17. It is generally believed that the analogy of 'virus' with regard to content propagation was coined by Margaret Jane Radin in her article "Human, Computers and Binding Commitment." See Radin, Margaret Jane. 2000. "Humans, Computers, and Binding Commitment." _Indiana Law Journal_ 75(4): 1125–1162. Available at: https://www.repository.law.indiana.edu/ilj/vol75/iss4/1.

18. The Free Art license and Creative Commons licenses are discussed in Chapter 3.

19. For recommendations on selecting a specific license, see the Free Software Movement's guide at: https://gnu.org/licenses/license-recommendations.html.

20. See The GNU Free Documentation License (GFDL) at: http://www.gnu .org/copyleft/fdl.html.

21. The GFDL can be used for any textual work regardless of its subject matter or format. See https://www.gnu.org/licenses/fdl-1.3.en.html.

22. See "Wikipedia: About" at: https://en.wikipedia.org/wiki/Wikipedia :About.

23. See Raymond's Shut Up and Show Them the Code (1999) and Stallman's Why "Free Software" Is Better Than "Open Source" (2002) as examples of the debate between Stallman and Raymond on the issue of freely available code.

24. At about the same time, Perens had conceived a similar concept for hardware devices and their interfaces that he called "open source hardware." The open source hardware initiative has not been as popular as open source software but the open hardware community is still active through the Open Source Hardware Association (https://www.oshwa.org).

25. See The Debian Free Software Guidelines (DFSG) at: https://www.debian .org/social_contract#guidelines.

26. Open Source Definition (https://opensource.org/osd).

27. For more information, see "Non-Software Licenses" at: https://choose alicense.com/non-software.

28. See "The License Review Process" at: https://opensource.org/approval.

29. See "Licenses & Standards" at: https://opensource.org/licenses.

30. The X11 license (https://directory.fsf.org/wiki/License:X11).

31. For explanation on why the term "MIT license" is misleading, see: https://www.gnu.org/licenses/license-list.html#Expat.

32. The Apache 2.0 license (https://www.apache.org/licenses/LICENSE-2.0).

33. Complete lists of all approved open source licenses sorted by name and by category are available at: https://opensource.org/licenses.

34. This saying refers to Linus's Law formulated by Raymond in his essay, and later a book, *The Cathedral and the Bazaar* (2001). This Law was named in honor of Linus Torvalds, the developer of the Linux kernel. A more complete statement reads: "Given a large enough beta-tester and co-developer base, almost every problem will be characterized quickly and the fix obvious to someone. Or, less formally, 'Given enough eyeballs, all bugs are shallow.' I dub this: 'Linus's Law'" (30).

35. The Free Software Foundation maintains a regularly updated directory of malicious functionalities that can be accessed at: https://gnu.org/malware.

Suggested Readings

Moglen, Eben. "Anarchism Triumphant: Free Software and the Death of Copyright." *First Monday* 4, no. 8 (1999). https://firstmonday.org/ojs/index.php/fm/article/download/684/594?inline=1.

Raymond, Eric S. *The Cathedral and the Bazaar: Musings on Linux and Open Source by an Accidental Revolutionary.* Sebastopol: O'Reilly Media, 2001.

Stallman, Richard M. *Free Software, Free Society: Selected Essays of Richard M. Stallman.* Boston: GNU Press, 2006.

Weber, Steve. *The Success of Open Source.* Cambridge: Harvard University Press, 2004.

Suggested Resources

Free Software Foundation (FSF)
https://www.fsf.org
A nonprofit organization for promoting the ideals of free software. Maintains The Free Software Definition, oversees the GNU Project, and provides support services related to education, copyright, and software verification and certification.

Open Source Initiative (OSI)
https://opensource.org
A nonprofit corporation for educating about and advocating for the benefits of open source software. Maintains the Open Source Definition (OSD), delineating 10 requirements for an open source license, conducts license review processes to ensure that new licenses conform to the OSD, and maintains a list of approved open source licenses, organized by category and alphabetically.

CHAPTER THREE

Open Content Licensing

Filling the Gap Between
"All Rights Reserved" and
"No Rights Reserved"

. . . creation always involves building upon something else.

There is no art that doesn't reuse. And there will be less art if every reuse is taxed by the appropriator.

—Lawrence Lessig (2001)

It is not uncommon for scholars to knowingly or unknowingly sign away all of their copyrights to publishers of their works. As a result, these scholars cannot freely distribute their own works, modify them, or allow open access for others to use them. Furthermore, they have to ask the publisher's permission for each and every use of their own work (which can be time consuming and expensive), since most commercial publishers still impose stringent conditions on the usage of the works they publish. Many scholars are unaware that they can release their work under an open content license, while still getting their work published. An open content license allows authors to easily communicate to the users of their work which copyrights they want to reserve for themselves and which copyrights they want to waive for the benefit of others. This provides authors with a legal mechanism to ensure that they retain copyright while allowing others to use their work under certain conditions.

The open content licensing model was inspired by the Free Software Movement, pioneered by Richard Stallman, and the Open Source Initiative, commonly credited to Bruce Perens and Eric Raymond.[1] Similarly to those other movements, the open content licensing model is driven by a strong desire to "place the interests of authors and users on an even playing field" (Kreutzer 2011, 118). It is based on a belief that the traditional copyright regime is one of the major obstacles to creativity and innovation and it seeks to ensure that there is a large pool of freely available works that other creators can use and build upon. By utilizing Stallman's idea of the four freedoms of a software user and Raymond's and Perens's pragmatic arguments for openness as a collaborative paradigm, the open content licensing model has developed a set of similar licensing principles but broadened the scope of content to include works other than software, such as scholarly research, literature, music, and art.[2]

Defining an Open Content License

The term "open content license" contains within it two distinct concepts—open content and licensing. The meaning of the term "license" is straightforward. The word "license" is derived from the Latin word "licere" ("to allow") and literally means "permission." In copyright law, a license is the legal permission given by the owner of a copyrighted work (a licensor) to the recipient of the license (a licensee) to exercise certain rights with respect to the copyrighted work. From this perspective, an open content license can be broadly defined as a legal document, in which the copyright holder specifies the conditions under which his or her work can be used, reused, and redistributed. Typically, a work licensed with an open content license can be used, reused, and redistributed with few or no restrictions, although the degree of openness in open content licenses can vary from very open to very restrictive. Some open content licenses simply allow copying, while others grant users permissions to adapt and modify the work. The more restrictive a license, the more difficult it is to reuse the work, in contradiction with the idea of openness. The most open kind of license is one in which the copyright holder waives all the ownership rights and places the work in the public domain.

To delineate the meaning of the term "open content" is more challenging. As Kreutzer (2011, 111) observes, "[h]ow the term open content is defined exactly remains an open issue." The term "open content" itself was coined by David Wiley, then a graduate student at Brigham Young University. Wiley invented this term in the context of his OpenContent Project[3] initiated in 1998 in order "to evangelize a way of thinking about sharing materials, especially those that are useful for supporting education" (Wiley 2003). Inspired by the Free Software Movement and the Open Source Initiative, particularly by the practical benefits of openness advocated by the Open Source Initiative (Wiley and Gurrell 2009), Wiley (n.d.) defined "open content" as "any copyrightable work (traditionally excluding software, which is described by other terms like 'open source') that is either (1) in the public domain or (2) licensed in a manner that provides everyone with free and perpetual permission to engage in the 5R activities." According to Wiley, these 5R activities include the following: 1) Retain (i.e., make and own copies of works); 2) Revise (i.e., modify and improve works); 3) Remix (i.e., combine two or more works); 4) Reuse (i.e., use works in a wide range of ways); and 5) Redistribute (i.e., share works with others)[4] (Ibid.). Even though the OpenContent Project is no longer actively maintained, Wiley's definition of open content continues to be widely cited in the literature and on the Web.

Another widely referenced definition of openness with respect to content was created by the Open Knowledge Foundation (OKF),[5] an international not-for-profit organization. Founded in 2004 by a British researcher, entrepreneur, and technologist, Rufus Pollock, OKF promotes the adoption of open knowledge practices and open data and maintains the Open Definition project,[6] which purports to "[make] precise the meaning of 'open' with respect to knowledge" (Open Knowledge Foundation, n.d.). Similarly to Wiley's concept of the 5Rs, the Open Definition was significantly influenced by the Free Software Movement and the Open Source Initiative. OKF explicitly states that the Open Definition is "substantially derivative" of the Open Source Definition created by Bruce Perens and that it is committed to continuing Richard Stallman's "ideals of software freedom" (Ibid.). The Open Definition project crystallizes the meaning of open in its key statement, which reads as follows: "Open means **anyone** can **freely access, use, modify, and share,** for **any purpose** (subject, at most, to requirements that preserve provenance and openness)" (Ibid.; emphasis in original). In comparison with Wiley's definition, the Open Definition offers a greater degree of elaboration on what an open content license *can* contain and what it *must* contain in order to qualify as an open content license. The full version of the Open Definition[7] provides a detailed set of criteria for open content licenses that can be summarized as the freedom to access, use, reuse, and redistribute content with no restrictions beyond the attribution and share-alike requirements. The Open Definition also includes a list of conformant and nonconformant open content licenses for creative works.

Another notable initiative that attempted to define the meaning of openness with regard to licensing was the Definition of Free Cultural Works (DFCW) project[8] launched in 2006 by a German journalist and software developer, Erik Möller, in the context of the Wikimedia project but no longer actively maintained. In its preamble, DFCW summarized the rationale behind its project as follows:

> Social and technological advances make it possible for a growing part of humanity to *access, create, modify, publish and distribute* various kinds of works—artworks, scientific and educational materials, software, articles—in short: *anything that can be represented in digital form.* Many communities have formed to exercise those new possibilities and create a wealth of collectively re-usable works. Most authors, whatever their field of activity, whatever their amateur or professional status, have a genuine interest in favoring an ecosystem where works can be spread, re-used and derived in creative ways. The easier it is to re-use and derive works, the richer our cultures become.
>
> (Definition of Free Cultural Works, n.d.; emphasis in original)

Similarly to the two aforementioned projects, DFCW was rooted in Stallman's idea of the four freedoms of a software user and the ideas of the Open Source Initiative. DFCW aimed to create the definitions of "free works" and "free licenses" that could be used as "a tool to determine whether a work or license should be considered 'free'" (Ibid.). According to DFCW, to be considered free, a work "*must* be covered by a Free Culture License, or its legal status *must* provide the *essential freedoms*" (Ibid.; emphasis in original). Analogous to Stallman's free software definition, these essential freedoms include:

1. "The freedom to use and perform the work";
2. "The freedom to study the work and apply the information";
3. "The freedom to redistribute copies";
4. "The freedom to distribute derivative works" (Ibid.).

A free work must also meet the following additional conditions:

*   Source data must be made available
*   A free format, i.e., a format not protected by patents, must be used for digital works
*   No technical restrictions should be used to impede the essential freedoms
*   No legal restrictions or limitations such as patents, contracts, or privacy rights must be imposed to limit the essential freedoms (Ibid.)

Compared to Wiley's definition of open content, DFCW is broader and more refined in that it refers to both copyrighted works and patents. It also delineates "permissible restrictions" on the use of works that do not "impede the essential freedom[s]," as well as "restrictions which are not permissible" because they "limit essential freedoms" (Ibid.).

Although the DFCW project was considered by some people a failure because "the community never widely agreed upon the term ["free cultural work"] or its definition" (Kreutzer 2011, 111), the DFCW definitions of "free works" and "free licenses" are still being recognized as viable by some open content communities. For example, Creative Commons (CC) identifies its Attribution (CC-BY) and Share-Alike (CC-BY-SA) licenses and its Public Domain Dedication tool (CC0) as compliant with DFCW.[9]

Key Open Content Licenses

The OpenContent and Open Publication Licenses

In 1998, David Wiley created and released his OpenContent License,[10] which was credited for being "the first proper free content license" (Grassmuck 2011, 30), although it was largely based on Stallman's General Public License.[11] In 1999, Wiley, in collaboration with Eric Raymond, Tim O'Reilly, and other open source activists, replaced the OpenContent License with the Open Publication License (OPL).[12] Similarly to Stallman's General Public License, the OPL permitted users to freely copy, redistribute, and modify OPL-licensed content. Unlike the General Public License, the OPL required acknowledgement of the original author(s) of the content and, if applicable, the publisher. The OPL also included some "good practice recommendations" (Open Publication License 1999) and two license options that a licensor could elect to invoke. The first option prohibited users of OPL-licensed content from distributing "substantively modified versions without the explicit permission of the author(s)" (Ibid.). The second option prohibited commercial use of OPL-licensed content "in standard (paper) book form" without obtaining prior permission from the copyright holder (Ibid.). The OPL "was widely and rightly criticized" because it did not require licensors to clearly and concisely indicate which of these two options they had chosen to invoke (Wiley and Gurrell 2009).

Neither the OpenContent License nor the Open Publication License have been maintained or modified since their last updates (in 1998 and 1999, respectively), although these licenses "remain online for archival purposes in their current locations" (Wiley 2003). In 2003, Wiley officially terminated his OpenContent Project and incorporated it into the work of Creative Commons, which, in his words, "was doing a better job of providing licensing options which will stand up in court" (Ibid.). The same year, Wiley joined Creative Commons as its educational use license project lead.

The Free Art License

The Free Art License[13] was created in 2000 by the Copyleft Attitude movement in France with the intention to license musical, visual, sculptural, and performing arts works. Similarly to Wiley's open content licenses, the Free Art License was inspired by and based on the General Public License designed by Richard Stallman for free software. Dusollier (2003, 285) speculates that the influence of the copyleft model on art was due to the fact that young artists who were already employing free software tools were "seduced by this alternative grass-root model, and quickly adopted a similar posture for the practice and diffusion of art."

The main rationale of the Free Art License, as stated in its preamble, is "to promote and protect creations of the human mind according to the principles of copyleft: freedom to use, copy, distribute, transform, and prohibition of exclusive appropriation" (Copyleft Attitude 2007). To achieve this goal, the Free Art License enables creators to specify the extent to which they allow the public to use their works (either initial work or subsequent works) while respecting the rights of the original authors. In particular, the Free Art License allows creators to grant the public the following rights:

• To copy or make reproductions of the artwork
• To distribute the artwork or perform it in public
• To modify the artwork

Like other copyleft licenses, this license requires that any changes made to the initial work be subject to the same terms and conditions as the Free Art License.

The OpenMusic Licenses

The OpenMusic Project[14] originated in Germany in 2001 with the goal "to show that successful methods and technologies of the Free Software world can be applied to other goods such as intellectual property" (OpenMusic, n.d.). The OpenMusic project offers two customized OpenMusic licenses, which largely replicate Stallman's General Public License in the realm of music by granting the public certain rights to freely use the musical works: 1) the Green License,[15] allowing almost any use, private or commercial, and 2) the Yellow License,[16] allowing any noncommercial use. There used to be two other OpenMusic licenses—the Red License, allowing only private use, and the Rainbow License, allowing to mix and match other OpenMusic licenses—but they appear to be no longer available.

Creative Commons Licenses

The Creative Commons, Inc.,[17] generally referred to as Creative Commons (CC hereafter), was founded in 2001 by Lawrence Lessig, professor at Stanford University's Law School, in collaboration with his peers, Hal Abelson and Eric Eldred. In his book *Remix: Making Art and Commerce Thrive in the Hybrid Economy*, Lessig expressed his frustration with the cumbersome negotiability of copyrighted content while, in his opinion, digital technology offered so many opportunities for creativity and innovation. He wrote: "Why should it be that just when technology is most encouraging of creativity, the law should be most restrictive? [. . .] The answer is: for no good reason, save inertia and the forces that like the world frozen as it is" (2008, 105). The goal of the CC initiative was "to increase the amount of openly licensed creativity in 'the commons'—the body of work freely available for legal use, sharing, repurposing, and remixing" (Creative Commons, n.d.). The CC initiative was largely supported by the Center for the Public Domain, a charitable foundation, currently ceased, which used to sponsor public domain spaces on the Web, offer free legal advice, and advocate for copyright reform.

In 2002, CC designed and released the first suite of its open content licenses. According to Lessig (2005), the basic idea behind the CC licenses (which, he accepted, was "stolen" from the Free Software Foundation) was "to produce copyright licenses that artists, authors, educators, and researchers could use to announce to the world the freedoms that they want their creative work to carry." CC licenses are intended for individual authors, companies, or institutions and can be described as generic open content licenses because they can be applied to any type of scholarly or creative work for which usage rights exist.[18] They allow creators to retain copyright and get credit for their work while concurrently allowing others to reuse their work under certain standardized conditions.

Each CC license includes three layers, as shown in Figure 3.1:

1. The Legal Code:[19] a "lawyer-readable" version of the license, written in a formal legal language that can be used in court.

2. The Commons Deeds: a "human readable" version of the license in simplified form using the CC icons.

3. The Machine Readable Code: a version license in a machine-readable format that helps computers understand what rights are granted by the license.

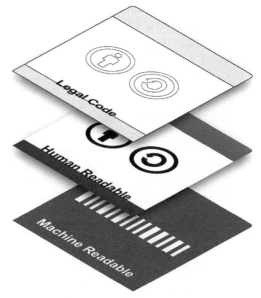

Certain features are common to all CC licenses. All CC licenses:

- Assert the licensor's copyright over the work

- Allow the licensor to determine the extent and the manner to which the licensor is willing to grant the public certain rights to the work

Figure 3.1 "The three layers of a CC license" by Creative Commons (2020), licensed under CC BY 4.0.

- State a set of rights granted by the licensor to the licensee

- Indicate that they do not affect other people's fair use, first sale, and free expression rights

- Last for the duration of the work's copyright

- Can be applied worldwide

- Are nonexclusive

- Are irrevocable[20]

All CC licenses prohibit the users:

- To do any of the things that the licensor has chosen to restrict without obtaining the licensor's permission

- To alter the terms of the license

- To use technological or other measures to restrict access to the work

- To remove copyright notices from all copies of the work

- Not to link to the license from copies of the work

When these requirements are met, all CC licenses grant the users the four baseline rights:

- To copy the work
- To redistribute the work
- To display or perform the work publicly, including digital performances
- To convert verbatim copies of the work into a different format

Figure 3.2 "Different license elements" by Creative Commons (2020), licensed under CC BY 4.0.

In addition to the four baseline rights and restrictions included in all CC licenses, creators can choose optional license elements represented by four visual icons, as shown in Figure 3.2.

The icon (a) means "Attribution" or "BY." This license element requires attribution to the creator of the work. The icon (b) means "Non-Commercial" or "NC." This license element prohibits the use of the work for commercial purposes. The icon (c) means "No Derivatives" or "ND." This license element prohibits redistribution of modified versions of the work.[21] The icon (d) means "Share Alike" or "SA." This license element requires that derivative works are redistributed under the terms of the original license.

These license elements can be mixed and matched to generate a CC license that suits the needs of an individual creator. The six icon-based CC licenses are shown in Figure 3.3.

These licenses grant the users the following rights:

a. **CC BY** (https://creativecommons.org/licenses/by/4.0)

Grants users the right to copy, redistribute, and reuse the work for any purpose, including commercially, provided that attribution is given to the creator.

b. **CC BY SA** (https://creativecommons.org/licenses/by-sa/4.0/)

Grants users the right to copy, redistribute, and reuse the work for any purpose, including commercially, provided that attribution is given to the creator and that any modified versions of the work are redistributed under the same license as the original work.

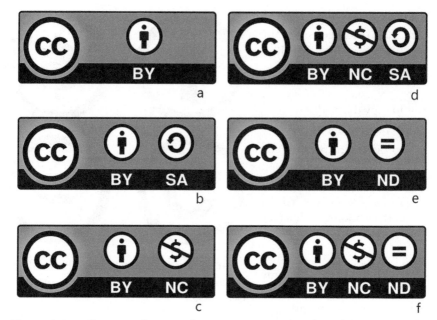

Figure 3.3 "The six BY licenses" by Creative Commons (2020), licensed under CC BY 4.0.

c. **CC BY NC** (https://creativecommons.org/licenses/by-nc/4.0/)

Grants users the right to copy, redistribute, and reuse the work for noncommercial purposes only, provided that attribution is given to the creator.

d. **CC BY NC SA** (https://creativecommons.org/licenses/by-nc-sa/4.0/)

Grants users the right to copy, redistribute, and reuse the work for noncommercial purposes only, provided that attribution is given to the creator and that any modified versions of the work are redistributed under the same license as the original work.

e. **CC BY ND** (https://creativecommons.org/licenses/by-nd/4.0/)

Grants users the right to copy, redistribute, and use the work for any purpose, including commercially, provided that attribution is given to the creator and that any modified versions of the work are not redistributed.

f. **CC BY NC ND** (https://creativecommons.org/licenses/by-nc-nd/4.0/)

Grants users the right to copy, redistribute, and reuse the work for noncommercial purposes only, provided that attribution is given to the creator and that any modified versions of the work are not redistributed.

The diversity of CC licenses constitutes an indispensable part of the CC approach toward licensing. According to Lessig, CC prefers to "listen to what creators and consumers say" in order to meet their diverse needs rather than "[march] in with a set of defined principles that come from who knows where, and [impose] those regardless of the views of those who live in that particular domain" (quoted in Poynder 2006).

Figure 3.4 "CC0 and Public Domain Mark" by Creative Commons (2020), licensed under CC BY 4.0.

In addition to the six core licenses, CC offers creators two public domain tools, as shown in Figure 3.4.

a. **CC0** (https://creativecommons.org/publicdomain/zero/1.0/) Known as the "public domain dedication" tool, CC0 (read as "CC zero") allows creators to waive all of their copyrights and dedicate the work to the public domain.[22]

b. **The Public Domain Mark (PDM)** (https://creativecommons.org/share -your-work/public-domain/pdm/)

   This tool functions as the "No Known Copyright" label.[23]

By any measure, CC licenses are the most widely used open content licenses in the world. At the time of this writing, there are more than 2 billion CC-licensed works available on the Internet.[24] While initially set up in the United States, CC has a number of affiliated networks across the globe. In 2013, CC created a suite of international licenses that can be adapted to suit different jurisdictions, regardless of the work's country of origin.[25]

Misconceptions about Open Content Licensing and Copyright

There are two common misconceptions about open content licensing and copyright. The first misconception is that it opposes or undermines copyright law. In fact, quite the opposite is true. Open content licensing, in all its forms, exists within the copyright law and relies on it for its validity. More specifically:

- Works released under an open content license must be copyrighted
- The licensor must be the copyright holder to the work being licensed
- The grant of rights included in the license must last for the duration of the work's copyright

- The types of use and reuse of openly licensed content are already permitted by copyright law
- Users who—intentionally or unintentionally—violate the license terms are treated as copyright infringers and, as such, become subject to liability for their offenses

Some jurisdictions require that an open content license must include a waiver of the copyright holder's moral rights. The United States, which recognizes moral rights on a limited basis, does not require a waiver of moral rights, unless the licensed content falls within the category of works that are afforded a limited recognition of moral rights.[26]

The second misconception about open content licensing and copyright is that works released under an open content license automatically belong in the public domain where these works exist in the "no rights reserved" context. Quite to the contrary: open content licenses are based on the "some rights reserved" approach, which acknowledges the rights of users to build upon the works of others, while protecting the rights of authors. This approach is particularly important in the digital environment, where it is easy to copy and distribute vast amounts of copyrighted materials without asking permission of the copyright holders. In this sense, the open content licensing model fills the gap between the default "all rights reserved" approach of copyright law and the "no rights reserved" rule of the public domain. Although the authors can waive all of their rights and place the work into the public domain by using, for example, the Creative Commons' public domain dedication tool CC0, the nature and goal of openly licensed content is different from that of the public domain, where no one owns or controls the content in any way.

Furthermore, at the heart of the concept of open content licensing are these three fundamental principles of copyright law:

1. The author of a creative and original work is that work's copyright holder as soon as the work is fixed in a tangible medium of expression.[27]

2. A copyright holder is automatically granted a "bundle" of exclusive rights, which include:

    - The right to reproduce copies of the work
    - The right to distribute copies of the work
    - The right to perform and display the work publicly
    - The right to make derivative works based on the original work[28]

3. A copyright holder has legal power to transfer some or all of these rights to others.

Open content licensing enables creators to retain some of these rights while relinquishing other rights to the public through licensing. In other words, open content licensing enables the authors to "unbundle" the "bundle" of their exclusive rights and articulate which rights they want to reserve for themselves and which rights they want to grant to others. This approach helps balance the creator's freedoms with the user's obligations in order to facilitate the environment where the sharing and building upon the works of others become a norm.

Benefits and Drawbacks of Open Content Licensing

Most benefits and drawbacks of open content licensing are essentially the same for both creators and users. As Kreutzer (2011, 116) puts it, "authors are 'creative users' or 'using creators'—especially in the digital world."

The benefits of open content licensing include:

- Access to a vast pool of royalty-free works that can be used, redistributed, and built upon
- Ability to control how the work can be used and reused by others
- Simplified distribution and sharing of copyrighted content without a "middleman," such as a publisher, an agent, or other distributor of works
- Transparent copyright management, minimizing risks from litigation for copyright infringement
- Availability of "human-readable" versions of licenses that are easy to understand by a lay person[29]
- Opportunity to showcase the work that can help authors attain recognition or enhance their reputation
- Opportunity to meet the open access requirements of funding agencies
- Reduced transaction costs compared to conventional licensing practices
- Worldwide validity of open content licenses

Drawbacks of open content licensing include:

- Perpetuity and irrevocability of open content licenses
- Possibility of violation of third parties' rights when republishing works, particularly the works that have been previously published commercially
- Inability to combine or merge content released under conflicting licenses, for example, under the licenses with divergent "Share Alike" provisions
- Inability to reuse content due to the "No Derivatives" requirement imposed by some licenses

- Restriction to noncommercial use imposed by some open content licenses
- Difficulty drawing a line between commercial and noncommercial use, as "no activity is completely disconnected from commercial activity"[30]
- Potential loss of commercial gain that might result from "giving away" some of the copyrights
- Difficulty tracking and correctly articulating required attributions when multiple works are combined into a single work (known as "attribution stacking")
- Difficulty tracking various work modifications
- Concerns that others might take advantage of the work by plagiarizing it, making a profit from selling it, or otherwise unethically exploiting it
- Difficulty of enforcing the license terms
- Potential interoperability between jurisdictions of different countries

As any forward-looking model, open content licensing has drawn both praise and criticism. Some proponents of this model describe it as "an exceedingly beneficial alternative model for the regulation of access to and use of works of authorship" (Kreutzer 2011, 119). Others hail it as a "re-imagined" copyright system where "authors are not individual rights-holders but contributors to a collective conversation" and "users are not trespassers but participants in a public dialogue" (Craig 2011, 57). Skeptics, on the other hand, consider the reliance of open content licensing on copyright as "ideological fuzziness" (Elkin-Koren 2005, 377) and an attempt "to subvert the [copyright] regime from within" by using copyright's own strategies (Dusollier 2007, 1394). Corbett (2011, 527) echoes this argument by stating that "a fatal disconnect between copyright law and civil society [. . .] cannot be remedied by strategies which rely upon copyright law for their very existence." Others argue that the open content licensing model is "suitable only for amateur or 'home-made' content from which creators did not intend to profit in the first place" (Bloemsaat and Kleve 2009, 248). Yet others criticize open content licenses for not being based on ethical principles of true openness and freedom, like Stallman's free software philosophy, but rather advocating an idea of reserving the rights of copyright holders instead of granting these rights to the users (Cramer 2006; Hill 2005).

Notes

1. The Free Software Movement and the Open Source Initiative are discussed in Chapter 2.

2. Even though an open content license can be applied to any type of material, only open file formats (versus proprietary or patented file formats) could ensure access to and reusability of the material. According to The Open

Definition, an open format is "a format with a freely available published specification which places no restrictions, monetary or otherwise, upon its use" (https://opendefinition.org/ofd/).

3. The term "OpenContent" in the name of the project is mashed together in the original.

4. Originally, there were the 4Rs (Reuse, Revise, Remix, and Redistribute). Wiley introduced the fifth R (Retain) seven years after he had introduced the idea of the 4Rs.

5. Open Knowledge Foundation (https://okfn.org).

6. The Open Definition (https://opendefinition.org).

7. The full version of the Open Definition is available at: https://opendefinition .org/od/2.1/en/.

8. Definition of Free Cultural Works (DFCW) (https://freedomdefined.org /Definition).

9. See Creative Commons. "Understanding Free Cultural Works" at: https:// creativecommons.org/share-your-work/public-domain/freeworks.

10. The archived version of the OpenContent License can be found at: http:// web.archive.org/web/20030806033000/http://www.opencontent.org/opl.shtml.

11. For a description of the General Public License, see Chapter 2.

12. The archived version of the Open Publication License can be found at: http://opencontent.org/openpub/.

13. The Free Art License is available at: https://artlibre.org/licence/lal/en/.

14. The term "OpenMusic" in the name of the project is mashed together in the original.

15. The Green License is available at: http://openmusic.linuxtag.org/green.html.

16. The Yellow License is available at: http://openmusic.linuxtag.org/yellow.html.

17. The Creative Commons Inc. (http://creativecommons.org)

18. Even though CC licenses can be applied to software, CC "strongly encourages" using the licenses specifically designed for software such as open source licenses (https://creativecommons.org/faq).

19. See Legal Code Defined at: https://creativecommons.org/legal-code-defined/.

20. See the Creative Commons FAQ, answering the question "What happens if the author decides to revoke the CC license to material I am using?" at: https:// creativecommons.org/faq/.

21. Proponents of "true freedom," including Richard Stallman, refuse to support Creative Commons because, they argue, the NonCommercial and No Derivatives clauses are incompatible with the concept of freedom (See GNU Operating System, *Various Licenses and Comments about Them* at: https://www .gnu.org/licenses/license-list.en.html#NonFreeDocumentationLicenses).

22. CC0 is not a license in itself, but a tool to use in certain jurisdictions, for example, in Germany and some other European countries, which limit or prohibit a complete waiver of copyright. For an explanation of how to use CC0, see https://creativecommons.org/share-your-work/public-domain/cc0/.

23. PDM is not a legal document. It simply indicates that a work is already free of known copyright restrictions.

24. See Creative Commons at: https://creativecommons.org.

25. See the Creative Commons FAQ, answering the question "What are the international ('unported') Creative Commons licenses, and why does CC offer 'ported' licenses?" at: https://creativecommons.org/faq/.

26. See 17 U.S. Code § 106A. Rights of certain authors to attribution and integrity at: https://www.copyright.gov/title17/92chap1.html#106a.

27. Exceptions to this principle include the following situations: when the work has been produced by a government agency or created for an employer ("work for hire") or when the author transferred the copyright to someone else, for example, to a publisher.

28. There are some exceptions and limitations to this power, such as fair use, library exception, the TEACH Act, and classroom exception, that permit certain uses of copyrighted works by individuals, libraries, and educators without obtaining permission from the copyright holders.

29. This argument applies primarily to Creative Commons licenses. In many cases, the wording of open content licenses requires legal interpretation, and this might discourage some people from making use of the work (Kreutzer 2011).

30. CC Wiki: Noncommercial Interpretation (https://wiki.creativecommons .org/wiki/NonCommercial_interpretation).

Suggested Readings

Creative Commons. *Creative Commons for Educators and Librarians*. Chicago: American Library Association, 2020.

Crews, Kenneth D. *Copyright Law for Librarians and Educators: Creative Strategies and Practical Solutions*. Chicago: American Library Association, 2020.

Guibault, Lucie, and Christina Angelopoulos, eds. *Open Content Licensing: From Theory to Practice*. Amsterdam: Amsterdam University Press, 2011.

Lessig, Lawrence. *The Future of Ideas: The Fate of the Commons in a Connected World*. New York: Vintage Books, 2002.

Suggested Resources

Creative Commons License Selector
https://creativecommons.org/choose/
A tool developed by Creative Commons. Enables users to select a Creative Commons license based on the needs and preferences of an individual creator.

CC Meta Search
https://search.creativecommons.org
A search engine developed by Creative Commons. Searches the Web for openly licensed and public domain works, including images, video, and audio. Search results can be filtered by commercial or noncommercial use, license, resource type, size, and source.

CHAPTER FOUR

Open Access (OA)

Redefining Scholarly Publishing

. . . if we envision the world communities of scientists as a complex network of distributed intelligence, open access now appears as one of the essential means to make it work in a fuller, more efficient, fashion. It also appears as a tool to move toward an even playing field in scientific research and education.

—Jean-Claude Guédon (2006, 28–29)

In October 2003, the Public Library of Science (PLoS) published the first issue of its open access journal *PLoS Biology*, in which Duke University researchers Miguel Nicoleis and Jose Carmena publicized their research findings about how they had trained monkeys with brain implants to move a robot arm with their thoughts, a discovery that might one day allow paraplegics to perform similar functions. That first issue of *PLoS Biology* received more than half a million hits throughout the world within a few hours after its publication, even bringing down the server temporarily. "Nothing else has ever argued so strongly for open-access publishing," observed the founders of PLoS, Michael Eisen, a biologist at Lawrence Berkeley National Laboratory; Harold Varmus, one of the 1989 Nobel laureates in Physiology or Medicine; and Patrick Brown, a biochemist at Stanford University, whose intention was "to do something that fundamentally changes the way scientific research is communicated" (Eisen 2003, 6). If open access succeeds, they continued, "everyone with an Internet connection will be a click away from a comprehensive online public library of scientific and medical knowledge" (Ibid.).

The advent of the open access publishing model is generally attributed to three forces:

1. A steady escalation in scholarly journal prices, known as the "serials pricing crisis," which forced many libraries to cancel their journal subscriptions.[1]
2. The increased migration of scholarly journal publishing from print to electronic formats that expedited and simplified the ways research could be disseminated to a worldwide audience.
3. The widespread use of restrictive copyright and licensing barriers and access control technologies that blocked access to electronic publications by unauthorized users and caused, in the words of Suber (2003), "the permission crisis."

These countervailing forces—some hindering and some facilitating knowledge distribution—resulted in a serious concern among scholars and librarians about the limitations of the traditional publishing system in which large commercial publishers hold a monopoly over the distribution of research findings. This monopoly has been cited as one of the major factors underlying an enormous increase in the cost of commercial journal subscriptions that has negatively affected the purchasing power of many academic libraries. Consequently, this situation limited the scholars' ability to reach an audience beyond the customers who can afford to pay for subscriptions and therefore excluded large parts of the research community from scholarly interaction, especially in developing countries (Guédon 2001, 2006; Martin 2014; Schlimgen and Kronenfeld 2004; Suber 2012). While many publishers and researchers still believe that there is no better way to disseminate research findings than through the traditional subscription-based model, a growing number of initiatives are advocating for a redefined publishing paradigm, known as open access.

In the simplest terms, open access (henceforth OA) means that full-text scholarly literature is available online, free of charge, and free of most legal and technological restrictions on access or use. As Peter Suber, one of the leading OA advocates, explains it, "The basic idea of OA is simple: Make research literature available online without price barriers and without most permission barriers" (2012, 8).

While a continuing move toward open access to knowledge is one of the most far-reaching transformations in current scholarly publishing, it is not an entirely new paradigm. Martin (2020, 8) writes:

> The age-old question of open access to knowledge descends from several traditions of scholarship. As Weller (2014, 139) affirms, "the story of open scholarship has been one of steady adaptation and growth rather than

sudden revolution." This story can be traced back to Gutenberg's invention of the printing press around 1445 that simplified duplication of scholarly materials previously only done by hand in monasteries and libraries. The Royal Society of London, established in 1662, put in place the first institutional mechanisms for promoting scientific activity, protecting the rights of authors, and governing science as public knowledge in early modern Europe. In particular, the Society's publication *Philosophical Transactions* encouraged scholars "to abandon their attachment to secrecy and to submit their work to the judgment of its fellows" (Eamon 1985, 344). Henry Oldenburg, the Society's secretary, who established a systematic correspondence with the scholars throughout Europe and provided a public forum for the announcement and discussion of new scientific discoveries, was among the first individuals to promote the idea of openness in scholarly communication (Hall 1965, 2002). The concept of openness in scholarship also descends from the ideas of French Encyclopedists of the eighteenth century who strived to disseminate existing knowledge to the public with the intention of improving society through education. The teachings of Rousseau, Montessori, and Dewey, who advocated openness as an important educational value, are also precursors of the concept of openness in scholarship.[2]

More recent steps toward OA can be traced back to the mid-1960s with the advent of computers being connected through a networked infrastructure. However, the OA publishing approach itself had started in the late 1980s to early 1990s when a few pioneering journals, such as *New Horizons in Adult Education, Psycoloquy,* and *The Public-Access Computer Systems Review,* among others, began offering free online access to research papers by utilizing volunteer labor and without an intent to generate profit (Bailey 2006). These journals allowed their authors to retain copyright to their papers, thereby applying an open content licensing approach,[3] which, a decade later, has been adopted by Creative Commons, Inc. (Ibid.). The OA publishing model had gained momentum in the early 2000s when three declarations, namely the Budapest Open Access Initiative, the Bethesda Statement on Open Access Publishing, and the Berlin Declaration on Open Access to Knowledge in the Sciences and Humanities, commonly known as the BBB declarations, transformed and shaped the publishing environment in successive decades.

The Budapest Open Access Initiative

The Budapest Open Access Initiative (BOAI)[4] issued a public statement that arose from a conference held by the Open Society Institute in Budapest in December 2001. The BOAI statement was released to the public on February 14, 2002, and initially was signed only by 16 publishers, scholars, and administrators.[5] It was the first document to define the term "open access" and encapsulate the key principles of OA laid out in the following paragraph:

> The literature that should be freely accessible online is that which scholars give to the world without expectation of payment. Primarily, this category encompasses their peer-reviewed journal articles, but it also includes any unreviewed preprints that they might wish to put online for comment or to alert colleagues to important research findings. [. . .] By "open access" to this literature, we mean its free availability on the public internet, permitting any users to read, download, copy, distribute, print, search, or link to the full texts of these articles, crawl them for indexing, pass them as data to software, or use them for any other lawful purpose, without financial, legal, or technical barriers other than those inseparable from gaining access to the internet itself. The only constraint on reproduction and distribution, and the only role for copyright in this domain, should be to give authors control over the integrity of their work and the right to be properly acknowledged and cited. (BOAI 2002)

The key principles of OA outlined in the BOAI statement can be summarized as follows:

1. OA literature primarily includes peer-reviewed journal articles but may also include preprints.
2. OA literature is available online and therefore either digitized or born digital.
3. OA literature is available free of charge.
4. Authors of OA literature are not expecting payment for their efforts.
5. OA literature can be used for any lawful purpose without any financial, legal, or technical constraints.
6. The only requirements for the use of OA literature are the proper attribution of the authorship and assurance of the work's integrity.

To achieve OA to peer-reviewed journal literature and preprints, the BOAI recommended (but not required) two strategies:

1. Publishing in open access journals (i.e., publishing in online journals that do not charge users subscription or access fees and where most restrictions on use and reuse have been lifted)
2. Self-archiving (i.e., depositing peer-reviewed journal articles and preprints in an OA repository, a digital platform that hosts and provides free access to research outputs)

The Bethesda Statement on Open Access Publishing

The Bethesda Statement on Open Access Publishing,[6] which originated at a 2003 meeting held at the Howard Hughes Medical Institute in Maryland, expanded the BOAI definition of OA.[7] According to the Bethesda Statement, an OA publication must meet the following two conditions:

1. "The author(s) and copyright holder(s) grant(s) to all users a free, irrevocable, worldwide, perpetual right of access to, and a license to copy, use, distribute, transmit and display the work publicly and to make and distribute derivative works, in any digital medium for any responsible purpose, subject to proper attribution of authorship, as well as the right to make small numbers of printed copies for their personal use.

2. A complete version of the work and all supplemental materials, including a copy of the permission as stated above, in a suitable standard electronic format is deposited immediately upon initial publication in at least one online repository that is supported by an academic institution, scholarly society, government agency, or other well-established organization that seeks to enable open access, unrestricted distribution, interoperability, and long-term archiving (for the biomedical sciences, PubMed Central is such a repository)." (Bethesda Statement on Open Access Publishing 2003)

The Bethesda Statement differed from the BOAI definition of OA in three important points:

1. It defined an additional user right with regard to OA publications: the right to make *derivative* works without requiring permission.

2. It specified that the user's "free, irrevocable, worldwide, perpetual" rights are granted to them by the copyright holder(s) under a license (e.g., under an open license).

3. It required (versus recommended) that the full versions of OA articles must be deposited "immediately upon initial publication" in online repositories maintained by "well-established" organizations (versus, for example, author webpages) for "long-term archiving."

The Berlin Declaration on Open Access to Knowledge in the Sciences and Humanities

The Berlin Declaration on Open Access to Knowledge in the Sciences and Humanities[8] was drafted at the 2003 Conference on Open Access to Knowledge in the Sciences and Humanities[9] hosted by the Max Planck Society and the European Cultural Heritage Online (ECHO) project. The definition of OA proposed by the Berlin Declaration was almost identical to the definitions offered by the two previous statements. However, it expanded the scope of those statements, which encompassed primarily peer-reviewed journal literature, to include OA for other types of research outputs such as "raw data and metadata, source materials, digital representations of pictorial and graphical materials and scholarly multimedia material" (Max-Plank Society 2003).

In 2005, at the follow-up conference, titled "Progress in Implementing the Berlin Declaration on Open Access to Knowledge in the Sciences and Humanities" and later nicknamed "Berlin 3," the conference participants issued an additional statement, which called upon research institutions to do the following:

1. "Implement a policy to *require* their researchers to deposit a copy of all their published articles in an open access repository.
2. *Encourage* their researchers to publish their research articles in open access journals where a suitable journal exists and provide the support to enable that to happen."

    (Max-Plank Society 2005; emphasis added)

To date, the BBB declarations remain the most influential documents that have informed subsequent OA statements issued by various organizations and advocacy groups, including the IFLA Statement on Open Access to Scholarly Literature and Research Documentation (2003),[10] Washington D.C. Principles for Free Access to Science (2004),[11] and Scientific Council Statement on Open Access by European Research Council (2006).[12,13]

Main Strategies for Attaining OA

There are three main strategies for attaining OA to scholarly literature: 1) publishing in an OA journal (gold OA), 2) publishing in a hybrid journal (hybrid OA), and 3) self-archiving (green OA).[14]

Gold OA

The gold OA approach means that full-text peer-reviewed journal articles are available online on the OA journal's website immediately upon publication, free of charge, and free of most restrictions on access or use. Some OA publishers, however, restrict public access to the full text of articles they publish for a specific period of time, often called an embargo period, which can last up to several months or longer. Most OA advocates do not recognize the embargo model as fully open.

Most OA journals are published online by born-OA publishers who produce only OA journals. Examples of born-OA publishers include BioMed Central (BMC),[15] a UK-based publishing house, publishing 300+ journals in all areas of science, medicine, technology, and engineering, and PLoS,[16] a California-based nonprofit company, publishing a suite of journals across all areas of science and medicine. OA journals can be also produced by commercial publishers who are willing to experiment with the OA publishing model. For example, large commercial publishers such as Elsevier, Oxford Academic, and Wiley have switched some of their established subscription-based journals to OA. Finally, OA journals can be produced by nontraditional publishers such as universities, research centers, learned societies, libraries, and individual scholars.[17]

While OA journals are intended to be free for readers, they are not free for OA publishers. The production costs of OA journals include the costs of maintaining a high-quality website, managing peer review and editorial control, and providing technical support. OA journal production costs can be covered, either partially or in full, by the money that comes from institutional membership fees, donations, advertising, and supplemental subscription-based products. Some OA publishers recover these costs through article processing charges (APCs) applied to each article they publish. APCs can be paid by authors or authors' institutions upon acceptance for publication or paid up-front by the authors' research sponsors. However, many OA journals do not charge any APCs, nearly all OA journals waive or substantially reduce APCs in cases of economic hardship, and most (if not all) OA journals offer waivers and discounts to authors based in developing countries. A growing number of academic and research libraries are establishing OA publishing funds (also called campus OA funds) to provide financial support for researchers who wish to publish in OA journals that charge APCs. Depending on the institution's financial capacity, OA publishing funds cover either fully or partially the journal's APCs.[18]

Hybrid OA

The hybrid OA approach refers to an optional model utilized by some commercial publishers who allow their authors to make individual articles, typically funded by APCs, freely available within their subscription-based journals. Examples of publishers utilizing the hybrid OA model include Wiley and Springer that offer their authors the OA publishing options, called, respectively, OnlineOpen and SpringerOpen. Some OA advocates do not recognize the hybrid OA model as open and consider it "double dipping," a process in which the publisher simultaneously profits from two income sources: APC payments and journal subscription charges (Anderson 2013; Björk and Solomon 2014; Pinfield, Salter, and Bath 2016). In response to these accusations, some hybrid journals issue "no double-dipping policies," according to which they decrease their subscription prices based on the number of OA articles published in their journal in previous years.[19]

Green OA

The green OA approach, or self-archiving, is a strategy used by authors to make the digital versions of their scholarly articles, typically in the form of preprints[20] or postprints[21] (collectively referred to as eprints), openly available in an institutional repository or an open access disciplinary archive. Eprints can be uploaded on the author's personal website, in a disciplinary OA repository, or in an institutional repository. Repositories that comply with the metadata harvesting protocol of the Open Archives Initiative (OAI)[22] are interoperable, which means that the repositories' content can be harvested into a single searchable archive where the search engine crawlers can more easily discover it and thus index it. In addition to scholarly articles, self-archived materials can include other documents that have not been published by traditional means such as working papers, technical reports, and conference presentations. Many researchers believe that these unpublished works offer a more immediate path to research findings than published products and thus are as valuable as the final publication itself because they "stimulate intellectual interest and further scholarly pursuits" (Regazzi 2015, 200).

Disciplinary OA repositories are typically sponsored by research organizations and include scholarly materials in one specific discipline or several associated disciplines. Examples of OA disciplinary repositories include arXiv.org[23] and PubMed Central.[24] arXiv.org is the longest-established disciplinary OA repository launched in 1991 and managed by Cornell University. arXiv.org facilitates long-term digital preservation of and open access to eprints in the fields of physics, computer science, mathematics, and quantitative biology. PubMed Central is maintained by the National Library of Medicine at the U.S. National Institutes of Health (NIH). It archives publications in the biomedical and life sciences. It also serves as the designated repository for research papers that fall under the

NIH Public Access Policy and similar policies from other funding agencies.

Institutional repositories (IRs) are typically maintained by academic or research libraries or library consortiums and archive the intellectual output of a single institution or a multi-institutional community. What distinguishes IRs from other types of OA repositories is a greater likelihood of their sustainability. In the words of Bailey (2005, 265), "Funding agencies may decide to stop supporting disciplinary archives with generous grants, or the individuals or organizations that offer them may lose interest. Once established as part of the institutional mission, IRs will persist." The major portion of an IR's content is concentrated on journal articles, book chapters, theses and dissertations, and other scholarly materials authored by the institution's faculty, staff, and students. Some IRs are also archiving and maintaining access to other types of materials such as datasets, presentations, learning and teaching materials, and digitized library materials. What is being included within an IR depends on a policy decision made by each individual institution. Examples of IRs include the DSpace@MIT,[25] an IR maintained by the libraries at the Massachusetts Institute of Technology (MIT), and MD-SOAR (Maryland Shared Open Access Repository),[26] a collaboratively managed repository of several universities and colleges in Maryland.

Even though there are several strategies for attaining OA to scholarly content, these strategies are not mutually exclusive. For example, a researcher may self-archive the same work as an eprint in a disciplinary or institutional repository and then publish the final version of that work in an OA or a hybrid journal. Using these strategies in combination increases the likelihood that the scholarly content will be found and used by other researchers.[27]

OA Monographs

Even though OA monograph publishing still remains in its early stages, it has been increasingly incorporated into the larger landscape of open scholarship (Grimme et al. 2019; Pyne et al. 2019). A few major academic publishers have begun to offer OA publishing options for monographs. For example, Springer offers its authors the opportunity to publish their books in the OA manner and encourages them to self-archive the final published PDF in their respective institutional repositories or in other OA archives.[28] Some university presses, such as UCL Press in the United Kingdom and Amherst College Press in the United States, have shifted their publishing models exclusively to OA in order to increase the visibility of their publications, including monographs. Libraries, university presses, and other organizations are partnering on initiatives to experiment with OA monograph publishing and financing models. For example, TOME (Toward an Open Monograph Ecosystem),[29] a pilot project of the Association of American Universities (AAU), Association of Research Libraries (ARL), and Association of University Presses (AUPresses), enables OA monograph publishing through TOME publication grants. Knowledge Unlatched,[30] a global library consortium, offers a crowdsourcing funding model for OA books. Research funders, most notably in Europe, are also developing policies for the support and funding of OA monographs to maximize the impact of the research they support. The European Research Council (ERC), the Wellcome Trust, and the Swiss National Science Foundation (SNSF), among others, mandate OA for monographs supported by their grants and they also provide financial assistance for OA monograph publication.

Notwithstanding these initiatives, OA monographs still constitute a smaller fraction of OA publications relative to journal articles (Grimme et al. 2019). As of late 2021, the Directory of Open Access Books (DOAB)[31] lists about 47,200 titles compared to nearly 7 million journal articles listed in the Directory of Open Access Journals (DOAJ). This situation has been attributed to several factors, including the diversity of book publishing practices and business models (sometimes referred to as "bibliodiversity"), higher publishing cost and higher associated book processing charges (BPCs) paid either by authors or their sponsors, and lower research funding available for disciplines in which monographs remain the predominant form of scholarship, such as in the humanities and most of the social sciences (cOAlition S 2021; Grimme et al. 2019; Pyne et al. 2019).

OA and Copyright

The transfer of copyright for a work from an author to the publisher as a condition of publication is still a common practice. When transferring copyright to the publisher, an author actually transfers the entire bundle of exclusive rights, namely the rights for reproduction, distribution, public performance and display, and creation of derivative works. This means that the publisher holds a monopoly over the distribution of the original work and that its use—and, consequently, its reach and impact—is limited for the author and the users alike because it is dependent on the publisher's permission. Unless specifically addressed in the publishing agreement, often called the copyright transfer agreement, this also means that the author loses control over the work and cannot freely distribute it, allow open access to it, or reuse portions of it in a subsequent work.

The practice of transferring the copyright exclusively to the publisher is most prevalent in the traditional subscription-based system, although some OA publishers require authors to sign away the copyright to the journal as well. The majority of OA journals, however, allow authors to retain the copyright to their work. Moreover, they encourage their authors (and, in some cases, require them) to release their works under an open content license, such as a Creative Commons (CC) license, to maximize the reuse of their work by others. In particular, use of the CC Attribution license (CC BY), which allows for unrestricted reuse of the content subject only to the attribution requirement, is strongly supported by many OA publishers. BMC, PLoS, Hindawi, and eLife, among other OA publishers, require use of the CC BY license as the default for works they publish. For example, PLoS states on its website that all PLoS authors must release their papers under the CC BY license so that "anyone can reuse [PLoS papers] in whole or part for any purpose, for free, even for commercial purposes [. . .] as long as the author and original source are properly cited" (PLoS ONE, n.d.). Although OA journal articles are free of most copyright restrictions, authors are advised to retain some of their copyrights to prevent, for example, the distribution of misattributed or distorted copies of their original papers.

Some commercial publishers are also adopting the use of CC licenses for the OA articles published in their hybrid journals. For example, OA articles published in SpringerOpen journals are released under the CC BY license, which allows these articles "to be freely downloaded from the SpringerOpen website, and to be re-used and re-distributed without restriction, as long as the original work is correctly cited" (SpringerOpen, n.d.). Wiley's OA journals and the hybrid journals with the OnlineOpen option (with the exception of a few society-owned journals) publish OA articles under the CC licenses.

The Scholarly Publishing and Academic Resources Coalition (SPARC) has developed the Addendum to Publication Agreement, a legal document that modifies a publisher's standard copyright transfer agreement.[32] If accepted by the publisher, the addendum allows the author to retain individual copyrights to a work, for example, the right to self-archive the work in an OA disciplinary or institutional repository or reuse portions of it in a subsequent work. Retaining the right to self-archive is becoming increasingly important to authors whose works fall under research funders' public access mandates that require grant recipients to share the published results of their research with the public. SHERPA/RoMEO,[33] a service managed by SHERPA (Securing a Hybrid Environment for Research Preservation and Access), can help authors address the uncertainty of copyright compliance when self-archiving. SHERPA/RoMEO includes publishers' policies on whether an author is permitted to self-archive, where, and under what conditions.

OA and Peer Review

Because the production cost of OA journals is often underestimated, the term "open access" is often used synonymously with the term "free." This misunderstanding has led some scholars to believe that OA journals are not peer reviewed and, therefore, of poor quality. This belief may affect the scholars' decision on where to submit their papers in favor of subscription-based journals.

Peer review is still considered one of the most common quality control mechanisms in scholarly journal publishing, including OA publishing. Similarly to traditional journals, reputable OA journals provide peer review and other editorial services, which are largely sustained by volunteer effort, in order to maintain the high quality and integrity of works they publish. Some OA journals provide a traditional "blind" peer review, in which both the author of the work and the reviewers remain anonymous, while other OA journals experiment with an open peer review, in which the reviewers' identities are disclosed and included in the peer review evaluations that might be published alongside the article.[34] OA disciplinary and institutional repositories do not conduct peer review but simply make their content freely available on the Web. However, these repositories often contain journal articles that were first published in peer-reviewed journals before being made accessible through a repository.

OA Policies and Mandates

Research funding agencies increasingly require their grant recipients to share the published results of their research and associated unclassified data with the public. Public access mandates not only help maximize the accountability and impact of the federal research investment, they also provide scholars with additional strategies for ensuring the widest possible dissemination and reuse of their research output, as well as its long-term storage and stewardship.

The Public Access to Science Act

In 2003, Minnesota Congressman Martin Sabo introduced in the House of Representatives a bill entitled the Public Access to Science Act. This bill aimed to address copyright restrictions in scientific publishing by proposing an amendment to Title 17 of the U.S. Code,[35] which outlines United States copyright law. According to Sabo's bill, the works resulting from scientific research "substantially funded by the Federal Government" must be excluded from copyright protection and become public domain (U.S. Congress 2003). Since scientific research is largely funded by tax dollars, Sabo argued, the results of this research "[belong] to, and should be freely available to, every person in the United States" (Ibid.). Although Sabo's bill was never voted on, it was the first legislative attempt to affect copyright law by expanding and speeding up public access to scientific research.

The NIH Public Access Policy

In 2008, the U.S. NIH implemented the Public Access Policy to ensure that the public has access to the published results of research projects funded by the NIH. The policy required all researchers to submit electronic versions of their final peer-reviewed manuscripts that arise from NIH funds to PubMed Central (PMC), a digital archive maintained by the National Library of Medicine. The manuscripts, including graphics, data, and other supplemental materials, must be deposited in PMC immediately upon acceptance for publication and made openly available on the Web no later than 12 months after publication[36] (National Institutes of Health 2008). Unlike Sabo's bill, the NIH Public Access Policy was implemented "in a manner consistent with [existing] copyright law" (Ibid.), which means that the copyright initially belongs to the author of an NIH-funded research article and then may be transferred to a journal in which the article is published. In 2013, NIH issued the document reinforcing its Public Access Policy. According to this document, titled "Changes to Public Access Policy Compliance Efforts Apply to All Awards with Anticipated Start Dates on or after July 1, 2013,"[37] NIH would withhold funds from researchers who do not comply with the Public Access Policy (National Institutes of Health 2013).

The approach taken by the NIH has been modeled by other federal funding agencies in the United States. For example, the National Science Foundation (NSF), the Howard Hughes Medical Institute, and the National Aeronautics and Space Administration (NASA) are among the agencies that have adopted similar policies necessitating public access to government-funded research.[38] Public access policies are also increasing in numbers in other countries. For example, the Australian Research Council, the Canadian Institutes of Health Research (CIHR), and the Wellcome Trust in the United Kingdom have implemented policies necessitating public access to government-funded research.

The America COMPETES Reauthorization Act of 2010

In 2010, President Barack Obama signed into law the America Creating Opportunities to Meaningfully Promote Excellence in Technology, Education, and Science (COMPETES) Reauthorization Act of 2010.[39] This act helped ensure broader public access to federally funded research by introducing two requirements: 1) it required the establishment of an Interagency Public Access Committee to coordinate "dissemination and long-term stewardship of the results of unclassified research, including peer-reviewed publications and digital data, supported by Federal science agencies" and 2) it directed the Office of Science and Technology Policy in the White House to develop policies that would facilitate online access to and long-term preservation of unclassified federal scientific collections "for the benefit of the scientific enterprise" (U.S. Congress 2011).

The Office of Science and Technology Policy Memorandum

In 2013, the Office of Science and Technology Policy (OSTP) released the memorandum entitled "Increasing Access to the Results of Federally Funded Scientific Research." This memorandum directed each U.S. federal agency with over $100 million in annual extramural research and development expenditures to develop a "clear and coordinated" policy to make the results of research funded by the federal government (including unclassified research published in peer-reviewed scholarly publications and digital data) freely available to the public "to the greatest extent and with the fewest constraints possible and consistent with law" (Holdren 2013). This memorandum also required federal agencies to ensure that results of federally funded research are stored for long-term preservation in a reputable digital repository maintained by the agency funding the research or through the partnership with other organizations such as scholarly associations, libraries, and publishers.

Plan S

Plan S was put forward in 2018 by cOAlition S,[40] an international consortium of research funding organizations. The goal of Plan S is to make scientific publications that result from research funded by members of the cOAlition S "immediately open access at the point of publication under open licenses" (cOAlition S, n.d.). At the time of this writing, Plan S is supported by 29 influential organizations, including Wellcome Trust, UK Research & Innovation, Bill & Melinda Gates Foundation, the Howard Hughes Medical Institute, and World Health Organization.

Effective 2021, the three main routes to Plan S compliance include:

1. Publication in an OA journal, defined by Plan S as a journal "where all peer-reviewed research articles are openly available from the point of publication."
2. Publication on an OA publishing platform such as the Wellcome Open Research and Gates Open Research platforms that aggregate openly available peer-reviewed articles.
3. Deposition of either the final published version of an article or the manuscript accepted for publication in an OA repository without an embargo period.

Regardless of the chosen route to Plan S compliance, cOAlition S members "strongly encourage" and, in some cases, require the deposition of all publications in an OA repository in order to ensure their digital preservation and to maximize their discovery. Under Plan S, authors retain copyright to their works but are required to release them under an open content license, preferably a CC Attribution license (CC-BY). As of 2021, only peer-reviewed articles fall under Plan S, although cOAlition S has already issued a set of recommendations regarding OA for academic books.[41]

Some private foundations are also establishing policies that are similar to those of federal research agencies, including the Andrew W. Mellon Foundation, Bill & Melinda Gates Foundation, William and Flora Hewlett Foundation, Gordon and Betty Moore Foundation, and Microsoft Research. For example, the Bill & Melinda Gates Foundation mandates that all published research resulting from its funding and all data related to the published research results be freely and openly accessible immediately after publication.[42] A growing number of universities have also been issuing OA mandates, according to which the faculty signing the resolutions agree to grant their respective universities a nonexclusive, irrevocable right to distribute their scholarly works worldwide for any noncommercial purpose. Among the institutions that have issued such mandates are Harvard University, Stanford University, and Trinity University.

OA Benefits

OA offers clear benefits to a diverse range of stakeholders, including researchers, publishers, libraries, and anyone who uses scholarly information for research or educational purposes. In the words of the BOAI (2002), OA ensures "completely free and unrestricted access to [peer-reviewed journal literature] by *all scientists, scholars, teachers, students, and other curious minds*" (emphasis added).

Arguments supporting the rationale for OA can be divided into three broad categories—ethical, pragmatic, and economical—thereby making OA "appealing to both altruists and bean counters" (Suber 2011, 182).

Ethical arguments make the case for OA as an essential human right defined by Article 19 of the Universal Declaration of Human Rights as the right "to seek, receive and impart information and ideas through any media and regardless of frontiers" (United Nations General Assembly 1948). OA has also been seen as an opportunity to address the inequality and exclusion implicit in the subscription-based journal publishing industry by treating knowledge as a public good rather than as a commodity. As Suber (2011, 182) states, "[open access] literature excludes no one, or at least no one with an Internet connection." From this perspective, OA is akin in spirit to the Free Software Movement.[43] The Free Software Movement championed by Richard Stallman in the 1980s had a strong humanitarian dimension since it emphasized the rights of software users and aimed to address the "injustice of proprietary software" that "doesn't respect users' freedom and community" (GNU Operating System, n.d.).

Pragmatic arguments for OA are typically more "researcher-centric" (Fecher and Friesike 2014). These arguments highlight such advantages of OA for researchers as the increased visibility and impact of their scholarship, higher citation counts and alternative usage metrics, and an opportunity to comply with the public access mandates issued by research funding agencies. OA also helps improve the credibility and reliability of researchers' scientific claims by making these claims openly available for comment, verification, and critique. Finally, OA fulfills the researchers' need for *timely* access to peer-reviewed publications in their field of study. The need for timely access to research is particularly important for biomedical scientists. As Dorothy Bainton, professor emeritus at the University of California at San Francisco, explains it, "Timely access to a broad range of current scientific publications is a necessity [. . .] for both our clinicians, so that they may care for patients with the most up-to-date data, as well as our scientists who are making the breakthroughs in such areas as cancer, infectious, cardiovascular and neurological diseases" (quoted in Davidson 2003, 4). Chemist Peter Murray-Rust provides an even more concise and straightforward argument in his tweet: "Open Access Saves Lives" (Murray-Rust @petermurrayrust 2020).

OA also offers economic benefits for researchers and readers alike. OA specifically serves those researchers who are employed by institutions with limited funding or who work outside academia and therefore are unable to acquire access to subscription-based journals through library support. OA provides developing-country researchers with greater access to the global peer-reviewed literature, thereby informing and advancing their research, as well as helping them distribute their own scholarship at little or no cost. By doing that, OA creates a more open, inclusive, and equitable worldwide scholarly communication system. As Crawford (2011, 3) argues, OA "serves the community by eliminating wealth as a precursor for access."

For publishers, OA helps reduce the production costs associated with digital rights and subscription management, licensing terms enforcement, and other measures that block access to unauthorized users. As Suber (2011, 182) points out, "[t]his exclusion costs the excluder money." OA also helps publishers reach a wider readership and potential authors faster than is feasible through subscriptions and controlled access. The costs of manuscript preparation, peer review, and dissemination in an OA journal that "dispenses with print and publishes directly to the Internet" are also much lower than in subscription-based journals (Ibid.). For those publishers who still produce print versions of their journals, OA reduces the production costs even further.

For academic libraries and institutions they support, OA provides an opportunity to address the serials pricing crisis by helping them lower their collection development expenses that can be allocated for other purposes. Moreover, OA contributes to the libraries' educational and preservation missions by helping them remove the "permission barrier" (Suber 2012) in the form of publisher copyright restrictions. For example, OA allows libraries to lawfully make multiple copies of research materials for course reserves without the need to pay copyright clearance fees or to migrate these materials to new platforms for long-term preservation.

For industries, OA accelerates the production process by making new research findings directly available to a wide range of stakeholders who can use them more effectively and more rapidly in future research and practice, thereby increasing return on the industries' financial investment. Lastly, OA helps return the results of research back to the taxpayers since a substantial subset of government-funded research is supported by public funds. Even though the majority of scientific research is funded by tax dollars, access to that research is not freely available to the taxpayers—it is restricted to those who can afford to pay for journal subscriptions.

OA Challenges

Even though OA publishing is becoming increasingly recognized as a valuable approach to knowledge distribution, it is still being rather slowly accepted in academia. This state of affairs is largely due to the fact that publication in traditional peer-reviewed journals, especially in globally circulated journals with high impact factors published in English, is still a major institutional criterion for professional recognition and career advancement (Altbach 2015; Björk 2004, 2013; Cadez, Dimovski, and Groff 2017; Maron et al. 2019). In some institutions, researchers work in environments where open scholarship is "not only not recognized, but actively discouraged" (Weller 2014, 189).

The shift toward OA publishing practices has been uneven among academic disciplines. This can be explained by the diversity of discipline-specific scholarly communication cultures, availability of funding to cover article processing charges, and varying degrees of pressure from funding agencies to provide public access to research publications (Björk and Korkeamaki 2020; Eve 2017; Severin et al. 2018). OA practices have gained wider acceptance in the biological and medical sciences, where research is traditionally reported in peer-reviewed journal articles and where timely access to the latest research findings can be crucial for making scientific breakthroughs (Martin 2014). Support from the government has also played an important role in advancing OA practices in biomedical disciplines, where public access to federally funded research has been increasingly mandated by major funding agencies.

On the other side of the disciplinary spectrum are the humanities, where the uptake of OA practices has been the lowest compared to other disciplines (Eve, 2014; Maron et al. 2016; Suber 2014). A potential factor influencing this situation is that the shelf life of monographs—the primary form of research output in the humanities—is much longer than that of journal articles and that the full cost of monograph publishing is much higher (Ibid.). Moreover, relatively few humanities scholars depend on external funding for their scholarship, and thus, they are less likely to be subject to public access mandates, not to mention that such mandates generally exclude monographs. Another potential factor affecting growth of OA in the humanities is that their journals tend to have higher rejection rates than journals in the sciences and, therefore, they must charge higher article-processing fees for every published paper (Suber 2014). Suber also notes that general skepticism about OA has been greater among humanists because they have so far had "fewer working examples [of OA] to dispel misunderstandings, generate enthusiasm and inspire commitment" (Ibid., xi).

In the social sciences, proliferation of OA practices has been consistently higher than in the humanities but lower than in the biomedical sciences (Liu and Li 2018; Severin et al. 2020). According to a recent study conducted by Crawford (2020), the number of OA journals within the social sciences accounted for 29% of all journals included in the Directory of Open Access Journals (DOAJ). However, researchers in the social sciences were among the earliest adopters of self-archiving in OA repositories (green OA) as a means of sharing their published and unpublished manuscripts via online repositories (Severin et al. 2020; Soderberg, Errington, and Nosek 2020). Economics, in particular, was one of the first disciplines to establish a preprint archive, RePec (Research Papers in Economics),[44] as early as 1993. Other prominent examples include the Social Science Open Access Repository,[45] SocArXiv,[46] and the Social Science Research Network (now known as SSRN)[47] founded in 1994 and acquired by Elsevier in 2016. Some authors speculate that the widespread use of self-archiving as the preferred route to OA might have lessened the social scientists' need to make the transition from "the faster, surer, and already more heavily traveled green road of OA self-archiving" (Harnad et al. 2004) to the gold road of publishing in OA journals (Pölönen and Laakso 2022; Severin et al. 2020).

Digital technologies themselves, while essentially enabling OA, impose some technological, economic, and sociocultural constraints on the greater use of OA resources. These constraints include nonexistent or unreliable Internet connections in some areas of the world, censorship or filtering restrictions on accessing certain types of web-based materials in some cultures, inadequate access for users with disabilities, and language barriers for non-English speakers (Suber 2012). Even though OA is not tied exclusively to particular environments or cultures, the degree to which OA access practices are adopted is still technology dependent, and thus, comparisons between scholarly cultures are inevitable.

For some scholars, however, the complete transition to OA is "less a battle with external forces usurping practice, but more an internal one, between existing practice and opportunities available" (Weller 2014, 150). Internal barriers to OA include psychological "threats" such as information overload due to the increasing availability of OA publications from a diverse range of sources (Veletsianos and Kimmons 2012) and the time and effort it takes "to make the cognitive leaps required for openness to a different mode of thought or a new body of knowledge" (Peters and Roberts 2011, 86–87). Also, the pressure on scholars to make claims to priority of discovery or invention can lead to temporary secrecy about ongoing research, especially in rapidly developing biomedical and engineering fields, where recognition and tenure often depend on who is the first to publish a new research finding and where there is fear of the ideas being "borrowed" by a competitor (Martin 2014).

Finally, the lack of clear understanding of the nature of OA that still exists in academia hinders the complete transition to OA in scholarly publishing. Suber (2009) argues that the OA movement has been held back by "persistent and harmful myths and misunderstandings," namely, the myths that OA bypasses peer review, invites plagiarism and misattribution, and violates copyright, among other misunderstandings.

OA and Predatory Publishing

Even though the proponents of OA consider the traditional commercial publishing system obsolete and believe that the future of scholarly publishing belongs to OA, more skeptical researchers are concerned about the risks posed by open practices and by what "unfettered openness" (Willinsky 2006) could mean for the future of scholarship. Like any innovative process, OA inadvertently generates opportunities for unethical practices such as predatory publishing. Predatory journals—also called parasitic or pseudo journals—are OA publications that exploit the "author-pays" publishing model to earn revenue. Predatory journals *appear* to operate as legitimate scholarly journals but fail to meet high professional standards of scholarly publishing, such as the provision of robust peer review and long-term preservation of published research. They undermine the credibility of the OA publishing model and corrupt the integrity of published research. Predatory publishing also results in a colossal loss of knowledge because predatory publishers could cease their operation at any time and all research published in their journals could disappear from the Web.

Predatory publishing is not an entirely new phenomenon. Before the Internet, it existed in the form of vanity book publishing, where authors paid the publisher up-front for the printing of their works "as is" with minimal or nonexistent quality control or editorial services. Elements of predatory publishing have also been present in "advocacy research" known for reporting only the findings that bolster the author's primary argument.

The coining of the term "predatory publishers" is typically attributed to Jeffrey Beall, a former Scholarly Initiatives librarian at the University of Colorado in Denver, who said: "The reason I call certain publishers predatory is because they *prey* on people. They try to trick honest researchers, and sometimes they are successful" (quoted in Vence 2017; emphasis added). Although, according to Beall's definition, the term "predatory" implies a *deliberate* intent to deceive, not all predatory journals are *deliberately* deceitful. Predatory journals—intentionally or unintentionally—provide a convenient publishing platform for authors who are willing to take "unethical shortcuts" (Beall 2012) in order to publish plagiarized and self-plagiarized work or work of questionable quality. As Anderson (2015) noted, "It's not just about whether authors are being fooled; it's also about whether predatory publishers help authors to fool others." Shen and Björk (2015) provide a similar argument, saying that "most authors are not necessarily tricked into publishing in predatory journals; they probably submit to them well aware of the circumstances and take a calculated risk that experts who evaluate their publication lists will not bother to check the journal credentials in detail."

Given the relative ease with which online journals are created, predatory journals can be run by a small publisher, a group of people, or even a single person. Predatory publishers are notorious for using aggressive email solicitations of potential authors with the promise of guaranteed manuscript acceptance (often dependent on the author's payment), expedited peer review, and speedy publication. They often charge authors publication fees that are typically much lower than the fees of reputable open access journals (Shen and Björk 2015) but might refuse to retract submitted articles, as they aim to publish as many articles as possible to make a profit. They often "prey" upon early-career researchers, who are unfamiliar with scholarly publishing standards and anxious to gain publication experience, as well as researchers affiliated with institutions located in developing countries, who might lack other publishing options (Beall 2012; Frandsen 2017; Shen and Björk 2015; Xia et al. 2015).

Identifying reputable OA journals and avoiding getting scammed by predatory publishers are challenging tasks for many researchers. There is still no agreed-upon definition or standardized criteria of predatory journals. Furthermore, profit-seeking behavior, superficial peer review, and publication of flawed research can be present in legitimate amateur journals as well as in established journals (Berger and Cirasella 2015).

The red flags of potential publishing fraud reported in the literature[48] include:

- Unprofessional journal appearance, including amateur website design and spelling and grammar errors on the journal's website
- Lack of transparency in policies and business practices, such as missing or fake information about editorial board members and unverifiable or false information about the journal headquarters
- Missing or fabricated International Standard Serial Number (ISSN)
- Use of bogus or inflated journal metrics
- False claims about being indexed in prestigious databases or about being included in the Directory of Open Access Journals (DOAJ)

The increased prevalence of predatory journals in the last decade (Cukier et al. 2020a, 2020b; Frandsen 2017; Grudniewicz et al. 2019; Shen and Björk 2015) has led to the development of various blacklists of predatory journals, as well as tools and guidelines intended to help researchers identify trustworthy journals. Jeffrey Beall created a list of OA journals suspected of predatory practices (known as the Beall's List), which is based on predefined criteria such as the lack of a peer review process and the provision of fake information about journal location and editorial boards.[49] Cabell's Scholarly Analytics,[50] a for-profit company, provides Predatory Reports that include information about potentially predatory journals. The DOAJ[51] maintains a publicly available spreadsheet of journals that falsely claim inclusion in the database.[52] Knowledge E,[53] a private company based in Dubai, the United Arab Emirates, created a tool called "Think. Check. Submit,"[54] which provides a step-by-step guide to evaluating the trustworthiness of a journal. The Committee on Publication Ethics (COPE),[55] a nonprofit organization dedicated to promoting ethical publishing practices, provides practical guidance for authors on publishing topics, including predatory publishing. Another source that can help researchers identify reputable OA journals is the Open Access Scholarly Publishers Association (OASPA),[56] an international community representing the interests of OA publishers. OASPA maintains a list of the OASPA-approved members that have passed an in-depth review conducted by the membership committee aiming to determine whether an OA journal "operates with integrity and is genuinely committed to open access publishing" (OASPA, n.d.). One of the OASPA membership criteria includes the presence of peer review policies, which the journal must clearly state on its website.

In addition to predatory journals, there are other types of scholarly "predators" to be aware of such as 1) journal "hijackers," who create a duplicate website for an established scholarly journal and then solicit article submissions for the authentic journal on the hijacked website; 2) predatory monograph publishers, who often target new thesis and dissertation authors to publish their work as books for a fee without a proper editorial process; and 3) predatory conference organizers, who solicit submissions and charge registration fees for poorly organized or nonexistent conferences. In addition to "organizing" poorly or nonexistent conferences, predatory conference organizers may promise researchers to publish their presentations as articles in the journal associated with the conference. Journals associated with predatory conferences are also predatory, and the conference organizers may later insist on additional article processing charges to publish the articles. Knowledge E has developed a guide for evaluating conferences called "Think. Check. Attend,"[57] which can help researchers to differentiate between an authentic conference and a predatory conference.

Notes

1. According to the Association of Research Libraries, libraries' expenditures for ongoing resources, including print and electronic journals, rose by 521% from 1986 to 2015 (Morris and Roebuck 2017). Furthermore, the average journal subscription cost continues to rise (Bosch, Albee, and Romaine 2019, 2020). Although library budgets have also increased during the last decades, they have failed to rise at a rate comparable to inflation (Verminski and Blanchat 2017).

2. More recently, Robert Merton, Basarab Nicolescu, Michael Gibbons, and Peter Suber can also be described as "open knowledge" thinkers.

3. Open content licensing is discussed in Chapter 3.

4. The Budapest Open Access Initiative (BOAI) (https://www.budapest openaccessinitiative.org).

5. To date, the BOAI statement has been signed by over 6,000 individuals and over 1,200 organizations from around the world. (https://www .budapestopenaccessinitiative.org/list_signatures).

6. The Bethesda Statement on Open Access Publishing (http://legacy.earlham .edu/~peters/fos/bethesda.htm).

7. In addition, the Bethesda Statement provided the supplementary statements from three groups of stakeholders—Institutions and Agencies; Libraries and Publishers; and Scientists and Societies.

8. The Berlin Declaration on Open Access to Knowledge in the Sciences and Humanities (https://openaccess.mpg.de/Berlin-Declaration).

9. This conference was later nicknamed the Berlin Conference (Berlin 1).

10. IFLA Statement on Open Access to Scholarly Literature and Research Documentation (https://www.ifla.org/publications/ifla-statement-on-open-access -to-scholarly-literature-and-research-documentation).

11. Washington D.C. Principles for Free Access to Science (https://archive .org/details/WashingtonD.c.PrinciplesForFreeAccessToScience-AStatement From).

12. ERC Scientific Council Statement on Open Access (https://erc.europa.eu /sites/default/files/press_release/files/erc_scc_statement_2006_open_access_0 .pdf).

13. For more information about OA initiatives, visit "Timeline of the Open Access Movement" (http://oad.simmons.edu/oadwiki/Timeline), a wiki maintained by the Open Access Directory and open for community editing.

14. The first use of the terms "gold OA" and "green OA" are generally attributed to Stevan Garnad who used these terms in his critique of Jean-Claude Guédon's article "The 'Green' and 'Gold' Roads to Open Access: The Case for Mixing and Matching" published in 2004 in *Serials Review* 30(4): 315–328. Garnad's critique of this article can be accessed at https://arxiv.org/abs/cs/0503021.

15. BioMed Central (BMC) (https://www.biomedcentral.com).

16. Public Library of Science (PLoS) (https://plos.org).

17. The Scholarly Publishing and Academic Resources Coalition (SPARC) provides guidance on starting a new OA journal or converting an existing subscription-based journal to OA distribution at: https://sparcopen.org/our -work/alternative-publishing-models/open-access-journal-publishing-resource -index/.

18. SPARC provides a guide for setting up an OA publishing fund as well as information regarding existing funds at: https://sparcopen.org/our-work/oa-funds/.

19. See, for example, Elsevier's no double dipping policy at: https://www .elsevier.com/about/policies/pricing.

20. A preprint is the version of an article that has been accepted by a publisher for publication but has not yet undergone formal peer review.

21. A postprint is either the version of an article that has been peer reviewed but not yet copyedited and formatted by a publisher or the final peer-reviewed version of an article after processing by a publisher such as copyediting and formatting changes.

22. The Open Archives Initiative (OAI) (http://www.openarchives.org/).

23. arXiv.org (www.arxiv.org).

24. PubMed Central (PMC) (http://www.ncbi.nlm.nih.gov/pmc/).

25. DSpace@MIT (https://dspace.mit.edu).

26. MD-SOAR (https://mdsoar.org).

27. There are also other, less common strategies for attaining OA to scholarly literature, namely, gratis OA, libre OA, and platinum OA. See the Glossary for definitions of these strategies.

28. Springer. "Publish an Open Access Book with Springer" (https://www .springer.com/gp/open-access/books).

29. TOME (https://www.openmonographs.org).

30. Knowledge Unlatched (https://knowledgeunlatched.org).

31. Directory of Open Access Books (https://www.doabooks.org).

32. The SPARC's Addendum to Publication Agreement is available at: https://sparcopen.org/wp-content/uploads/2016/01/Access-Reuse_Addendum.pdf.

33. SHERPA/RoMEO (http://www.sherpa.ac.uk/romeo).

34. Open peer review is discussed in Chapter 8.

35. The text of Title 17 of the United States Code is available at: https://www.copyright.gov/title17/.

36. Researchers can self-submit their manuscripts directly to PMC via the NIH Manuscript Submission System (NIHMS) (http://nihms.nih.gov/db/sub.cgi). Some journal publishers will automatically deposit NIH-funded articles to PMC on behalf of researchers without a charge no later than 12 months after publication. A list of such publishers can be found at https://publicaccess.nih.gov/submit_process_journals.htm. A selected number of publishers, especially those that produce hybrid journals, will deposit NIH-funded articles to PMC for a fee upon special arrangement with the authors. A list of publishers that make such arrangements can be found at https://publicaccess.nih.gov/select_deposit_publishers.htm.

37. "Changes to Public Access Policy Compliance Efforts Apply to All Awards with Anticipated Start Dates on or after July 1, 2013" (https://grants.nih.gov/grants/guide/notice-files/NOT-OD-13-042.html).

38. SPARC maintains two community-based resources: 1) for tracking U.S federal funder article sharing policies (http://datasharing.sparcopen.org/articles); and 2) for tracking U.S federal funder data sharing requirements (http://datasharing.sparcopen.org/data).

39. This Act, first passed in 2007, was largely based on the 2007 report by the National Academies titled *"Rising Above the Gathering Storm: Energizing and Employing America for a Brighter Economic Future,"* which aimed to boost the economic competitiveness of the United States by increasing federal government support for basic research and STEM education.

40. cOAlition S (https://www.coalition-s.org).

41. cOAlition S statement on Open Access for academic books (https://www.coalition-s.org/coalition-s-statement-on-open-access-for-academic-books/).

42. Bill & Melinda Gates Foundation Open Access Policy. Available at: https://www.gatesfoundation.org/How-We-Work/General-Information/Open-Access-Policy.

43. The Free Software Movement is discussed in Chapter 2.

44. RePec (http://repec.org).

45. Social Science Open Access Repository (https://www.gesis.org/en/ssoar/home).

46. SocArxiv (https://osf.io/preprints/socarxiv).

47. SSRN (https://www.ssrn.com/index.cfm/en).

48. See, for example, Cukier et al. 2020a, 2020b; Shen and Björk 2015; Strinzel et al. 2019.

49. Although Beall's List was taken down in 2017, its archived version is still available at https://beallslist.net.

50. Cabell's Scholarly Analytics (https://www2.cabells.com).

51. Directory of Open Access Journals (DOAJ) (http://www.doaj.org/).

52. The DOAJ's spreadsheet is available at https://docs.google.com /spreadsheets/d/1Y_Sza4rPDkf-NNX9kwiErGrKeNTM75md9B63A_gVpaQ /edit#gid=0.

53. Knowledge E (https://knowledgee.com).

54. Think. Check. Submit. (https://thinkchecksubmit.org).

55. The Committee on Publication Ethics (COPE) (https://publicationethics .org).

56. Open Access Scholarly Publishers Association (OASPA) (https://oaspa .org).

57. Think. Check. Attend. (http://thinkcheckattend.org).

Suggested Readings

Suber, Peter. *Open Access.* Cambridge: MIT Press, 2012.

Willinsky, John. *The Access Principle: The Case for Open Access to Research and Scholarship.* Cambridge: MIT Press, 2006.

Suggested Resources

CHORUS (Clearinghouse for the Open Research of the United States)
https://www.chorusaccess.org
A nonprofit organization facilitating discovery, access, and preservation of peer-reviewed publications that result from federally funded research.

Directory of Open Access Books (DOAB)
https://www.doabooks.org
A searchable directory of OA books and OA publishers established and maintained by OAPEN Foundation at the National Library in The Hague. In addition to listing individual book titles and publishers, DOAB makes the metadata of all its titles available as open data.

DOAJ (Directory of Open Access Journals)
http://www.doaj.org/
A directory of OA journals that aims to include only OA journals using a quality control system such as peer review. Maintained by the Lund University Libraries, Sweden.

Open Access Button
https://openaccessbutton.org
A free tool allowing users to report when they are denied access to full-text research articles because of paywalls and, when possible, retrieving the open access versions of these articles on behalf of the users.

Open Access Disciplinary Repositories
http://oad.simmons.edu/oadwiki/Disciplinary_repositories
An extensive list of open access repositories organized by discipline. Part of the Open Access Directory (OAD), a community-based wiki dedicated to promoting open access resources.

OpenDOAR (Open Directory of Open Access Repositories)
https://v2.sherpa.ac.uk/opendoar/
An international directory of OA repositories that can be searched by subject, location, software platform, and type of content.

ROARMAP (Registry of Open Access Repository Mandates and Policies)
http://roarmap.eprints.org
An international registry of OA mandates and policies adopted by research funders, research institutions, and universities around the world.

SHERPA/Juliet
https://v2.sherpa.ac.uk/juliet/
A service of SHERPA (Securing a Hybrid Environment for Research Preservation and Access) providing information on research funders' requirements on open access publication and data sharing.

SHERPA/RoMEO
https://v2.sherpa.ac.uk/romeo/
A service of SHERPA (Securing a Hybrid Environment for Research Preservation and Access) providing information on publishers' self-archiving policies. RoMEO stands for Rights MEtadata for Open archiving.

Unpaywall
https://unpaywall.org
A free service locating and providing access to paywalled articles that have been legally archived and made freely available in institutional repositories and other websites.

CHAPTER FIVE

Open Educational Resources (OER)

Linking Openness and Education

Education is about sharing knowledge; thus, openness is inherent in education.

—Catherine Cronin (2017, 16)

Open scholarship and open educational resources are often discussed in various forums as separate concepts, although these concepts do overlap and share some principles and ideals. They both start with the same ideas regarding freedom, collaboration, and sharing. Similarly to the ethos of open scholarship, open educational resources aim to improve the value of knowledge, its ownership, and worldwide distribution by lowering or eliminating the cost and permission barriers for educational materials. As Marshall Smith, director of the William and Flora Hewlett Foundation Education Program, states, "[a]t the heart of the open educational resources movement is the simple and powerful idea that the world's knowledge is a public good and that technology in general and the World Wide Web in particular provide an extraordinary opportunity for every-one to share, use, and reuse that knowledge" (Smith and Casserly 2006, 10). These ideas can be traced back to the Enlightenment with its quest for openness, freedom, and knowledge for all (Peters 2017) and the ideas of French Encyclopedists of the eighteenth century (Diderot, Voltaire, Montesquieu, and D'Alembert, among others) who strived to disseminate existing knowledge to the public with the intention of improving society through education (Martin 2017).

Envisioning Openness in Education

In recent decades, the idea of openness in education has attracted considerable attention and debate. However, no single agreed-upon theory (or an explicit single definition) of open education has so far been presented in pedagogical, political, economic, or scholarly discourses. Depending on the context, the term "open education" has been used either metaphorically or implicitly as a broad descriptor of "partly interchangeable, complementary or conflicting conceptions" (Hug 2017, 388). These conceptions encompass a wide variety of approaches to teaching and learning, such as the use of openly licensed educational resources, application of open pedagogical models, establishment of institutional policies regarding open educational materials, and utilization of associated digital and distributed networked technologies.

The concept of open education is broad and inconclusive as well. It can refer to a pedagogical practice, a philosophical idea, a social movement, a technological advancement, or an application of the open licensing model to educational resources. As Hanick and Hofer (2017) state, "Open education is simultaneously content and practice."

From the pedagogical perspective, the concept of open education can be traced back to the teachings of Rousseau, Montessori, Dewey, and Piaget, who advocated openness and student-centered learning as important educational values. Open education has also been associated with the theory of connectivism, introduced by George Siemens in 2005, which emphasized the role of autonomy, community participation, and openness as important prerequisites to learning (Siemens 2005). Open education has also been interpreted as open pedagogy, one of the tenets of which is the rejection of the idea of "disposable assignments" seen only by a student author and an assignment grader and, as such, "[adding] no value to the world" (Wiley October 21, 2013). In lieu of "disposable assignments," the proponents of open pedagogy advocate the idea of "renewable assignments," which employ social networks and participatory technologies to empower students as co-creators of knowledge and enhance teacher-student collaboration (Cronin 2017; Van Allen and Katz 2019).

From the philosophical standpoint, open education has been associated with the educational concept of *Bildsamkeit*,[1] referring to a process through which an individual makes use of his freedom to develop a personality (Hug 2017), and with the German philosophical tradition of *Bildung*,[2] referring to the process of an individual's intellectual and spiritual self-formation, which results from the constant interaction between the individual and the world. With respect to *Bildung* and open education, Deimann (2013) called them "kindred spirits" and argued that *Bildung* can provide open education with a theoretical framework because these two concepts share moral values of inclusivity and unrestricted access to knowledge.

Open education has also been regarded as a political and social movement, which is "firmly and explicitly grounded in concerns about social justice" (Jhangiani and Green 2018, 141). As a movement, open education aspires to enhance and equalize access to knowledge on a global scale. It adheres to the fundamental human rights and freedoms embodied in the Universal Declaration of Human Rights—the right to education (Article 26) and the freedom "to receive and impart information and ideas through any media regardless of frontiers" (Article 19) (United Nations General Assembly 1948).

The notion of open education as a technological advancement has been attributed to a relatively recent period. Weller (2011, 24) states that the open education movement can be viewed as "a response to, or at least as part of, a broader social change made possible by digital technologies." Indeed, digital technologies, particularly the Internet, whose influence on knowledge sharing has been compared to that of the printing press, help equalize educational opportunities by not only providing a global audience with rapid and often free access to information but also by enabling a more efficient coproduction of educational resources and programs. In this regard, it is not surprising that open education has often been confused with open learning, a collective term describing the model through which higher education institutions operate exclusively on a distance education model versus a campus-based education model. Similarly to open learning, open education is thought to be intrinsically associated with and dependent on information communication technologies for access to educational resources and learning and teaching tools.

Finally, the terms "open education" and "open educational resources" (OER hereafter) have often been used interchangeably, although these two terms are not synonymous. The Scholarly Publishing and Academic Resources Coalition (SPARC) calls OER "the foundation of open education" (SPARC, n.d.). More precisely, however, OER should be seen as a distinct, more structured subset of open education that aims to simultaneously achieve three goals: 1) offer substantial cost savings to students, 2) enable educators to retain key copyrights to the educational materials they create, and 3) remove or significantly lower permission barriers to copyrighted educational resources.

Defining OER

Unlike the concept of open education, the concept of OER is clearly defined. Simply put, it refers to learning content that can be freely and openly used and reused by anyone without the need to request permissions from copyright holders or to pay license fees or royalties. Learning content can include any material designed for use in teaching and learning.

OER can be compiled as individual textbooks or collections of textbooks, organized as online courses, or produced as separate components (e.g., textbook chapters, lecture notes, learning modules, and lesson plans). In addition to learning content, OER can incorporate tools and implementation resources. Tools include a wide variety of authoring tools and collaboration platforms that enable the production, editing, use, and reuse of OER.[3] Tools can also include content management and learning management software that support the creation and delivery of learning content. Implementation resources include open licensing tools and design and interoperability standards that enable open sharing, use, and reuse of OER.

Typical OER are digital (either "born digital" or converted to digital formats through the process of digitization) and can include text, files, images, video, and audio of any digital size. However, OER can be present in any format, including print and multimedia formats. Given that in some developing countries (versus developed countries), Internet connectivity and access to computer technology are limited, a higher percentage of OER in these countries are more likely to be created and shared with users as print resources, rather than as digitized or "born digital" materials. In some countries, culture-specific non-Western approaches to teaching and learning can also make people reluctant to use digital resources in an educational setting.

Most OER originate in colleges and universities, nonprofit educational organizations, and academic libraries and can be produced by individual authors, academic units, or a group of peers. Currently, insufficient data are available regarding who the primary creators and users of OER are. However, it can be presumed that most OER are produced by faculty in higher education institutions and are primarily used by educators and students in these institutions, although OER can be produced and used in all sectors of education, as well as outside formal educational settings.[4]

Although the majority of OER initiatives have taken place in the United States and European countries, OER projects are growing rapidly in other parts of the world. Open Education Consortium, an international community of organizations from all educational sectors, has been actively promoting OER and making them accessible on a global level.

Arguments for OER

OER have been developed primarily (but not exclusively) in response to the high cost of commercial college textbooks that constitute a substantial portion of the expenses facing college students. While college instructors select and use a wide range of instructional materials for their classes, required textbooks are still the most common method for distributing course material to students, especially at the undergraduate level.

The high cost of required textbooks has been consistently reported as a major barrier to student access to materials (Seaman and Seaman 2017, 2018, 2020). Nicole Allen, a Student Public Interest Research Groups (SPRIGs) advocate, called textbooks "the top hidden expense of college" (quoted in Sandman 2013). Even though textbook prices vary by publisher and discipline, the price tag for many textbooks for introductory subjects is often over $200 (Allen 2016). By the end of a semester, the cost of the very same textbooks "drops to pennies" (Ibid.). The College Board estimated that the average public college student should budget between $1,240 and $1,460 for textbooks and supplies per year (Ma et al. 2019). Furthermore, the cost of college textbooks produced by commercial publishers has been steadily increasing. According to the Bureau of Labor Statistics, consumer prices for college textbooks increased 88% from 2006 to 2016, which is over three times the rate of inflation since 1977 (Bureau of Labor Statistics 2016). Even though the cost of some textbooks has recently started to decline (Bureau of Labor Statistics 2021), many faculty members still consider textbook prices "obscene" and "outrageously expensive" (Seaman and Seaman 2020).

Commercial textbook prices take a toll not only on the students' budget but also on their academic achievement. High textbook prices put some students in the position of choosing which courses to take based on the cost of textbooks or choosing to take fewer courses or drop courses altogether (Martin et al., 2017). Due to high cost, some students opt for older textbook editions or free copies of commercial textbooks illegally downloaded online (DeMartini, Marshall, and Chew 2018; Dennen and Bagdy 2019; Seaman and Seaman 2020).

OER advocates explored the use of textbooks and other instructional materials freely available online as a potential solution to the problem of high textbook costs.[5] It was estimated that students who used OER in place of traditional textbooks produced by commercial publishers saved on average $116.94 per course (Nyamweya 2018). Based on this estimate, replacing all their courses with OER would save undergraduate students thousands of dollars over their four-year academic career. OER initiatives such as OpenStax CNX[6] and the Achieving the Dream Open Education Resource (OER) Degree Initiative[7] report saving U.S. students millions of dollars in instructional material costs (Griffiths et al. 2020; Ruth 2019). OER offer potential financial benefits to faculty also. For example, instead of purchasing costly instructional materials such as quizzes, homework sets, and exam packs supplied by proprietary publishers, faculty can adopt or adapt openly and freely available instructional materials or create their own OER.

A fair amount of empirical studies have also examined the relationship between the use of OER and learning outcomes. Most of these studies detected no significant differences in learning outcomes between students who were enrolled in courses with commercial textbooks and those enrolled in courses using OER. However, results across these studies indicated that OER were at least as good as commercial course materials while simultaneously reducing the financial burden on students, particularly those students who would not otherwise have access to the course materials due to the cost barrier (Allen et al. 2015; Clinton and Khan 2019; Engler and Shedlosky-Shoemaker 2019; Jhangiani et al. 2018; Lawrence and Lester 2018; Medley-Rath 2018). A recent survey that asked postsecondary faculty to rate the quality of OER they had adopted for their courses came to a similar conclusion that OER can be both free of cost and support positive student learning outcomes. According to the survey results, the majority of faculty rated the quality of OER as equal to that of non-OER alternatives and indicated that they would use OER again for their courses (Seaman and Seaman 2020). Some studies indicated that students in courses utilizing OER had higher retention rates, performed better on exams, and received higher final grades (Hilton and Laman 2012; Pawlyshyn et al. 2013). Considerably fewer studies reported the decrease in learning performance of students using OER in place of commercial textbooks (see, e.g., Gurung 2017).

Arguments for OER tend to focus on the financial benefits to college students. Because of that some people mistakenly regard OER simply as any educational resource available for free on the Internet. Even though many websites allow free online access to their digitized educational content, the content itself might be restrictively licensed and thus cannot be reused and modified.[8] In the context of OER, "free of cost" is not synonymous with "open." According to Downes (2007), there is a significant difference between "open" and "affordable" and between "open" and "accompanied with a non-monetary tariff." Downes questions that resources requiring "some sort of payment by the user—whether that payment be subscription fees, contribution in kind, or even something simple, such as user registration—ought to be called 'open'. Even when the cost is low—or 'affordable'—the payment represents some sort of opportunity cost on the part of the user, an exchange rather than sharing" (32).

OER advocates argue that incorporating OER into higher education has a transformative effect beyond cost savings and that any definition of OER as merely being free of cost to users oversimplifies the vision and goals of the OER movement. What differentiates an OER from other free educational resources is its open license. The Open Education Consortium states that openness in education is not simply a matter of access to educational content, but rather "the ability [of individual users] to modify and use materials, information and networks so education can be personalized to individual users or woven together in new ways for large and diverse audiences" (Open Education Consortium, n.d.).

The users' ability to reuse, revise, remix, and repurpose educational materials is central to the concept of OER. To be considered an OER, a resource must either reside in the public domain (meaning that anyone can use it without any copyright restrictions), or it must be released under an open content license[9] (meaning that anyone can use and reuse the resource for any purpose as long as the license conditions are met by the user).

From the beginning, the OER movement has been inspired by the Free Software Movement[10] pioneered by Richard Stallman (Dinevski 2008; Martin 2020; Tuomi 2013). According to Stallman (2006, 133), a software program is free if the program's user has the four essential freedoms:

1. "The freedom to run the program in any way, for any purpose;
2. The freedom to change the program to suit the user's needs;
3. The freedom to redistribute copies of the program to help others;
4. The freedom to distribute copies of the improved version of the program to give others a chance to benefit from the changes."

David Wiley, one of the leading figures in the OER movement, introduced the concept of "the 5Rs of openness," which echoes Stallman's idea of the four freedoms. According to Wiley, an OER is any copyrightable educational resource that either resides in the public domain or is licensed in such a way that it provides others "with free and perpetual permission" to engage in the following 5R activities:

1. "Retain—make, own, and control a copy of the resource (e.g., download and keep your own copy)

2. Revise—edit, adapt, and modify your copy of the resource (e.g., translate into another language)

3. Remix—combine your original or revised copy of the resource with other existing material to create something new (e.g., make a mashup)

4. Reuse—use your original, revised, or remixed copy of the resource publicly (e.g., on a website, in a presentation, in a class)

5. Redistribute—share copies of your original, revised, or remixed copy of the resource with others (e.g., post a copy online or give one to a friend)" (Wiley March 5, 2014)[11]

Wiley's concept of the 5Rs of openness is at the very core of OER. It shifts the emphasis from freedom of access, which by itself is not sufficient, to the freedom of use and reuse of information, thus further reducing barriers to sharing, remixing, and redistributing of educational resources. This, however, does not mean that there are not any restrictions with regard to the use and reuse of OER. Unless an OER has been designated as being in the public domain by the author, its use might be restricted. For example, the author might specify that its use requires attribution, or that it must be noncommercial, or that the work must be shared under the same license.

Authors can easily mark an OER with the rights they want to reserve by using an open content license such as a Creative Commons (CC) license.[12] Creative Commons offers licenses with different degrees of openness. The degree of openness varies depending on the exact terms attached to a particular license. The Creative Commons Attribution license (CC BY) is often the license of choice for OER creators. This license allows for maximal use, reuse, and repurposing of an educational resource while giving the credit (attribution) to the creator(s) of that resource. However, when there are multiple reuses of the same resource by multiple people, the application of the CC BY license might become confusing. In those cases, the use of the least restrictive "no copyright reserved" designation—CC0 (reads as "CC zero")—may be more appropriate, as it provides a simple way to place the work in the public domain.

In Figure 5.1, CC licenses are arranged according to the degrees of their "freedom"—from the least restrictive CC0 designation, which allows creators to waive all the rights to their work and place it in the public domain, to the two most restrictive licenses: CC BY ND, which does not allow others to make any changes to a work, and CC BY ND NC, which does not allow others to make any changes to a work or use it commercially.

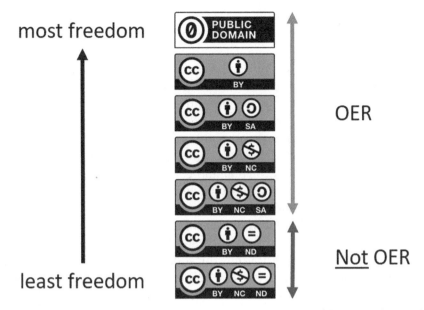

Figure 5.1 "OER and Creative Commons licenses" by Cable Green, licensed under CC BY 4.0.

Based on an interpretation of the degrees of "freedom" represented in Figure 5.1, the CC BY ND and CC BY ND NC licenses are not OER-compatible licenses because the ND ("No Derivatives") clause does not allow others to revise or remix the OER.

The OER Movement

The OER movement is of fairly recent origin. On April 4, 2001, the Massachusetts Institute of Technology (MIT) announced in *The New York Times* that MIT would offer all of its courses freely available online to anyone around the world at no charge (Goldberg 2001). In his announcement, Charles Vest, the MIT president at that time, declared that this initiative, later dubbed MIT OpenCourseWare (OCW), was "a natural fit to what the Web is really all about" (Ibid.). Vest (2004, B20) gave five reasons for MIT to "give away all its course materials via the Internet": 1) to advance education and widen access to information, 2) to offer MIT faculty a greater opportunity for using and reusing each other's work, 3) to preserve a record of MIT's evolving curriculum, 4) to keep in touch with MIT alumni and help them stay current in their fields, and 5) to help MIT students become better prepared for their classes.

The MIT OCW initiative[13] had quickly become the focus of a global discourse in the sphere of education. In early July 2002, representatives of universities and of international and nongovernmental organizations from around the world convened at the Forum on the Impact of Open Courseware for Higher Education in Developing Countries, held in Paris, to discuss OCW issues and opportunities.[14] At this forum, the participants agreed to "develop together a universal educational resource available for the whole of humanity, to be referred to henceforth as Open Educational Resources," defined as "[t]he open provision of educational resources, enabled by information and communication technologies, for consultation, use and adaptation by a community of users for noncommercial purposes"[15] (UNESCO 2002).

Since that landmark forum, other OER-related meetings have taken place around the world (primarily among the United Nations Educational, Scientific and Cultural Organization [UNESCO] member states) and have adopted a number of documents that continued to shape and strengthen the OER movement. Among the most influential are the following statements:

- *The Cape Town Open Education Declaration*

  This declaration was adopted in 2007 by the participants of a meeting hosted by the Shuttleworth Foundation and the Open Society Institute and held in Cape Town, South Africa. The Cape Town Open Education Declaration, released officially in January 2008, called on educational stakeholders to freely share their resources through open content licenses in order to "facilitate use, revision, translation, improvement and sharing [of these resources] by anyone"[16] (Cape Town Open Education Declaration 2007).

- *The Paris OER Declaration*

  This declaration (also known as the Paris Declaration) was adopted in 2012 at the First World Open Educational Resources (OER) Congress held at the UNESCO Headquarters in Paris. The Paris Declaration called on the UNESCO member states to take action in the following 10 areas:

  1. "Foster awareness and use of OER;
  2. Facilitate enabling environments for use of Information and Communications Technologies (ICT);
  3. Reinforce the development of strategies and policies on OER;
  4. Promote the understanding and use of open licensing frameworks:
  5. Support capacity building for the sustainable development of quality learning materials;
  6. Foster strategic alliances for OER;

7. Encourage the development and adaptation of OER in a variety of languages and cultural contexts;

8. Encourage research on OER;

9. Facilitate finding, retrieving and sharing of OER;

10. Encourage the open licensing of educational materials produced with public funds" (UNESCO 2012).

- *The Ljubljana OER Action Plan*

   This action plan was adopted in 2017 at the Second World Open Educational Resources (OER) Congress, cohosted by UNESCO and the government of Slovenia and held in Ljubljana, Slovenia. The Ljubljana OER Action Plan aimed "to meet the challenges of mainstreaming OER content and practices into education systems worldwide" and recommended all educational stakeholders take specific actions in the following five areas:

   1. "[B]uilding the capacity of users to find, re-use, create and share OER";

   2. Addressing "language and cultural issues";

   3. "[E]nsuring inclusive and equitable access to quality OER";

   4. "[D]eveloping sustainability models";

   5. "[D]eveloping supportive policy environments" (UNESCO 2017).

- *Recommendation on Open Educational Resources (OER)*

   This document was adopted in 2019 at the UNESCO's 40th General Conference, held in Paris, France. It defined the following five strategic objectives:

   1. "Building capacity of stakeholders to create access, use, adapt and redistribute OER;

   2. Developing supportive policy;

   3. Encouraging inclusive and equitable quality OER;

   4. Nurturing the creation of sustainability models for OER; and

   5. Facilitating international cooperation" (UNESCO 2019).

While legally nonbinding, these documents demonstrate the commitment of the OER movement to global knowledge sharing and distribution. They also attest that the OER movement is strongly supported by a broad range of governments and organizations. The organizations particularly known for their OER advocacy and support include:

- *William and Flora Hewlett Foundation*[17]

   A nonpartisan, private charitable organization. To date, the William and Flora Hewlett Foundation is the largest financial supporter of the OER movement, including its funding support for MIT's OCW, the Open

Education Consortium, the OCW at Utah State University, and OpenStax CNX at Rice University.

- *The Andrew W. Mellon Foundation*[18]

  A private philanthropic foundation providing grants to institutions of higher education, libraries, museums, and other organizations to support initiatives in the arts and humanities, including OER initiatives. Jointly with the William and Flora Hewlett Foundation, it provided initial funding support for MIT's OCW and has awarded a number of multimillion-dollar grants to other higher education institutions to support their OER initiatives, such as the OER initiatives at Michigan State University and the University of Virginia.

- *SPARC (Scholarly Publishing and Academic Resources Coalition)*[19]

  An international coalition of academic and research libraries "committed to making Open the default for research and education" (SPARC [@SPARC_NA], n.d.). SPARC's Open Education initiative offers professional development and outreach opportunities; publishes *OER Digest*, a biweekly newsletter on OER updates; and provides platforms, such as Connect OER and OER Policy Tracker, that help find and share information about OER initiatives and policies in higher education institutions across North America.

- *Open Education Consortium (OEC)*[20]

  An international, nonprofit network of open education organizations and institutions established as OpenCourseWare Consortium in 2005 and renamed Open Education Consortium in 2014. One of the OEC's goals is to "build capacity to find, reuse, create and share Open Educational Resources (OER)" (Open Education Consortium, n.d.). OEC holds conferences and meetings focused on open education, provides relevant tools and resources, and cohosts educational webinars with the Community College Consortium for Open Educational Resources (CCCOER).

Challenges to a Wider Adoption of OER

Despite the continuing growth of the OER movement and its role in reducing the price and permission barriers in education, the movement confronts a number of challenges that hinder a more widespread adoption of OER across the world. These challenges include:

- *Low awareness of OER*

  Although awareness of OER among faculty is on the rise, the majority of faculty members are still unaware of the benefits of creating or repurposing OER (Seaman and Seaman 2020).

- *Concerns about OER quality*

  Concerns about the quality of OER and uncertainties about the appropriateness of their learning content and instructional design have often been cited as a barrier to a wider OER adoption by postsecondary faculty (see, for example, Belikov and Bodily 2016; Jhangiani et al. 2016; Kortemeyer 2013; Seaman and Seaman 2017).

- *Production cost*

  The production cost of creating an OER is often underestimated. Although OER are (mostly) free for the user, they are not free for the producer. There are real costs on the part of an institution that hosts and provides access to OER, including the cost of software, hardware, maintenance, and staff training. There may also be indirect costs involved in the production and maintenance of OER such as licensing fees for the software needed to use the resource or copyright clearance fees associated with the use of copyrighted material. As Wiley (2007, 19) points out, "[s]ustaining work the results of which are given away for free is difficult."

- *Low incentives*

  Low incentives for faculty to become engaged in OER have been cited as another barrier to a wider adoption of OER in higher education institutions. Time and energy spent in creating new OER or modifying existing OER are substantial and often viewed by faculty as an additional burden rather than an exciting opportunity to enhance their own teaching and scholarship (D'Antoni and Savage 2009; Seaman and Seaman 2020). Some institutions offer financial support in the form of grants to compensate faculty for their time and effort in incorporating OER into their courses.

- *Absent or inadequate academic reward system*

  Even though many faculty members who incorporate OER into their courses do so for altruistic reasons, low institutional and peer recognition has been reported as an underlying inhibitor of OER adoption. In many institutions, the development of OER still carries little or no weight in the tenure and promotion process, which can make some faculty reluctant to get involved in OER projects (Durham and Braxton 2019; Seaman and Seaman 2020).

- *Lack of technical skills and training*

  Lack of technical skills and training as a barrier to OER adoption is a recurrent theme in the OER-related literature. Creating, repurposing, or using OER effectively requires certain digital and media literacy skills that faculty might not yet be comfortable with[21] (Hassall and Lewis 2017; OECD 2007).

- *OER discoverability*

  Locating quality OER can be a challenging task, as OER can reside in various places.[22] Some OER can be part of OER repositories, library collections, federated databases, or institutional repositories, or they can be simply available on the Web, where they can remain practically invisible to the user not familiar with effective search and discovery tools.[23] OER potential for discovery can be further challenged by the lack of expertise (or time) on the part of OER authors to produce comprehensive and meaningful metadata for their works (OECD 2007). As Grégoire and Dieng (2016, 70) observe, "capturing key metadata can make a world of difference between an OER that remains obscure and one that becomes popular." Adding metadata to an OER can be time-consuming. Furthermore, the author adding metadata to a resource does not know how that resource might be used by others, and therefore, the resource might be searched from a totally different perspective than that of the author (OECD 2007). The lack of a common taxonomy for OER that can effectively work across different cultures and languages is another barrier to OER findability (Ibid.).

- *Intellectual property and copyright issues*

  Resolving intellectual property and copyright issues linked to the use of third-party materials has been one of the most challenging and costly processes in OER projects. In some cases, the cost of obtaining permissions for use of third-party copyrighted content is nearly half of the cost of the whole OER initiative (Albright 2005; OECD 2007). Low awareness about or understanding of open content licensing, which is central to the OER concept, remains a significant inhibitor for faculty who are either unwilling or unprepared to deal with open licensing procedures (Seaman and Seaman 2020).

- *Language and culture barriers*

  The vast majority of OER are produced by Western societies and available only in the English language (Cobo 2013; OECD 2007; Rets et al. 2020; Rossini 2010). Willems and Bossu (2012, 191) note that while "English is considered an international language due to its usage in knowledge dissemination [. . .], the majority of learners worldwide come from non-English-speaking backgrounds." The OER linguistic "imbalance" presents obstacles to effective use and reuse of OER in non-English-speaking countries (Banzato 2012; Wen-Hao, Meng-Fen, and Shen 2012). Furthermore, this "imbalance" imposes a risk of creating "a one-way street with developed countries responsible for producing OER and the less developed countries confined to consumption" (Albright 2005, 14). In addition, authors of English-language OER tend to adhere to Western pedagogical theories, and this situation can limit the relevance of OER in non-Western settings. As Albright (2005, 12) puts it, "OER are cultural as much as educational, in that they give users an insight into culture-specific methods and approaches to teaching and learning." The challenge of OER's "cultural hegemony" (D'Antoni and Savage 2009) is further aggravated by the inadequate technological infrastructure in less developed countries, such as limited access to computers or poor Internet connectivity, as well as the lack of familiarity or confidence with computer technology in some remote regions (an issue known as "the global digital divide").

OER Quality

Because the term OER has often been used together with the terms "free" and "online," it is not surprising that some people assume that OER are not of comparable quality to proprietary educational materials because they are not peer reviewed, lack editorial direction, might have been remixed by others, and allow anyone to modify existing content with an open license.[24] The assumption that "free" means "low quality" has been challenged by OER advocates, most notably, by David Wiley. In his blog posts, "Stop Saying 'High Quality'" and "No, Really—Stop Saying 'High Quality,'" Wiley cautions about equating the idea of "high quality" of an OER with the traditional authoring and editorial process. He writes:

> [. . .] I fully believe that resources created through the "traditional process" *can* effectively [support] learning. But there are two things I don't believe:
>
> 1. That conformance to the traditional process *guarantees* that every resource created that way will effectively support learning, and
> 2. That the traditional process is the *only* process that can result in resources that effectively support learning.
>
> (April 1, 2015; emphasis in original)

Answering the question about what constitutes quality in an OER is not as simple as it sounds. Quality in general is a subjective and contextual matter and thus difficult to measure in absolute terms. Measuring the quality of an OER is just as challenging. Perceptions of the quality of an OER vary depending on its intended use, type of user, or the particular phase of the OER is in its life cycle. An OER can be evaluated in terms of presentation design, suitability for a particular teaching practice, or effectiveness as a learning tool. With regard to reuse, an OER can be evaluated in terms of usage rights, accessibility options, resource size, or ease of adaptation. Furthermore, the very same OER can be of "high quality" for one user and of "low quality" for another. Tovar et al. (2015, 7) provide the following example to illustrate this point: "An OER [can be] highly rated as excellent quality by students in their remedial learning, but [...] teachers elsewhere [can] find [the same OER] terribly difficult to adopt, change the language, and relocalise to another culture and context. So on one level the OER is high quality but on another higher level this same OER is low quality and unusable."

Some research in this area (see, for example, Jung, Teruyoshi, and Latchem 2016; Kawachi 2014; Tovar et al., 2015) takes the work of Harvey and Green (1993) as the starting point. In their article "Defining Quality," Harvey and Green describe five dimensions of quality in relation to higher education: 1) quality as being exceptional, 2) quality as perfection or consistency, 3) quality as fitness for purpose, 4) quality as value for money, and 5) quality as transformation. Of these five dimensions, the conception of "fitness for purpose" appears to be most appropriate to use in evaluating the quality of an OER because it defines OER quality as being relevant to the user's needs, whether the user is a learner or a teacher. As Tovar et al. (2015) argue, "fitness for purpose" depends on whose perspective is being considered. Similarly, Bethard et al. (2009, 221) conclude that "quality is the matter of perspective" and that quality "depends on the alignment between the user constituency being served, the educational setting where deployed, and the intended purpose of the resource."

There have been multiple efforts, ranging in scope and specificity, to develop OER quality criteria. For example, Uvalić-Trumbić and Daniel (2014, 13) simply suggest that "the quality criteria used to assess the quality of any educational materials can be applied to OER." Wiley (March 27, 2015) argues that "the core issue in determining the quality of any educational resource is the degree to which it supports learning" and that "the true desideratum of educational materials is 'effective'" (emphasis in original). In a like manner, Clements, Pawlowski, and Manouselis (2015, 1104) state, in rather general terms, that quality in the context of OER means that "a teacher finds a *suitable* resource for his/her teaching" (emphasis added).

Although the educators adopting or adapting OER are themselves the best judges of the quality of a particular OER, some educators, particularly those who have had minimal or no teaching training or experience, are not always able to assess the pedagogical effectiveness of OER they are using in their courses (Miao, Mishra, and McGreal 2016). Likewise, learners who use OER individually are not always knowledgeable enough to evaluate the quality or accuracy of OER they access.

In order to assist educators with OER quality assessment, a number of OER evaluation rubrics have been developed by individual researchers and by educational organizations. For example, the Learning Object Review Instrument (LORI) developed by Nesbit, Belfer, and Leacock (2009) has been used to evaluate the quality of a wide variety of OER. Achieve,[25] a nonprofit educational organization, has created the Rubrics for Evaluating Open Education Resource (OER) Objects,[26] as well as an online OER evaluation tool[27] (hosted on OERCommons.org) that offers users a five-star rating system to evaluate OER.

OER quality assessment can also be achieved through peer review, similarly to the traditional evaluation model of scholarly publications. For example, OER submitted to MERLOT[28] (the acronym for Multimedia Educational Resources for Learning and Online Teaching) are subject to a written review by at least two reviewers who are experts in a relevant discipline. These reviewers evaluate the material submitted to MERLOT according to the predefined criteria that address the following three aspects of an OER: quality of content, potential effectiveness as a teaching tool, and ease of use.

Another means of assessing the quality of an OER is by relying on the reputation of the institution that hosts the content. Prominent institutions presumably have some internal quality control procedures before they release their OER, although these procedures are not always transparent to the users of their resources. Some institution-based OER projects—for example, OpenLearn,[29] the learning platform developed by the Open University[30] in the United Kingdom—use the prestige of participating institutions to assure that the resources on their website are of good quality.

Finally, the OER evaluation process can be complemented by informal mechanisms such as "public review," wherein quality can be discerned based on comments and ratings provided by the user community or on the number of downloads for each resource on the website. For example, OER Commons,[31] an OER repository developed by the Institute for the Study of Knowledge Management in Education (ISKME), enables users to rate and comment on the resources in its collection. A similar approach is the postpublication peer review, in which the editorial process is open to any user. For example, OpenStax CNX,[32] the Rice University–based publisher of open textbooks, invites users to submit suggestions and corrections on their open textbooks to the OpenStax CNX team, which then reviews them and makes necessary changes.

Types of OER Projects

OER projects show a great diversity in terms of the size of the operation, the type of production, and the degree of integration of users in the production process. Some of these projects are highly structured and centralized, while others are less formally structured and almost fully decentralized (Wiley 2007). They also vary in terms of cost recovery, operational sustainability, technical maintenance, content organization, and staffing (Downes 2007).

The two most common models of OER projects are the producer-consumer model and the coproduction model. In the producer-consumer model, an institution provides all the services and produces all the content, which can then be used and reused by both internal and external consumers. One of the most prominent examples of this model is the MIT OpenCourseWare,[33] which is entirely institution-based in the sense that all materials originate from MIT faculty and the services are almost exclusively provided by MIT paid employees (Wiley 2007). In the coproduction model, an OER project involves external contributors of content and depends, to a large degree, on voluntary work of community members. An example of this model is MERLOT, which includes professional staff members, who are responsible for the project's overall management, the site maintenance, and editorial processes, and a community of volunteers, who contribute materials, promote MERLOT services to others, and assist professional staff members with developing practices and policies that govern the project's operation. MERLOT also engages the user community to evaluate its content by submitting ratings and comments about the resources.

Some institution-based OER initiatives use a hybrid approach to the organization and provision of services in that they rely on both the paid staff and volunteers, such as student volunteers, to advance their OER programs (Wiley 2007). An example of such an initiative is the OER@ USU program[34] at Utah State University (USU), which is "a hybrid of centralization and decentralization of both organization and services" (Ibid., 7). This program provides access to a collection of USU's OpenCourseWare; textbooks authored by USU faculty; educational materials used in USU's courses; and supplemental educational materials such as learning modules, laboratory experiences, curricular, and exams. These resources are available through the USU's institutional repository, DigitalCommons@USU, which runs on bepress's Digital Commons platform and is maintained by the USU Libraries. Unlike MIT, USU doesn't make all its courses freely available online.

Sustainability of OER Projects

Sustainability, which is closely linked to the project's funding model, is key to the long-term survival of any OER initiative not only in monetary terms but also in terms of the goals and imperatives of an individual institution. Downes (2007, 33–34) defines sustainability as having "long-term viability for all concerned," "[meeting] provider objectives for scale, quality, production cost, margins and return on investment" and being "capable of promoting wider objectives."

Wiley (2007) identified two unique sustainability challenges facing OER projects that need to be addressed in a systematic way: 1) sustaining the production and sharing of OER and 2) sustaining the use and reuse of their OER by end users. In order to address the first challenge, the project needs to rely on a funding model that can sustain the project's operations while simultaneously enabling it to meet its goals (Ibid.). De Langen (2013, 58) argues that "if open is defined in a strict sense, meaning that no kind of payment takes place between the users and the suppliers of OER, the only sustainable business model is the one based on grants and subsidies." However, studies on OER sustainability show that OER projects can be sustained financially in a number of ways. For example, Downes (2007) identified nine funding models for sustainable OER projects:

1. *Endowment model*

   A project is sustained on interest earned from base funding.

2. *Membership model*

   A coalition of interested organizations contributes funding for the project, either as a one-time contribution or on a subscription basis.

3. *Donations model*

   A project is funded by private or community donations, which, in turn, are managed by a nonprofit foundation.

4. *Conversion model*

   Additional services (such as technical support) or advanced features associated with the project "convert" users into paying customers.

5. *Contributor-pay model*

   Financial responsibility is placed on OER contributors, who are responsible for maintaining and updating their own resources.

6. *Sponsorship model*

   Income is generated from advertisements.

7. *Institutional model*

   A project is funded by the institution.

8. *Governmental model*

   A project is funded by an associated government body.

9. *Partnerships and exchanges model*

   A project relies on exchange of resources among project partners rather than on money.

Dholakia, King, and Baraniuk (2006) identified two additional funding models for sustainable OER projects—substitution model and segmentation model. With the substitution model, funds for an OER project are reallocated from funds for other technology software and infrastructure, such as course management systems or virtual learning environments. With the segmentation model, specific user "segments" are targeted and charged a higher price for value-added versions of a product, while a basic version of the product is offered for free. All sorts of combinations of these models might also be used.

Addressing the second sustainability challenge—to achieve the OER project's goals—is more difficult. According to Wiley (2007, 19), the project's chances of surviving long-term and meeting its goals can be increased if:

1. There is a clear understanding of the project's goals.
2. Joint decisions are made about the following aspects of the project:
    *   The project's size, structure, and degree of centralization of the organization
    *   Types of resources the project will offer and the types of formats in which these resources will be shared
    *   Types of reuse by the end user
    *   Nonmonetary incentives to engage project participants
    *   Cost-reduction measures
    *   A funding model that will most likely enable the project to meet its goals in an ongoing manner

It is clear that the issue of OER sustainability is relative and that cost-saving benefits of OER for the user do not directly translate into the financial sustainability of an OER project. Depending on the context, some OER projects may be more sustainable than others in terms of their financial circumstances, goals, and nonmonetary values.

Notes

1. The concept of *Bildsamkeit* was introduced by a German philosopher Johann Gottlieb Fichte and developed further by Hegel, Herbart, Schleiermacher, and, later on, by Dewey and Vygotsky, among others (Uljens and Ylimaki 2017).

2. *Bildung* is the philosophical tradition of what is commonly called 'post-Kantian German idealism.' The idea of *Bildung* has particularly risen to prominence with the writings of German philosopher Wilhelm von Humboldt. Humboldt described *Bildung* as the process of personal intellectual and spiritual self-formation, which results from the constant, multi-faceted interaction between the individual and the world in such a way that the individual's innate

talents could unfold. This never-ending process allows the individual to have all the world's experiences that enable him to "place the mark of his intellect on the world" in order to make both the world and himself "a bit more similar" (Humboldt 1960, 511, 327).

3. Some OER repositories include OER publishing tools in the suite of their services. See, for example, the OER Commons' Open Author tool (https://www.oercommons.org/authoring-overview) and MERLOT's Content Builder (https://www.merlot.org/merlot/login.htm).

4. Creative Commons (2020) suggests that higher education faculty are more likely to produce and use OER versus educators in primary and secondary schools because they "have the time, resources, and support to produce and revise educational resources; own the copyright to the content they create (though this depends on their contract with the college or university); and make unilateral decisions regarding what content is used in their courses" (108).

5. Under this interpretation, online OER are available to the user at no cost. However, while online OER are technically free of cost, there may be costs associated with their use such as photocopying and printing materials or using e-readers and print-on-demand books, although these costs are relatively low.

6. OpenStax CNX (https://cnx.org).

7. Achieving the Dream Open Education Resource (OER) Degree Initiative (https://www.achievingthedream.org/resources/initiatives/open-educational-resources-oer-degree-initiative).

8. It is, however, worth noting that even though these resources only offer the basic level of openness (i.e., freedom from cost), they are still important in terms of cost savings.

9. Open content licenses are discussed in Chapter 3.

10. The Free Software Movement is discussed in Chapter 2.

11. Originally, there were the 4Rs (Reuse, Revise, Remix, and Redistribute). Wiley introduced the 5th R (Retain) seven years after he had introduced the idea of the 4Rs.

12. For description of various CC licenses, see Chapter 3.

13. The idea of OpenCourseWare actually originated at the University of Tübingen in Germany with its 1999 Tübinger Internet Multimedia Server project (Fernández 2016, 886). However, this idea achieved a wider recognition only with the launch of the MIT OCW initiative in 2002.

14. This forum was preceded by a forum held in San Diego in December of 2001. The San Diego forum examined broad OCW issues, including intellectual property, technology, and access issues and concerns related to OCW effective language translation and cultural adaptation.

15. UNESCO's original definition of OER suggested that information and communication technologies are one of the main drivers that had enabled OER to emerge in its current form. However, UNESCO's definition of OER has evolved over time. In its *Recommendation on Open Educational Resources (OER)*, published in 2019, UNESCO defines OER as "learning, teaching and research materials *in any format*

and medium that reside in the public domain or are under copyright that have been released under an open license, that permit no-cost access, re-use, re-purpose, adaptation and redistribution by others" (UNESCO 2019) (emphasis added).

16. The Cape Town Open Education Declaration expanded on UNESCO's definition to include open education in general. This declaration stated that "open education is not limited to just open educational resources. It also draws upon open technologies that facilitate collaborative, flexible learning and the open sharing of teaching practices that empower educators to benefit from the best ideas of their colleagues. It may also grow to include new approaches to assessment, accreditation and collaborative learning" (Cape Town Open Education Declaration 2007).

17. William and Flora Hewlett Foundation (https://hewlett.org).

18. The Andrew W. Mellon Foundation (https://mellon.org).

19. SPARC (https://sparcopen.org).

20. Open Education Consortium (https://www.oeconsortium.org).

21. In 2016, the International Organisation of La Francophonie (IOF) published the *OER Trainer's Guide* (https://unesdoc.unesco.org/ark:/48223/pf0000266161), which aimed to identify and describe specific knowledge and tools pertaining to each of the capabilities listed in the OER Competency Framework (https://unesdoc.unesco.org/ark:/48223/pf0000266159_eng). Although slightly outdated, this guide is a good starting point of reference regarding specific steps for creating, co-creating, and publishing OER.

22. Most OER published online under Creative Commons licenses are indexed by Google. They can be found via the Google Advanced Search, where the search can be narrowed down by usage rights. A word of caution: even a correctly conducted advanced search does not guarantee that found resources are free to use or reuse. Each resource should be individually checked on its original site to verify the resource's licence.

23. Some institutions have tried to address the issue of OER discoverability by launching search tools that enable users to find OER in any subject area. One of the most notable examples of such tools is Mason OER Metafinder (https://mom.gmu.edu) from the George Mason University Libraries that searches across 20+ OER repositories simultaneously.

24. The last few years, however, have seen a number of changes in faculty's perceptions of OER quality. According to the recent survey by Bay View Analytics, which asked postsecondary faculty to rate the quality of OER they had adopted for their courses, faculty rated the quality of OER as being equal to that of non-OER alternatives (Seaman and Seaman 2020). It is worth mentioning that concerns about uneven quality hold true for some commercial textbooks also. Faculty expressed general concerns about "the dumbing down of [commercial] textbooks," describing them as being "outrageously expensive" while being "mostly encyclopedic and filled with a lot of superfluous information that daunts most students" (Ibid., 16).

25. Achieve (https://www.achieve.org).

26. The Rubrics for Evaluating Open Education Resource (OER) Objects (https://www.achieve.org/files/AchieveOERRubrics.pdf).

27. The *Achieve Open Educational Resources Evaluation Tool Handbook* provides guidance on how to use this tool. See https://www.achieve.org/files/AchieveOEREvaluationToolHandbookFINAL.pdf.

28. MERLOT (https://www.merlot.org).

29. OpenLearn (https://www.open.edu/openlearn).

30. The Open University (http://www.open.ac.uk).

31. OER Commons (https://www.oercommons.org).

32. OpenStax CNX (https://cnx.org).

33. MIT OpenCourseWare (https://ocw.mit.edu/index.htm).

34. OER@USU (https://oer.usu.edu/oer_at_usu).

Suggested Reading

Wesolek, Andrew, Jonathan Lashley, and Anne Langley (eds.). *OER: A Field Guide for Academic Librarians*. Forest Grove: Pacific University Press, 2018. https://scholarworks.boisestate.edu/fac_books/511.

Suggested Resources

Mason OER Metafinder
https://mom.gmu.edu
A search engine developed by the George Mason University Libraries that searches across 20+ OER repositories simultaneously.

MERLOT (Multimedia Educational Resource for Online Teaching and Learning)
https://www.merlot.org
A searchable OER referatory developed by the California State University Centre for Distributed Learning and designed primarily for students and faculty in higher education. MERLOT is a referatory in that it provides links to various OER that reside elsewhere on the web rather than hosting the content itself. MERLOT allows users to search multiple OER collections, as well as the entire Web, from a single search bar. MERLOT also offers the tools for creating OER materials and course ePortfolios.

OER Commons
https://www.oercommons.org
An OER repository created by the Institute for the Study of Knowledge Management in Education (ISKME). In addition to providing access to an extensive collection of OER in various subject areas, OER Commons provides collaborative workspaces for users to create, curate, discuss, and share OER and OER-related news and events.

OpenLearn
https://www.open.edu/openlearn
An online learning platform developed by The Open University in Great Britain. In addition to providing access to open courses from The Open University, OpenLearn offers videos, games, and other topical and interactive educational content.

OpenStax CNX
https://cnx.org
The Rice University–based OER initiative (formerly Connexions). OpenStax CNX provides access to open educational content in a variety of disciplines at all educational levels—from children to professionals—and includes contributors from around the world. OER in OpenStax CNX are organized into "Pages" that are further organized into "Books." Per OpenStax's self-description, these resources are "easily accessible online and downloadable to almost any device, anywhere, anytime."

CHAPTER SIX

Open Data

Facilitating Replication and Verification of Research Findings

> Scientific publication is not an exercise in informing others of new findings, it is an active dialog designed to identify errors and maximize the integrity of the knowledge.
>
> —Victoria Stodden (2014, 229)

Data serve as the primary source of information underlying scientific discoveries and are one of the most valuable assets of any research project. Collecting, generating, evaluating, and manipulating data, whether through observation, experiment, surveys, simulation, or some other means, are among the key activities that consume much of researchers' time and energy. Researchers also devote substantial time and effort on searching for preexisting data that are needed for replication, verification, or secondary analysis of their findings. Preexisting data that are unavailable to other researchers might need to be collected again, and that might be impossible to accomplish in some cases such as with observational data. In the context of computational research, where data are produced primarily in digital form and intrinsically depend on the speed with which computer technology moves forward or becomes obsolete, the data might eventually become inaccessible, corrupted, or even completely lost.

Open data, on the other hand, can address many of these issues. The goal of open data is to prevent duplication in the collection of data, ensure authenticity and reproducibility of research findings, and combat the loss and obsolescence of digital data.

What Are Open Data?

Yu and Robinson (2011) suggest that the term "open data" was used for the first time in the 1970s in a series of NASA's international policies dealing with remote sensing. According to other sources, the term was coined in 1995 in a document from a U.S. scientific agency dealing with the disclosure of geophysical and environmental data (Chignard 2013). While the origins of the term "open data" are still a matter of some debate, the conceptual meaning of open data has been explained rather consistently by various authorities.

The *Open Data Handbook* defines open data as "data that can be freely used, re-used and redistributed by anyone—subject only, at most, to the requirement to attribute and sharealike" (Open Data Handbook, n.d.). The Open Definition, a document produced and maintained by the Open Knowledge Foundation (OKF), elaborates on this definition by adding that open data must be 1) legally open, i.e., available under an open content license, and 2) technically open, i.e., "machine-readable, available in bulk, and provided in an open format" (Open Definition, n.d.). According to the Panton Principles, open data are data that are "freely available on the public internet permitting any user to download, copy, analyse, reprocess, pass them to software or use them for any other purpose without financial, legal, or technical barriers other than those inseparable from the internet itself" (Murray-Rust et al. 2010). In a similar vein, *The Open Science Training Handbook* defines open data as data that can be "freely accessed, reused, remixed and redistributed, for academic research and teaching purposes and beyond" and that "ideally, [. . .] have no restrictions on reuse or redistribution, and are appropriately licensed as such" (Bezjak et al. 2018).

Open Data Principles

To facilitate and promote open access to data, a number of community-based initiatives around the world produced guiding principles on data sharing and data stewardship.

The FAIR Principles

The FAIR principles, a set of 15 "aspirational" recommendations developed by a team of stakeholders from academia, government, industry, and scholarly publishing, provide guidance on enhancing the reusability of scientific data without dictating any specific technological implementations.[1] According to these principles, scientific data should be FAIR (standing for **f**indable, **a**ccessible, **i**nteroperable, and **r**eusable) in order to be maximally suitable for reuse. Boeckhout, Zielhuis, and Bredenoord (2018, 932) summarize the key ideas of the FAIR principles as follows:

> "**Findability.** Datasets should be described, identified and registered or indexed in a clear and unequivocal manner;
> **Accessibility.** Datasets should be accessible through a clearly defined access procedure, ideally using automated means. Metadata should always remain accessible;
> **Interoperability.** Data and metadata are conceptualized, expressed and structured using common, published standards;
> **Reusability.** Characteristics of data and their provenance are described in detail according to domain-relevant community standards, with clear and accessible conditions for use" (emphasis added).

It should be noted, however, that FAIR data are not *necessarily* open data. As Mons et al. (2017, 51) observe, "FAIR is not equal to Open." The FAIR principles do not advocate for free and unrestricted access to scientific data. They are quite compatible with models of restricted or controlled data access and release, as there may be legitimate concerns with regard to openly releasing sensitive, private, or proprietary data (Boeckhout, Zielhuis, and Bredenoord 2018; Mons et al. 2017; Wilkinson et al. 2016). Instead, the FAIR principles place a strong emphasis on openly available metadata so that computers can find and use data to the greatest extent possible. In this sense, the FAIR principles are balancing the values of openness and interests of confidentiality and intellectual property by offering effective practical means for furthering data sharing and data reusability.

The Panton Principles

The Panton Principles,[2] a set of four guiding principles for open data, were created by a team of open science advocates led by Peter Murray-Rust, a chemist at the University of Cambridge. These principles were originally drafted by Murray-Rust and his peers at the Panton Arms, a pub on Panton Street in Cambridge, United Kingdom, and that fact gave the name to the principles. The Panton Principles are based on the two foundational ideas of open science: 1) the idea that scientific advances are "based on building on, reusing and openly criticising the published body of scientific knowledge" and 2) the belief that "[f]or science to effectively function, and for society to reap the full benefits from scientific endeavours, it is crucial that science data be made open" (Murray-Rust et al. 2010).

The four Panton Principles can be summarized as follows:

1. Data should be accompanied by a precise and irrevocable statement that clearly describes the terms and conditions for the data reuse and repurposing.
2. Data should be licensed under a data-appropriate license.
3. Data should *not* be licensed under a license that prohibits the commercial use of data or the creation of derivative works [emphasis added].
4. Publicly funded data should be placed in the public domain (Ibid.).

In addition to these recommendations, the Panton Principles provide specific guidance for scientists on licensing their data and for placing their data in the public domain.

The 8 Principles of Open Government Data

The 8 Principles of Open Government Data[3] were drafted at the 2007 meeting in Sebastopol, California, by a group of activists, including Lawrence Lessig, Tim O'Reilly, Carl Malamud, and Aaron Swartz, who called themselves the Open Government Working Group (Chignard 2013). According to these principles, government data could be considered open if the data are:

1. *Complete* ("All public data are made available.")
2. *Primary* ("Data are published as collected at the source.")
3. *Timely* ("Data are made available as quickly as necessary to preserve the value of the data.")
4. *Accessible* ("Data are available to the widest range of users for the widest range of purposes.")
5. *Machine Processable* ("Data are reasonably structured to allow automated processing of [the data].")
6. *Nondiscriminatory* ("Data are available to anyone, with no requirement of registration.")
7. *Nonproprietary* ("Data are available in a format over which no entity has exclusive control.")
8. *License-Free* ("Data are not subject to any copyright, patent, trademark or trade secret regulation.") (Open Government Working Group 2007)[4]

The Open Government Working Group also declared that "[c]ompliance must be **reviewable**," which means that:

- "A contact person must be designated to respond to people trying to use the data.
- A contact person must be designated to respond to complaints about violations of the principles.
- An administrative or judicial court must have the jurisdiction to review whether the agency has applied these principles appropriately" (Ibid.; emphasis in original).

Open Data Policies and Mandates

The need for "opening up" research data, especially the data derived from publicly funded research, has been widely discussed since the 1985 report by the National Research Council entitled *Sharing Research Data.* This report proclaimed that "without the availability of data, the diversity of analyses and conclusions is inhibited, and scientific understanding and progress are impeded" (National Research Council 1985, 9–10). To address the need for open provision of data, research funding agencies began formulating data sharing policies in the mid-1990s. In 1996, the leaders of the international Human Genome Project drafted a set of principles (known as the Bermuda Rules) at a Bermuda Summit sponsored by the Wellcome Trust, the largest funder of biomedical research in the United Kingdom (Marshall 2001). The Bermuda Rules required that all human genome data sequenced under the public effort should be freely and openly posted online within 24 hours of sequencing in order "to encourage research and development and to maximize [the data's] benefits to society" (National Human Genome Research Institute 1996). The Bermuda Rules replaced a 1992 guideline stating that such data were made publicly available within six months (Ibid.), and therefore, they set a precedent for rapid data release in genomics and other research fields.[5]

At present, an increasing number of federal and private research funding agencies require that data produced in the course of the research project they fund are made freely and openly available for other researchers and the public. For example, the National Science Foundation (NSF) has announced a policy mandating that the publicly funded research data are made available to other researchers and to the public in freely accessible repositories, unless privacy or safety concerns prevent data sharing (National Science Foundation 2020). The National Institutes of Health (NIH) has had a data sharing policy since 2003 for applications with costs greater than $500,000 (National Institutes of Health 2003). On October 29, 2020, NIH released the "Final NIH Policy for Data Management and Sharing," which will take effect on January 25, 2023, and apply to all research funded or conducted by the NIH. According to this policy, all grant awardees must submit a Data Management and Sharing Plan outlining how research data will be managed and shared and how that data "should be made accessible as soon as possible, and no later than the time of an associated publication, or the end of performance period, whichever comes first" (National Institutes of Health 2020). The Bill & Melinda Gates Foundation mandates that all published research resulting from its funding and all data related to the published research results be freely and openly accessible immediately after publication (Bill & Melinda Gates Foundation, n.d.).

In Europe, various research funders have implemented similar policies on data sharing. The *Recommendation on Access to and Preservation of Scientific Information*, issued by the European Commission in 2018, requests that the European member states ensure that "research data that results from publicly funded research becomes and stays findable, accessible, interoperable and re-usable ('FAIR principles') within a secure and trusted environment" (European Commission 2018). The United Kingdom's seven Research Councils require that publicly funded research data "should be made openly available with as few restrictions as possible in a timely and responsible manner" (UK Research and Innovation 2018). Horizon 2020, the European Union's Research and Innovation program, implemented by the European Commission in 2014, mandated open access to all scientific publications generated by the Horizon 2020 projects and to all data underlying the published research results, with the possibility to opt out from the Horizon's 2020 "Open Research Data" pilot (European Commission "Horizon 2020," n.d.). In Horizon Europe, a seven-year research and innovation investment program that had succeeded Horizon 2020 in January 2021, the requirement for responsible data management based on FAIR principles is made separate from the requirement for open access to research data (European Commission "Horizon Europe," n.d.). According to this requirement, research data should be made open by default in line with the "as open as possible, as closed as necessary" principle (Ibid.) The use of certified repositories for research data, such as the European Open Science Cloud (EOSC)[6] that provides a portal for European researchers to access, process and share their data, is required in some Horizon Europe programs (Ibid.).

The sharing of publicly funded research data is further facilitated by documented procedures known as data management plans (DMPs). DMPs describe how research data will be generated or collected and how that data will be stored and shared in openly accessible repositories after the research project ends. DMPs help ensure that publicly funded research data are made freely available to other researchers and the public, unless privacy or safety concerns prevent data sharing. Major research funders, such as the National Science Foundation, NIH, and National Endowment for the Humanities, among others, require that DMPs are provided as part of research proposals and requests for funding. In Horizon Europe, DMPs have become mandatory for all its research projects as well, even if research data are not made open to the public for privacy or security reasons.

Open Government Data

The demand for open provision of data is also evident at the government level. In 2017, the Open, Public, Electronic and Necessary (OPEN) Government Data Act was introduced to the U.S. House of Representatives.[7] If signed into law, the OPEN Government Data Act would require federal agencies, excluding some government entities, to make government data "available in an open format [. . .] under open licenses" "[w]hen not otherwise prohibited by law, and to the extent practicable" (U.S. Congress 2017b). Similarly, the President's Management Agenda, released by the White House in 2018, outlines the importance of government data accountability and transparency (White House 2018). The agenda includes the Federal Data Strategy, which directs the federal government to do the following:

1. "[Improve] dissemination, [make] data available more quickly and in more useful formats;
2. [Maximize] the amount of non-sensitive data shared with the public;
3. [Leverage] new technologies and best practices to increase access to sensitive or restricted data while protecting the privacy, security, and confidentiality, and interests of data providers" (Ibid.).

Another important legislation includes the Grant Reporting Efficiency and Agreements Transparency (GREAT) Act, signed into law in 2019. The GREAT Act requires the creation and use of data standards for all information reported by recipients of federal awards. One of such data standards is the requirement that recipients of federal grants publish their data as open data "on a single public portal" (U.S. Congress 2019).

Journal Data Sharing Policies

In 2007 the scientists Gentleman and Lang introduced the concept of a compendium as a collection of the components of a research project that are needed for the understanding and replication of research findings by others. According to this concept, the key components of any research project are text, code, data, and auxiliary software necessary to re-create research computation (Gentleman and Lang 2007). The majority of published research, however, still does not include data, upon which the research claims rely (Stodden 2020). Unavailability of data used to generate published research findings, which often results in failures to verify and reproduce these findings, is "engendering a credibility crisis" in the sciences (Stodden, Guo, and Ma 2013).

To address this issue, the Transparency and Openness Promotion (TOP) Committee, consisting of scholarly journal editors, disciplinary experts, and funding agency representatives, developed the journal editorial guidelines aimed to promote and support transparency and reproducibility of research findings. The TOP Guidelines,[8] initially published in the journal *Science* by researchers at the Center for Open Science (Nosek et al. 2015), include eight modular standards, each with three levels of increasing rigor, with which journals can comply with transparency and openness in their editorial practices. In addition to the TOP Guidelines, the Center for Open Science introduced a new metric, the TOP Factor,[9] which rates the degree to which research journals comply with the TOP Guidelines.

A number of individual journals and journal clusters are already implementing the TOP Guidelines in their editorial policies by requiring authors to provide the data supporting research claims to journal editors and peer reviewers at the time of manuscript submission. Data can then be either published alongside the article in the form of an "enriched publication" or archived in an open data repository prior to manuscript submission. For example, the journal *Science* requires authors to make data, code, and other materials, upon which the manuscript is based "available to any reader of a *Science* Journal" (Science, n.d.). The journal *Nature*, likewise, makes the "prompt" availability of scientific data, code, and associated protocols to "readers without undue qualifications" a condition for publication in all *Nature* journals (Nature, n.d.). In parallel to these initiatives, other journals and journal communities have adopted similar policies that either require or encourage data sharing as part of the publication process.[10] For example, many journals in ecology and evolutionary biology adopt the Joint Data Archiving Policy (JDAP) requiring that "data supporting the results in the paper be archived in an appropriate public archive" (Dryad 2020). Some journals display "digital badges" on published articles to highlight and reward the articles that provide open access to supporting data (Hrynaszkiewicz 2020). According to several studies, the use of digital badges as an incentive for authors has been associated with increased data sharing (Ibid.).

Large commercial scholarly publishers such as Elsevier, Springer Nature, Taylor & Francis, and Wiley have also introduced data sharing policies. Unlike the publishers of *Science* and *Nature*, these publishers aim to accommodate data sharing requirements across various disciplines by offering their journals a number of policy types—from a basic policy with minimal requirements to share data upon request to a more stringent policy mandating data sharing as a condition for publication.

Some journal publishers require authors of manuscripts to submit a data availability statement indicating where the data supporting original research in their manuscripts can be found. If the manuscript is accepted for publication, the data availability statement is published as part of the article. Presently, all BioMed Central, Public Library of Science, and Nature journals require data availability statements. Springer Nature journals either require or encourage the provision of data availability statements in articles they publish. Some publishers provide guidance on preparing data availability statements, including Nature (Nature 2016) and Springer Nature (Springer Nature, n.d.).

A number of journal editors have also initiated data sharing policies. For example, the International Committee of Medical Journal Editors (ICMJE) requires its member journals, which include such flagship journals as the *British Medical Journal (BMJ)*, the *Journal of the American Medical Association (JAMA)*, *Lancet*, and the *New England Journal of Medicine*, to provide data sharing statements for clinical trials (Taichman et al. 2017). This decision was based on the ICMJE's belief that "there is an ethical obligation to responsibly share data generated by interventional clinical trials because trial participants have put themselves at risk" (Ibid.).

A small number of data journals, publishing peer-reviewed papers that describe datasets, and a number of journals with the most stringent data sharing policies have taken additional measures for strengthening data transparency and data reproducibility. These journals require their peer reviewers to complete an additional mandatory task for every paper in their journals—a data peer review—to ensure the authors' compliance with the journal's data sharing policies. Examples of journals with data peer review policies include *Scientific Data* published by Springer Nature and *GigaScience* published by Oxford University Press. Some other journals—for example, *Biostatistics* and *Breast Cancer*—employ additional editorial staff to conduct data reviews for all submitted papers.

Journal data sharing policies help accomplish a number of goals. They encourage more transparent practices by researchers (Giofrè et al. 2017; Nuijten et al. 2017) and enable other researchers "to interpret, replicate and build upon the methods or findings reported in the article" (Nature

2020). These policies help researchers comply with the funding agencies' mandates requiring data transparency and availability as a condition of grants. They also help increase the number of citations that journal articles receive and therefore increase both the authors' research impact and the journal's reputation (Piwowar, Day, and Fridsma 2007; Piwowar and Vision 2013). Journals with stringent data sharing policies have "significantly higher" impact factors compared to journals with more relaxed or no data sharing policies (Vasilevsky et al. 2017). Finally, journal policies that *mandate* data sharing by authors (compared to journal policies that simply *encourage* data sharing) greatly contribute to long-term availability of data (Vasilevsky et al. 2017; Vines et al. 2013).

The implementation and implications of different or conflicting journal data policies, however, may be confusing to researchers (Hrynaszkiewicz et al. 2020; Naughton and Kernohan 2016). An alternative approach to this problem was taken by the Data Policy Standardisation and Implementation Interest Group of the Research Data Alliance (RDA), which introduced a standardized research data policy framework supporting all journal and publisher data sharing requirements (Hrynaszkiewicz et al. 2020).

Open Data Repositories

Open data repositories have become a popular solution for finding, storing, and sharing research data, including raw data that have not yet been verified and analyzed. Open data repositories can be associated with government organizations, institutions, libraries, research sponsors, and commercial or nonprofit enterprises. Examples of open data repositories include Data.gov,[11] which serves as a catalog of the U.S. government-generated data collections; Google Earth,[12] which includes worldwide geographical data; and World Bank Open Data,[13] which provides access to economic and historical data from countries around the world.

There are many "general-purpose" repositories that archive diverse types of research data such as Dryad,[14] figshare,[15] and Zenodo.[16] There are also many discipline-specific open data repositories. As of this writing, there are nearly 2,800 disciplinary repositories listed in re3data.org,[17] an international registry of research data repositories.

Open data repositories enable researchers to locate, utilize, and repurpose data instead of collecting or generating new data. They also allow researchers to securely deposit their own data for long-term preservation and reuse. Data repositories typically assign digital object identifiers

(DOIs) to all uploaded datasets so that these datasets can be uniquely identified and cited. Some repositories create metadata for deposited datasets and offer metadata curation services. Others assist researchers with the migration of their datasets to up-to-date formats. Some data repositories are integrated with journal manuscript submission systems that enable authors to deposit data into the repository during the manuscript submission process. Publishers and research funders often provide lists of recommended data repositories in their data sharing policies. Researchers might also share their datasets through their institutional repositories.[18]

Licensing Open Data

The U.S. copyright law does not protect raw facts themselves, including raw data (U.S. Copyright Office 2020). However, a compilation of raw facts (e.g., a dataset), if this compilation "as a whole constitute[s] an original work of authorship," does not fall under the same law and may be protected by copyright[19] (Ibid., 2). The author of a dataset is automatically by law that dataset's copyright holder and, as such, has a legal power to release that dataset under an open license.[20] An open license enables the author of a dataset to clearly define the terms under which the dataset can be used and shared. An open license also helps the dataset users understand what they can legally do with that dataset. Some institutions or institutional departments require or strongly encourage using an open license as a matter of institutional policy or a condition of funding.

Open Data Commons,[21] a project of the OKF, provides two licenses that are designed specifically for datasets (referred to as databases):

- *Open Data Commons Attribution License (ODC-By)*[22]

  The ODC-By license allows users to copy, distribute, and use the database; produce works from the database; and modify, transform, and build upon it for any purpose. The only requirement the ODC-By license imposes on users is that they must acknowledge any public use of the database or works generated from the database.

- *Open Data Commons Open Database License (ODbL)*[23]

  The ODbL grants users the same freedoms and has the same attribution requirement as the ODC-By license but includes two additional conditions: 1) *Share-Alike* (a derived database must be released under the same license as the original) and 2) *Keep-Open* (technological restrictions such as digital rights management [DRM] mechanisms can be applied to the database or a derived database only as long as a version without such restrictions is also made available).

The Open Government Licence (OGL)[24] was developed by the National Archives in the United Kingdom and is intended for the UK's public sector and government information, including data. The OGL is a non-copyleft license, and its terms are similar to those of the Creative Commons' CC-BY license.[25] The OGL requires users to attribute the information source and information provider. It allows commercial uses and the creation of derivative works under the condition that derivative works do not suggest having official status. The OGL is compatible with the CC-BY and ODC-By licenses. Although not explicitly stated, the OGL is designed primarily for use in the UK, as implied by its wording.[26]

Analogously to open content licensing,[27] data licensing is prone to similar pitfalls, including:

- Inability to combine or merge datasets released under conflicting licenses, for example, under the licenses with divergent Share-Alike provisions
- Inclusion of the No Derivatives requirement that restricts data reuse
- Restriction to noncommercial use imposed by some licenses
- Difficulty drawing a line between commercial and noncommercial use of data
- Problem with tracking and correctly articulating required attributions when multiple datasets are combined into a single work ("attribution stacking")
- Difficulty tracking various dataset modifications
- Difficulty of enforcing the license terms
- Potential interoperability between jurisdictions of different countries

Dedicating Data to the Public Domain

Another way for researchers to make their datasets open is to dedicate them to the public domain, which means waiving all copyrights to those datasets. As with any copyrighted work, datasets can be released to the public domain only by the copyright holder or someone with a right to act upon the copyright holder's behalf.

There are two tools that can help researchers certify their dataset(s) as part of the public domain:

- CC0[28]

  CC0 (read as "CC zero") is the Creative Commons' public dedication tool, which allows researchers to waive all of their copyrights to their datasets and dedicate them to the public domain.[29] CC0 is not a license in itself, but a tool to use in jurisdictions that limit or prohibit a complete waiver of copyright, for example, in Germany and some other European countries.

• *The Public Domain Dedication and License (PDDL)*[30]

The PDDL document, created by Open Data Commons, is specifically intended for "permanently and irrevocably" dedicating datasets to the public domain. The PDDL terms are similar to those of CC0 in that they impose no requirements or restrictions on the use of the PDDL-licensed dataset or data.

Barriers to Data Sharing and Reuse

While many researchers embrace the *idea* of data sharing, a wide range of concerns and practical challenges may deter them from actually sharing their own data or reusing the data generated by others. Some of these concerns are rooted in the traditional academic culture and disciplinary norms and practices, while other concerns stem from researchers' individual perceptions associated with data sharing and reuse.

A number of recent surveys (Beno et al. 2017; Berghmans et al. 2017; Stieglitz et al. 2020; Tenopir et al. 2020) that collected information on researchers' data sharing practices identified a number of key barriers to data sharing and reuse. These include:

• Considerable time and energy associated with uploading, organizing, and describing raw data
• Low career advancement benefits of data sharing
• Anxieties about getting "scooped" by competitors
• Uncertainties about copyright and licensing issues associated with data sharing
• Concerns about privacy and security of data that involve information about human subjects and other sensitive information, such as data about nesting sites for endangered bird species and archaeological excavation sites
• Fear of data errors and discrepancies or false conclusions drawn from the data
• Concerns about releasing low-quality data
• An unevenly developed market for publishing research data

The barriers to data reuse include:

• Difficulty finding relevant high-quality research data
• Frustration about large volumes of available data

- Lack of expertise necessary to make use or make sense of available data
- Low incentives to make use of open data
- Concerns that high-impact journals will reject papers that report findings based on secondary analysis of open data
- Need to pay a fee or register before being able to download the data
- Difficulty understanding the data licensing terms explaining how the data can be used and reused
- Technical issues such as the lack of supporting infrastructure, well-developed metadata standards, and software tools for processing the data

There is also considerable heterogeneity among academic disciplines with regard to sharing research data. Different disciplines generate various types of data and have different norms and procedures for sharing their data. For example, researchers in the life sciences share their data more readily than researchers in the medical and social sciences, where there are privacy and security constraints with regard to sensitive data (Berghmans et al. 2017; Stieglitz et al. 2020). Although researchers in the humanities have significantly lower concerns about data privacy and data security, data sharing in the humanities disciplines is still relatively limited (Ibid.).

Notes

1. The FAIR Principles were originally described in Wilkinson et al. "The FAIR Guiding Principles for Scientific Data Management and Stewardship." *Scientific Data* 3, Article 160018 (2016):1–9. https://doi.org/10.1038/sdata.2016.18.

2. The Panton Principles (http://pantonprinciples.org).

3. The 8 Principles of Open Government Data (https://opengovdata.org).

4. Additional seven principles, which "the working group did not consider but might have," are available at https://opengovdata.org.

5. The Bermuda Rules were later described in various genome data policy statements issued by the National Human Genome Research Institute (NHGRI) in the United States.

6. European Open Science Cloud (EOSC) (https://eosc-portal.eu).

7. The OPEN Government Data Act builds upon the Digital Accountability and Transparency Act (the DATA Act) (https://www.congress.gov/113/plaws/publ101/PLAW-113publ101.pdf), signed by President Barak Obama into law in 2014. The DATA Act required the U.S. government to disclose its spending data, including information on contracts, loans, grants, and other financial assistance awards.

8. TOP Guidelines (https://www.cos.io/our-services/top-guidelines).

9. TOP Factor (https://www.topfactor.org).

10. Examples of journals with data sharing policies include the *American Economic Review*, *Clinical Infectious Diseases*, and the *Journal of Evolutionary Biology*.

11. Data.gov (http://www.data.gov).

12. Google Earth (http://www.google.com/earth/index.html).

13. World Bank Open Data (http://data.worldbank.org).

14. Dryad (https://datadryad.org).

15. figshare (https://figshare.com).

16. Zenodo (http://zenodo.org).

17. re3data.org (https://www.re3data.org).

18. Institutional repositories are discussed in Chapter 4.

19. Unlike the U.S. Copyright Law, the European Intellectual Property Law does have a legal right (referred to as a sui generis property right or, more simply, a database right), which protects mere compilations of raw facts such as, for example, the white pages of telephone books. The database right recognizes the effort invested in making such compilations (the 'sweat of the brow' doctrine), even when these compilations do not involve a 'creative' aspect.

20. According to the Panton Principles, open data should be licensed only under a data-appropriate license. They strongly discourage the use of Creative Commons (CC) licences as well as the use of the General Public License (GPL), the GNU Free Documentation License (GFDL) or one of the BSD licenses. The latter stands for Berkeley Software Distribution license and is a permissive or "non-copyleft" license, which allows greater liberties in mixing proprietary and free software.

21. Open Data Commons (https://opendatacommons.org).

22. Open Data Commons Attribution License (ODC-By) (https://opendata commons.org/licenses/by/1-0).

23. Open Data Commons Open Database License (ODbL) (https://opendata commons.org/licenses/odbl/1-0).

24. Open Government Licence (OGL) (http://www.nationalarchives.gov.uk /doc/open-government-licence/version/3).

25. Creative Commons (CC) licenses are discussed in Chapter 3.

26. Open Definition, a project of the Open Knowledge Foundation, provides links to data licenses that are created by other countries, including Canada, Germany, and Taiwan. See: http://opendefinition.org/licenses/#Data.

27. The open content licensing model is discussed in Chapter 3.

28. CC0 (https://creativecommons.org/publicdomain/zero/1.0).

29. For explanation of how to use the CC0 tool, see: https://creativecommons .org/share-your-work/public-domain/cc0/.

30. The Public Domain Dedication and License (PDDL) (https://opendata commons.org/licenses/pddl/1-0/).

Suggested Resources

data.gov
http://www.data.gov
An online repository of open datasets generated by the U.S. government that can be searched by topic, location, data format, and other parameters. Includes a collection of tools, case studies, and policies related to government data governance, management, sharing, and use.

DMP Tool
https://dmptool.org
A free web-based service of the University of California Curation Center of the California Digital Library. Provides templates that help meet institutional and funder requirements for data management and data sharing.

Fedora (Flexible Extensible Digital Object and Repository Architecture)
http://www.fedora-commons.org
An open source, digital object repository system that allows for long-term storage and retrieval of data and metadata.

Guide to Open Data Licensing
https://opendefinition.org/guide/data/
A guide produced by Open Definition, a project of Open Knowledge Foundation. Explains how to license data and discusses intellectual property rights associated with data.

Open Data Repositories
http://oad.simmons.edu/oadwiki/Data_repositories
An extensive list of open data repositories organized by discipline. Part of the Open Access Directory (OAD), a community-based wiki dedicated to promoting open access resources.

re3data.org
https://www.re3data.org/
An international registry of discipline-specific research data repositories. Covers all academic disciplines.

SHERPA/Juliet
https://v2.sherpa.ac.uk/juliet/
A service of SHERPA (Securing a Hybrid Environment for Research Preservation and Access) providing information on research funders' requirements on open access publication and data sharing.

CHAPTER SEVEN

Citizen Science (CS)

Transcending the Boundaries between Professional and Nonprofessional Science

Citizen science is, at once, a practice with a long history, a growing movement, a fledgling professional field, a global endeavor, and a powerful bridge between scientific research and the larger society that can benefit from it.

—Storksdieck et al. (2016)

What Is Citizen Science?

Citizen science (CS hereafter) refers to an active, voluntary involvement of nonscientists in scientific research. The distinction between scientists and nonscientists is generally based on the acquisition of formal training and credentials, although the assumption that citizen scientists are always nonprofessionals is not always appropriate because many CS participants are experts in their respective fields. A core tenet of CS is that "science is not the sole providence of professional scientists" (National Academies of Sciences, Engineering, and Medicine 2018, 28). This tenet is closely related to a broader ethical principle—the right to science and culture—established in Article 27 of the Universal Declaration of Human Rights, which states that "[e]veryone has the right to freely participate in the cultural life of the community, to enjoy the arts and to share in scientific advancement and its benefits" (United Nations General Assembly 1948).

Being poised at the intersection of professional science and civic engagement, CS has also been variously called civic science, community-based monitoring, crowd science, participatory sensing, and crowdmapping, among other names. According to the National Advisory Council for Environmental Policy and Technology (NACEPT) of the U.S. Environmental Protection Agency (2016, 1), all these terms have a common emphasis on "openness, democratization of science, and the mobilization of diverse people and communities."

The origins of the term "citizen science" are contested in the scholarly literature. According to some authors, this term was first used in 1978 by a biochemist, Erwin Chargaff, who argued that science should be dominated by dedicated amateur scientists devoted to a true pursuit of knowledge (Fecher and Friesike 2014). Other authors attribute the coining of this term to Alan Irwin (1995), who used it to describe "science which assists the needs and concerns of citizens [. . .] [and] implies a form of science developed and enacted by citizens themselves" (xi). Yet others credit Rick Bonney (1996) for introducing the term to refer to research projects at the Cornell Lab of Ornithology, where engaged nonprofessional volunteers took part in avian research. Officially, the term "citizen science" was added to the Oxford English Dictionary only in 2014[1] and was defined as "[t]he collection and analysis of data relating to the natural world by members of the general public, typically as part of a collaborative project with professional scientists" (Oxford English Dictionary, n.d.). At the government level, CS was defined as "a form of open collaboration in which individuals or organizations participate voluntarily in the scientific process in various ways, including: (A) enabling the formulation of research questions; (B) creating and refining project design; (C) conducting scientific experiments; (D) collecting and analyzing data; (E) interpreting the results of data; (F) developing technologies and applications; (G) making discoveries; and (H) solving problems" (U.S. Congress 2017a).

As a concept, CS is still evolving. It represents a multidimensional approach that shares some characteristics with open scholarship, including collaborative knowledge production, data sharing, and the involvement of diverse groups in the research process. At one end of the conceptual spectrum, CS is seen as a simple crowdsourcing technique, which allows professional scientists to recruit a large number of volunteers who do not consider themselves "epistemic equals to scientists" (Cornwell and Campbell 2012, 115) and who contribute "needed services, ideas or content" to large-scale projects through "microtasking" without necessarily engaging with the underlying scientific concepts (Eitzel et al.

2017). An example of such a project includes the Christmas Bird Count,[2] the first documented and the longest-running CS project initiated and administered by the National Audubon Society in 1900. In this annual project, thousands of volunteer birdwatchers across the United States, Canada, and other countries in the Western Hemisphere count birds over a 24-hour period in order to provide bird population information for conservation biologists. Some authors, however, argue that CS as a crowdsourcing technique is more than a source of "free labor" but also a practice involving learning (Jordan et al. 2011) and co-creation of new knowledge (Kasperowski and Hillman 2018; Kasperowski and Kullenberg 2019).

At the other end of the conceptual spectrum is "extreme" CS, a bottom-up, community-driven approach to research in which the boundaries between amateurs and professionals are broken down and in which members of the public become equal contributors to scientific research. In extreme CS, community members, including disadvantaged and marginalized communities, initiate a research project with the dual goal—to find solutions to a specific problem relevant to their lives (often triggered by an environmental risk or health hazard) and to benefit from addressing that problem (English, Richardson, and Garzón-Galvis 2018; Haklay 2013; Stevens et al. 2014; Woolley et al. 2016). An example of an extreme CS project is a project initiated by the indigenous communities in the Congo Basin rainforest of Central Africa that aimed to monitor commercial poaching, which was problematic for those communities because of overhunting (Rowland 2012). One of the strong supporters of extreme CS (including the project just mentioned) is the Extreme Citizen Science research group at the University College London in the United Kingdom (UCL ExCiteS).[3] The UCL ExCiteS research group works with diverse communities "at the extremes of the globalised world—both because of non-literacy and the remote or forbidding environments they inhabit" (Stevens et al. 2014, 20). This group also develops technologies to simplify the collection, sharing, and visualization of geographic information gathered by nonliterate and illiterate users, who have little or no prior technology experience.[4]

Related to the notion of extreme CS is the idea of CS as public resistance (Kullenberg 2015). The practice of CS as public resistance aids concerned citizens in responding to their local problems related to health, environment, or conservation. Similarly to extreme CS, this practice takes place outside of academic institutions and empowers diverse communities to set research agenda and collect scientific data independently from professional scientists and then actively participate in policy and political decision processes (Ibid).

Between these two ends of the CS conceptual spectrum there are other interpretations of CS. Some authors view CS as a civic education tool helping the public develop scientific literacy skills outside a formal academic setting (Bonney et al. 2009; National Academies of Sciences, Engineering, and Medicine 2018). Others consider CS a fledgling academic field in its own right (termed "a science of citizen science" by Francois Taddei [quoted in Rowland 2012]), which concerns not only CS projects but also "warrants consideration as a distinct discipline or field of inquiry" (Jordan et al. 2015, 208). One of the earliest and, by far, one of the most influential interpretations of CS is the view of CS as "scientific citizenship"—a science that addresses the needs of citizens and involves them in the scientific research process (Irvin 1995, 2001). In "scientific citizenship," the gap between professional and nonprofessional knowledge begins to close because scientists and citizens work together on shared problems (Ibid.).

A Brief History and Current State of CS

CS is a practice with a long history, although, until recently, it existed without a specific definition or conceptualization. The practice of systematically gathering data and observations of natural phenomena by members of the public has existed for most of recorded history and helped create large collections of flora and fauna data, fossils, and other specimens that are still valuable today (Miller-Rushing et al. 2012). Prior to the professionalization of science in the mid-nineteenth century, which has produced the two "mutually exclusive" types of researchers—professionals and amateurs (Strasser et al. 2019, 58)—almost all of the scientific research was conducted by individuals who were not trained as scientists in the contemporary sense and who conducted their scientific investigations aside from their main occupation (Silvertown 2009; Vetter 2011). For example, Benjamin Franklin, Gregor Mendel, and Charles Darwin were not trained as scientists and made their living in other, "paid" professions. The idea of "gentleman science," where people with time and means contributed to science as hobbyists, also bears resemblance to the notion of CS (National Academies of Sciences, Engineering, and Medicine 2018). As Kasperowski and Kullenberg (2019, 2) point out, "[i]t is actually professional science that is 'the new thing', and the citizen scientists have been there all along in the shadows."

Although the professionalization and institutionalization of science have marginalized the role of nonscientists in conducting scientific research (Miller-Rushing et al. 2012), the last three decades have seen a significant proliferation of CS projects and a greater attention to CS as a means of tackling research questions (Bonney et al. 2014). The growth of CS as a common practice potentially available to anyone can be attributed to multiple factors, including 1) increased recognition among professional researchers that citizen scientists represent a source of free labor, resources, and computational power that can help them fulfill their research goals; 2) a growing number of research funder mandates requiring their grant holders to demonstrate societal relevance of their research and undertake project-related public outreach and engagement in science; 3) the increased availability and widespread use of the Internet, geographic information system (GIS)–enabled applications, and smartphones that facilitate the collection, processing, and visualization of large amounts of data; 4) the reduced cost, ease of use, and improved accuracy of environmental sensors; 5) the proliferation of online social media sites, providing the infrastructure for sustaining large networks of citizen scientists; and 6) an ample number of published studies demonstrating the value and quality of CS data (Bonney et al. 2014; Cohn 2008; Dickinson et al. 2012; English, Richardson, and Garzón-Galvis 2018; Newman et al. 2012; Silvertown 2009).

In recent years, CS has become increasingly recognized by U.S. federal agencies as part of the rethinking of how scientific research relates to broader societal goals. The 2015 memorandum "Addressing Society and Scientific Challenges through Citizen Science and Crowdsourcing," issued by John Holdren, assistant to the president for science and technology, stated that CS projects "enhance scientific research and address societal needs, while drawing on previously underutilized resources," and "[connect] members of the public directly to Federal agency missions and to each other" (Holdren 2015, 1). This memorandum directed federal agencies to take specific steps for building capacity for CS, including identifying agency coordinators for CS projects and cataloging agency-specific CS projects in an online database. The same memorandum directed the agencies to apply the following three principles in CS project design: 1) data quality (data collected by citizen scientists should be "credible and usable"); 2) openness (datasets, code, and applications generated by CS projects should be "transparent, open, and available to the public, consistent with applicable intellectual property, security, and privacy protections"); and 3) public participation (participation in CS projects "should be fully voluntary, and volunteers should be acknowledged for their contributions") (Ibid., 2). As a result of this memorandum, federal agencies released a variety of CS-related resources, including the official government CS portal CitizenScience.gov,[5] which provides access to a

searchable catalog of federally supported CS projects, a toolkit for assisting practitioners with designing and managing CS projects, and a gateway to a large community of CS practitioners. Government support of CS
is also exemplified by the U.S. Crowdsourcing and Citizen Science Act,
introduced in 2017, with the goal of fostering the integration of CS in federal programs. This act granted federal agencies "direct and explicit
authority" to use CS to advance each agency's missions (U.S. Congress
2017a).

A continuing growth and formalization of CS are evidenced by the
recent establishment of CS associations around the world, including the
European Citizen Science Association,[6] the Australian Citizen Science
Association,[7] and the U.S.-based but globally open Citizen Science Association.[8] These associations develop international collaborations and
share CS best practices through their websites, conferences, and an open
access peer-reviewed journal *Citizen Science: Theory and Practice*. The
global reach of CS is further manifested by the formation of the Citizen
Science Global Partnership,[9] a network-of-networks launched in 2017 in
collaboration with the United Nations Environment Programme (UNEP)
and supported by the United Nations Educational, Scientific, and Cultural Organization (UNESCO) with the aim of supporting global coordination of CS projects. Horizon 2020,[10] the European Union's largest
research and innovation funding program, has also invested heavily in
CS as an approach for tackling societal problems.

Benefits of CS

CS offers substantial benefits to professional scientists, volunteers taking part in CS projects, and society at large. For scientists, CS effectively
combines public outreach and engagement objectives with the research
objectives of the scientists themselves (Silvertown 2009). By drawing on
volunteer labor, scientists are capable of tackling research questions at
scales that would be impossible to achieve through professional science
alone (Miller-Rushing et al. 2012; Sauermann and Franzoni 2015). Specifically, CS provides professional scientists with a valuable source of "free
labor," especially for those tasks that require a considerable expenditure
of time and effort, such as the collection of vast amounts of field and
observational data across a wide array of locations or over spans of time,
or both (Cohn 2008; Silvertown 2009; Stilgoe 2009). Enlisting large numbers of volunteers in the data collection process can also free up scientists'
time to conduct other, more specialized, complex activities such as
data analysis and interpretation (Resnik, Elliott, and Miller 2015).

Furthermore, the contribution of volunteers working in archives ("citizen archivists"), who transcribe, tag, index, and make accessible and searchable millions of documents archived by research institutions, enable scientists to compare historical records with current observations and gain insights into the impacts of changes in climate, land use, and socioeconomic factors on the environment and people (Miller-Rushing et al. 2012). Finally, CS allows scientists to benefit from the wealth of indigenous knowledge, unique skills, novel approaches, and diverse perspectives that volunteers contribute to projects, all of which can help increase the relevance of research questions and improve study outcomes (Danielsen et al. 2018; Sauermann and Franzoni 2015).

Volunteers benefit from taking part in CS projects in a number of ways as well. Benefits for CS volunteers include learning and career development opportunities, personal enjoyment, improved well-being, enhanced appreciation of their local environment, strengthened "sense of place" (Haywood 2014), satisfaction through contributing time and labor to scientific research, and the potential to address local issues and influence policy decisions (Haklay 2013; Robinson et al. 2018).

CS projects also offer benefits to society at large. CS challenges the knowledge monopoly of professional science by providing the public with an opportunity to influence the direction of research projects and make these projects more responsive to the needs of specific communities, including the needs of marginalized or disadvantaged groups (Fals-Borda and Rahman 1991; Irwin 1995; Ottinger 2009; Wynne 1996). Relatedly, Novak et al. (2018) point out that members of the public are more likely to accept the solutions resulting from a research project when they are actively involved in the research and solution-seeking processes.

Challenges of CS

While an increasing engagement of the public in scientific research appears to be a win-win scenario, it also presents many challenges. The key concern expressed by researchers with regard to CS is problems with data quality and data integrity that could potentially undermine the validity of CS projects (Cornwell and Campbell 2011; Dickinson et al. 2012; Riesch and Potter 2014). Although problems with data quality and data integrity can occur in any type of research, including federally funded science (Shamoo and Resnik 2009), scientists are concerned that volunteers without a research background may not have the necessary skills to collect, record, classify, or manage data properly. Scientists are also concerned that CS volunteers may fabricate, manipulate, or distort data in order to meet deadlines or sway particular research outcomes (Resnik, Elliott, and Miller 2015) or use unreliable data collection and data analysis techniques, either because these techniques are less expensive or because they are more likely to detect potential hazards (Ottinger 2009).

Another concern about data that often arises in CS projects is how to make data collected by citizen scientists openly available to the public without breaching data privacy and data confidentiality (English, Richardson, and Garzón-Galvis 2018). Many CS projects generate sensitive data, such as the precise global positioning system (GPS) coordinates of a discrete location, data about a protected or vulnerable species, private health data, or data enabling the identification of specific people or routines (Bowser-Livermore and Wiggins 2015). Sharing these data publicly can potentially harm the environment or the community whom citizen scientists intend to protect or serve. Related concerns may arise when CS project coordinators fail to adapt appropriate ethical standards involving research with human subjects or when they do not provide proper project oversight and may unintentionally expose participants to potential harm or unnecessary risks, for example, in participant-led health research or studies partaking in self-experimentation (Vayena and Tasioulas 2013).

Intellectual property issues also arise in some CS projects. Individual citizens or entire communities may claim ownership over the data they generated, especially if the project was time and effort intensive and resulted in a scientific publication (Riesch and Potter 2014). Relatedly, some communities may expect to have control over how the data they collected are shared and used, especially when such data concern traditional, "culturally embedded" information provided by the members of indigenous populations—for example, the information about local species, ecology, climate, and traditional medicinal practices (Shiva 2016).

Other concerns about CS include:

- The lack of a meaningful research impact or learning opportunities for citizen scientists when they are used simply as free workforce (Irwin 2001; Powell and Colin 2009).

- Inequality and exclusion that may take place when CS projects include volunteers who already have necessary resources in terms of time and technology but fail to engage members of underserved and marginalized communities (Nascimento et al. 2018).

- Barriers in access to computers, the Internet, and mobile phones or lack of technological skills in their use, any of which may prevent the members of disadvantaged communities from engaging in CS projects (English, Richardson, and Garzón-Galvis 2018).

- Power imbalances that occur when community-based participatory research projects are systematically being unfunded or ignored by formal research bodies (Nascimento et al. 2018).

- Sociocultural barriers, bias, and mistrust that prevent some communities (e.g., low-income communities and communities of color) from participating in community-driven CS projects (Shavers, Lynch, and Burmeister 2002; Wing et al. 2008).

- Conflicts of interest that may arise when individuals or groups use CS projects as an opportunity to advance their political objectives (Nature 2015).

- The potential for exploitation that occurs when researchers seek to monetize or otherwise profit from the free labor contributed by citizen scientists without equitably sharing with them the benefits or rewards received from the research project (Riesch and Potter 2014).

- Insufficient coordination and lack of clear definitions of the roles and responsibilities across different CS governance levels (Nascimento et al. 2018).

- Lack of comprehensive evaluation frameworks of CS projects and programs (Kieslinger et al. 2018).

To address these concerns and help guard against unintended negative consequences of CS, the European Citizen Science Association, in collaboration with an international community of CS researchers and practitioners, developed the Ten Principles of Citizen Science, the document that defines the characteristics of high-quality CS projects.[11] This document, published in 2015, provides researchers, project leaders, and decision makers with a set of core principles that can help them with developing CS projects. Currently available in 31 languages, the Ten Principles can also be used as a framework for comparing and assessing new or existing CS initiatives around the world.

Types of CS Projects

CS engages volunteers in a wide variety of projects, predominantly in the natural and environmental sciences, including projects on invasive species, habitat assessment, climate change, ecological restoration, and air and water quality improvement (Cohn 2008; Cooper et al. 2007; Silvertown 2009; Tauginienė et al. 2020). CS also increasingly engages volunteers in the social sciences, geography, epidemiology, and humanities (Kullenberg and Kasperowski 2016; Tauginienė et al. 2020). The number of CS project participants can range from a single person or a few individuals gathering local research data to thousands of volunteers participating in a large-scale national or international research project. Typically, citizen scientists work on a project alongside and under the direction of professional scientists or scientific organizations and contribute to that project in various ways, such as formulating research questions, collecting and processing data, conducting scientific experiments, and developing low-cost technologies and applications. Volunteers are involved in CS projects not as "subjects" of the research, but as participants, although the level of their participation depends on the nature of the project and can be either passive or active (Holdren 2015). Some CS projects relate to participants' hobbies such as bird watching and stargazing, while others focus on addressing specific societal needs related to health risks or environmental threats (Sauermann and Franzoni 2015). The goals of CS projects vary and can include enlisting the public in research activities for which professional scientists may not have the time or resources to pursue (Silvertown 2009), enhancing public understanding of science and developing scientific literacy (Bonney et al. 2009; Bonney et al. 2016), and engaging concerned communities in research and decision-making around local issues (Kullenberg 2015; Ottinger 2009). Incentives for participation in CS projects vary also and may include intellectual curiosity, educational goals, social and environmental justice, and socialization with like-minded people (Bowser et al. 2020; Jennett et al. 2016; Rotman et al. 2012).

CS projects have been classified in various ways: by disciplinary field (e.g., astronomy and ornithology), duration of participation (e.g., one-time activity or multiple activities over a long period of time), type of participation (e.g., in-person, online, and hybrid), and mode of communication (e.g., in-person, telephone, social media, and in writing) (National Academies of Sciences, Engineering, and Medicine 2018).

Bonney et al. (2009) group CS projects into three types—contributory, collaborative, and co-created—based on the level of public involvement in the research process. In contributory projects, participants simply collect data for a scientific study, although they may sometimes help analyze the data and disseminate research results. An example of a contributory project is FeederWatch,[12] a project conducted by the Cornell Lab of Ornithology, for which participants identify and count the birds that visit their backyard feeders during winter. In collaborative projects, participants assist with the analysis and interpretation of data and sometimes are also involved in the dissemination of research results. An example of the collaborative project is the Invasive Plant Atlas of New England (IPANE),[13] which involves the public in identifying and mapping invasive plants.

Co-created CS projects are initiated, designed, and conducted almost entirely by community groups in order to address the concerns of a particular community. In co-created CS projects, participants are involved in all stages of a scientific study, which may be conducted largely or totally independently of professional scientists. Examples of co-created projects are the projects conducted by ReClam the Bay (RCTB),[14] a nonprofit environmental organization, which engages volunteers in monitoring the water quality and restoring shellfish in the Barnegat Bay watershed in New Jersey.

Wiggins and Crowston (2011) categorize CS projects into five types—action-oriented, conservation, investigation, virtual, and educational. Action-oriented projects employ participatory action research methods to address local concerns, such as the project initiated by Sherman's Creek Conservation Association (SCCA)[15] to improve water quality in Sherman's Creek watershed in Perry County, Pennsylvania. Conservation projects are primarily focused on natural resource management issues, for example, the survey-based marine debris project aimed at identifying the distribution and type of beach litter in Monterey Bay in California (Rosevelt et al. 2013). Investigation projects focus on research goals requiring data collection from a specific physical environment. An example is the Snowtweets project,[16] initiated by the University of Waterloo in Canada, which aims to measure the snow depth in various locations around the world. Virtual projects are entirely web-based, such as Project Implicit,[17] which invites participants to examine their hidden bias via online sessions. In educational projects, the primary goals are learning and educational outreach, such as the Fossil Finders project,[18] where participants learn about Devonian fossils.

Haklay (2013) classifies Internet-based CS projects (dubbed by Grey [2011] "citizen cyberscience") into three categories: volunteered computing, volunteered thinking, and participatory sensing. In volunteered computing projects, large numbers of participants across the globe utilize the processing power of personal computers and the Internet to receive and send data. An example of a volunteered computing project is the SETI@home project,[19] which uses Internet-connected computers to search for extraterrestrial intelligence. In volunteered thinking projects, participants are trained to perform a particular task online. For example, in the Stardust@home project,[20] participants are trained to use the virtual microscope to identify traces of intercellular dust. In participatory sensing projects, participants use their mobile phones or other data-recording devices to collect environmental data—for example, in the NoiseTube project,[21] which monitors noise pollution.

The use of digital games for collecting research data, classifying images, and solving scientific problems is perhaps the most recent CS phenomenon. Volunteers can play CS-based digital games either independently or as part of a team. Typically, they are not required to have prior scientific knowledge, although some background knowledge in a game-relevant field can be beneficial (Ponti et al. 2018). One of the earliest CS-based digital games is Foldit,[22] developed by the Center of Game Science at the University of Washington in 2008. Foldit is a puzzle-based video game that uses "crowd intelligence" to predict protein molecule structure, a process that can aid scientists in preventing or treating important diseases, as well as in discovering new proteins, which can help in converting plants to fuel. Another example of a CS-based digital game is Eyewire,[23] a puzzle game from Sebastian Seung's lab at Princeton University, in which players are asked to identify connected regions in 3D-transformed functional magnetic resonance imaging (fMRI) images. Data produced by Eyewire allow researchers to understand how the human retina processes visual information and that, in turn, can help ophthalmologists improve blindness therapies and develop retinal prostheses.

Another, currently marginal, enabler of citizen engagement in science is do-it-yourself (DIY) science. Nascimento, Pereira, and Ghezzi (2014, 30) describe a DIY scientist as a person who "tinkers, hacks, fixes, recreates and assembles objects and systems in creative and unexpected directions, usually using open source tools and adhering to open paradigms to share knowledge and outputs with others." While DIY science projects primarily include amateurs and hobbyists, these projects also increasingly involve professional scientists who conduct research outside their institutional or laboratory settings, such as in their homes, Makerspaces, Techshops, Hackerspaces, and other informal locations (Novak et al. 2018).

Notes

1. See OED's "New Words List June 2014" at: https://web.archive.org/web/20160509083230/http://public.oed.com/the-oed-today/recent-updates-to-the-oed/previous%20updates/june-2014-update/new-words-list-june-2014#new_sub_entries.

2. Christmas Bird Count (https://www.audubon.org/conservation/science/christmas-bird-count).

3. UCL ExCiteS (https://www.geog.ucl.ac.uk/research/research-centres/excites).

4. See ExCiteS Software at: https://www.geog.ucl.ac.uk/research/research
-centres/excites/software.

5. CitizenScience.gov (https://www.citizenscience.gov).

6. European Citizen Science Association (https://ecsa.citizen-science.net).

7. Australian Citizen Science Association (https://citizenscience.org.au).

8. Citizen Science Association (https://www.citizenscience.org).

9. The Citizen Science Global Partnership (http://citizenscienceglobal
.org).

10. Horizon 2020 (https://ec.europa.eu/programmes/horizon2020/en).

11. This document is available at: https://zenodo.org/record/5127534#.Ya9
-7y2ZMnV.

12. FeederWatch (https://feederwatch.org).

13. Invasive Plant Atlas of New England (IPANE) (https://ipane.org).

14. ReClam the Bay (RCTB) (https://reclamthebay.org).

15. Sherman's Creek Conservation Association (https://www.facebook.com
/ShermansCreekConservationAssociation).

16. Snowtweets (http://snowtweets.uwaterloo.ca).

17. Project Implicit (https://implicit.harvard.edu/implicit/research).

18. Fossil Finders (https://www.fossilfinders.org).

19. SETI@home (https://setiathome.berkeley.edu).

20. Stardust@home (https://stardustathome.ssl.berkeley.edu).

21. NoiseTube (http://www.noisetube.net).

22. Foldit (http://www.Fold.it).

23. Eyewire (https://eyewire.org).

Suggested Resources

Citizen Science Association (CSA)
https://www.citizenscience.org
A U.S.-based but globally open association whose mission is to "[advance] knowledge through research and monitoring done by, for, and with members of the public." CSA holds biennial conferences; conducts skills-based webinars; forms field-building working groups; maintains a discussion listserv; and publishes monthly newsletters and an open access, peer-reviewed online journal, *Citizen Science: Theory and Practice.*

CitizenScience.gov
https://www.citizenscience.gov
An official U.S. government portal that provides access to a searchable catalog of federally supported CS projects, a toolkit for assisting practitioners with designing and managing CS projects, and a gateway to a large community of CS practitioners.

Citizen Science: Theory and Practice

https://theoryandpractice.citizenscienceassociation.org

An open access peer-reviewed online journal published by Ubiquity Press on behalf of the Citizen Science Association. Provides a venue for CS researchers and practitioners around the world for sharing best practices in designing, implementing, leading, assessing, and sustaining CS projects.

SciStarter

https://scistarter.org

A U.S.-based directory of CS projects and related activities and an online CS hub that helps users find, join, track, and contribute to hundreds of research projects and events.

Zooniverse

https://www.zooniverse.org

The world's largest online platform for CS research across a wide range of disciplinary fields hosted and operated by the Citizen Science Alliance and sponsored by several federal government organizations, including the National Science Foundation (NSF) and the National Aeronautics and Space Administration (NASA). Includes Project Builder, an online tool for creating CS projects.

CHAPTER EIGHT

The Many Paths to Openness

*Expanding the Sphere
of Open Scholarship*

Crossing boundaries is a defining characteristic of our age.
—Julie Thompson Klein (1996, 1)

Although the move toward openness in scholarship has found the most resonance in the six paradigms discussed in previous chapters, it has also been manifested by the emergence of other approaches to conducting research "in the open." These approaches are no longer restricted to traditional scholarly communication mechanisms but are present at nearly every stage of knowledge production and knowledge distribution—from idea creation to measuring the impact of research results. Some of these approaches have already gained traction within the scholarly community, others have received less attention from scholars, and yet others have been subject to debate.

Open Peer Review

Peer review is still the most commonly used approach for quality validation in academia, even though it has been criticized for being "inherently conservative" (Holbrook 2010) and not necessarily determining the true merit of a work (Hames 2007; Rowland 2002). Peer review is a process in which two or more experts from the same or related field of study (referred to as "peers") apply stringent criteria in evaluating the quality of manuscripts submitted for publication in a journal or other scholarly publication (e.g., an anthology or encyclopedia). The goal of peer review is to determine whether the submitted manuscripts are within the publication's scope, meet the research standards established for a given discipline, and are meritorious enough to deserve publication. In some cases, peer review is also used in the review of applications for tenure, promotion, and fellowship; in evaluating the work performance of individual faculty members; and in assessing strengths and weaknesses of specific academic departments or entire institutions in comparison to other departments or institutions. Since the middle of the twentieth century, peer review has also been widely employed in the evaluation of grant proposals (Holbrook 2010; Spier 2002).

A traditional peer review model operates in an anonymous, or blind, fashion. In single-blind peer review, the identities of the reviewers are concealed from the reviewee. In double-blind peer review, the identity of the reviewee is concealed from the reviewers as well. In triple-blind peer review, the identities of all parties involved in the review process are concealed from each other, including the reviewees, the reviewers, and the handling editor(s). Many people believe that such reciprocal anonymity reduces bias in the evaluation process, encourages unfiltered criticism, protects reviewers from potential retaliation, and ensures an overall objective review focused on research itself rather than being directed for or against the researcher.

Unlike the blind model of traditional peer review, open peer review (OPR) does not "mask" (McCormack 2009) the identities of authors or reviewers. In the broadest sense, OPR is a process in which the names, affiliations, and credentials of both reviewers and reviewees are disclosed to one another and sometimes to the community at large.

Although the discussions about "opening up" the peer review process can be traced back to the 1980s (McGiffert 1988), there is still no agreement upon the exact definition of OPR or a standardized model for its implementation. OPR is used as an umbrella term for a variety of overlapping, and sometimes contradicting, approaches for conducting peer review "in the open." In most cases, OPR refers to the process of peer review in which the identities of both reviewee and reviewers are disclosed to each other. In other cases, it refers to the practice of publishing reviewer reports alongside journal articles. Yet in other cases, OPR describes the crowdsourced model in which the publisher invites post-publication comments and ratings from the experts in relevant fields or even from any reader. OPR may also refer to a hybrid peer review process, which employs various combinations of the previously mentioned models.

Among the earliest adopters of OPR were the two open access journals: *Journal for Interactive Media in Education*, launched in 1996 by the Open University (United Kingdom), and *Atmospheric Chemistry and Physics*, launched in 2001 by the European Geosciences Union (Ford 2013; Pöschl and Koop 2008). Among other open access publishers who have been offering either optional or mandatory versions of OPR are BioMed Central,[1] Public Library of Science (PLoS),[2] Frontiers,[3] and PeerJ.[4] By far, one of the most prominent players in the OPR initiative is F1000Research,[5] an open access publishing and OPR platform for scientists and clinicians. F1000Research offers a fully transparent peer review in which any reader can see reviewer names and all the peer review reports and comments.

A small number of commercial publishers have also experimented with OPR, adopting different levels of transparency. For example, Nature has conducted several OPR trials for its journals since 2007 (Wolfram et al. 2020). In 2018, Wiley, in collaboration with Clarivate Analytics, launched its first OPR journal *Clinical Genetics* as part of its Transparent Peer Review pilot project and added 39 more journals to this pilot by the end of 2019 (Graf 2019).

At present, there is little consensus among scholars and publishers alike about whether OPR is significantly superior to the traditional blind peer review. Most arguments for OPR are ethical in nature, in line with the concept of openness in scholarship, advocating for social justice, transparency, and collaboration as the main principles. Proponents of OPR posit that it is unfair to expose scholars to the judgment of those who hide behind the "mask" of anonymity and whom the authors cannot hold accountable for hostile, erroneous, or unfair comments. They argue that by "unmasking" the identities of authors and reviewers, OPR helps scholars attain greater justice and fairness in scholarly publishing. As Smith (1999, 4) puts it, "a court with an unidentified judge makes us think immediately of totalitarian states and the world of Franz Kafka."

Other arguments for OPR are more pragmatic. They are based on a belief that the abolishment of anonymity in peer review improves the quality of reviews, enables an easier detection of scholarly misconduct, exposes potential conflicts of interest, and results in an overall greater responsibility and accountability on behalf of both authors and reviewers (Boldt 2011; Bornmann et al. 2011; Maharg and Nigel 2007; Perakakis et al. 2010; Prug 2010). Some scholars claim that open, robust discussions between authors and reviewers (as well as between authors and readers in case of the crowdsourced review model) help generate, refine, and disseminate new ideas and strengthen communities of practice (Ford 2013). OPR is also believed to help reviewers receive academic credit for their often "invisible labor" (Boldt 2011), make review reports more "constructive and civil" (Bernstein, Rachel 2015), mitigate reviewers' "unnecessarily vitriolic comments" enabled by anonymity (Clobridge 2016), and "flatten the hierarchy" of traditional peer review, in which senior academics tend to review the work of junior scholars (Maharg and Nigel 2007).

Although some people find the benefits of OPR compelling, others are concerned about the potential negative consequences associated with the abolished reviewer anonymity. Some of these concerns cited widely in the literature include:

- Difficulty finding reviewers who feel comfortable with self-identification
- Increased likelihood of cautious, bland reviews due to the reviewers' reluctance to criticize the work of influential scholars, colleagues, or more senior academics
- Potential of pleasing authors with a previous track record, with the expectation of reciprocated favors over time
- Greater likelihood of gender bias or bias based on nationality, race, and institutional affiliation as a consequence of author and reviewer identification
- In case of crowdsourced reviews, problematic validity of comments due to the questionable expertise of reviewers

Due to the absence of a consensual view on whether OPR surpasses the traditional research validation processes, a number of journals employing OPR in their day-to-day practices still constitute a small percentage of the overall number of scholarly journals. A recent study by Wolfram et al. (2020) identified 617 journals, primarily in the medical and natural sciences, which employed some form of OPR by the end of 2019. The same study revealed that 81% of these journals have been produced by only five publishers: BioMed Central, Frontiers, Kowsar, Multidisciplinary Digital Publishing Institute (MDPI), and SCIENCEDOMAIN International (SDI).

Invisible Colleges

The term "invisible colleges" refers to informal communication networks of scholars who belong to the same field of study or share research interests. The concept of invisible colleges originated in the seventeenth century in the Royal Society of London, where invisible colleges served as an influential channel of scholarly information exchange that took place outside an academic institution (Crane 1972). In the past, activities of invisible colleges consisted of unofficial reviews of scholarly manuscripts (typically by the means of marginal note-taking) and personal meetings of scholars who gathered together to discuss research topics or witness experiments (Ibid.). Because some of these meetings took place in London's coffeehouses, they became known as "penny universities," as one penny was the price of a cup of coffee (Ellis 1956).

Nowadays, the concept of invisible colleges has taken on a new dimension. The activities of today's invisible colleges take place predominantly through social networking sites[6] and include commenting, bookmarking, recommending, blogging, and microblogging. Because the new model of invisible colleges utilizes social media platforms as a means of scholarly exchange, it has also been referred to as social scholarship. Cohen (2007) defined social scholarship as "the practice [. . .] in which the use of social tools is an integral part of the research and publishing process . . . [and which is characterized by] openness, conversation, collaboration, access, sharing and transparent revision."

Twitter,[7] in particular, has emerged in recent decades as one of the most popular social media outlets for scholars (Van Noorden 2014). The brevity of tweets allows scholars to go through a vast amount of information at a glance and filter posts to match their research interests. Twitter also includes the capacity to follow discussions on research-related topics, share and comment upon preprints and published articles, and live-tweet from conferences and workshops. Furthermore, Twitter helps gauge research impact and public attention based on the number of "tweetations" (journal citations in tweets) (Eysenbach 2011) and that, in turn, may even predict citation rates of published research (Chan et al. 2018; Eysenbach 2011; Peoples et al. 2016).

Among other popular social networking sites used by scholars are ResearchGate, Academia.edu, Mendeley, and LinkedIn. ResearchGate[8] is a European for-profit social networking site, which is primarily oriented toward the science, technology, and medical fields (Manca 2018; Ortega 2015; Thelwall and Kousha 2017). The users of ResearchGate can publicize their scholarly outputs, upload and make freely available the full text of their papers (infringing, in some cases, on publishers' copyright policies [Jamali 2017]), collect altmetrics data surrounding the usage of their work, create profile pages, and connect with their peers.

Academia.edu[9] is a U.S.-based social networking site for scholars, dubbed the "Facebook for academics." Academia.edu has a substantial overlap in functionality with ResearchGate, although it targets scholars in the social sciences, arts, and humanities as its primary audience (Manca 2018; Thelwall and Kousha 2014). Academia.edu users can create a profile page describing their research interests and work in progress, upload their papers, gather usage data to measure research impact of their work, and use social networking features to communicate with other scholars.

Mendeley[10] is a company based in London, United Kingdom, and currently owned by Elsevier. Although Mendeley focuses primarily on helping scholars manage their references rather than on publicizing their own research, it does include a social networking component. For example, Mendeley users can create a research profile, start or join a public or private group, and find scholars with similar interests via public groups.

LinkedIn[11] is a private company, currently headquartered in California, United States. It provides a social media platform used primarily by job seekers and employers. LinkedIn aims to connect people through professional relationships, especially through indirect "connections" that may include the user's past and present colleagues, as well as prospective employers. While LinkedIn does not provide academic-oriented services per se, it offers scholars an option to include a list of publications in their profile; create "connections" to other scholars; "endorse" each other's professional skills; form interest groups; share posts within their network; and write, edit, and publish articles through the LinkedIn Publishing platform.

Ample literature has been written about the benefits (as well as the risks) of social networking sites for scholars.[12] The benefits for scholars include:

- Helping scholars stay abreast of new publications, research news, grant opportunities, project calls, events, and relevant science policies
- Enabling greater visibility of individual scholars and their scholarship
- Facilitating rapid exchange of ideas among researchers
- Encouraging discussions and experimentation
- Allowing researchers to connect with potential collaborators and people with similar research interests and ideas
- Helping gain insights about someone's personality based on their social media activities

Despite these benefits, some scholars are reluctant to engage in social media activities and even consider the use of social networking sites to be risky. Some researchers believe that social media activities do not meet the high standard of scholarship and can potentially harm their academic image or create tension between casual socializing and professional communication (Veletsianos and Kimmons 2013). Others believe that the premature release of new ideas and findings on social media platforms can be dangerous, as it might negatively impact the research community and the public at large (Sherbino et al. 2015). Some are concerned about the potentially low quality or inappropriateness of content posted on social media sites and the opportunity for manipulating social media interactions such as recruiting friends or students to tweet, like, or save particular publications or otherwise "buying" social media follows and likes (Priem 2013; Sherbino et al. 2015). Yet others are challenged by the sheer amount of information available through social networking sites, the speed and dynamic culture of social media, and the time and effort required for social media activities such as following, commenting, and writing "concise, smart, and interesting posts" (Jaring and Bäck 2017).

A significant variation exists in how researchers in different disciplines participate in social media activities. Ortega (2015) found that researchers in the biomedical and technological fields connect with other researchers through social media less frequently than researchers in the social sciences. In the rapidly developing biomedical and technological fields, where patents, tenure, and promotion often depend on who is the first to publish research findings, there is significant fear that new ideas can be "stolen" and published by a competitor (Waldrop 2008; Weller 2011). For social scientists, the use of social networking sites has been less controversial (Ortega 2015). This is particularly true with regard to researchers conducting sociological and behavioral studies, for whom social networking sites allow one to analyze user-generated information; recruit potential participants for their studies; and collect research data on how different people and social groups interact, feel, and reason in different settings (Garaizar et al. 2012).

Even though the scholars' attitude toward the use of social networking sites varies, these sites still serve as an important source of information for many researchers. They also provide opportunities for greater openness and transparency in scholarly communication practices than if they took place in a more formal setting or were considered traditional academic metrics for career advancement (Martin 2014).

Altmetrics

Citations in peer-reviewed journals referencing other articles have traditionally been used as core indicators for assessing the scholarly impact of those articles. According to Merton's normative theory, citations represent an intellectual or cognitive influence of the cited author on the author(s) of another publication (Merton 1973). Articles that are cited are considered to have greater impact than those articles that are not cited

(Meho 2007; Nicolaisen 2007; Smith 1981; Van Raan 2004). In the words of Blaise Cronin (1981, 16), citations are "frozen footprints in the landscape of scholarly achievement [. . .] which bear witness of the passage of ideas."

In recent decades, citation impact indicators have increasingly been used for evaluating the performance of individual researchers, academic departments, institutions, and research proposals (Cabezas-Clavijo et al. 2013; Moed 2016). Examples of commonly used citation impact indicators are the Hirsch Index (or the h-index), which evaluates the cumulative impact of an author's research productivity, and the journal impact factor, which measures a journal's average number of citations per article. While citations provide insight into the merit of individual publications, the validity of citations as a true measure of research impact has been debated for the following reasons:

- Citations may take several years to accrue, and thus they fail to demonstrate the impact of more recent research (Aksnes, Langfeldt, and Wouters 2019).

- Citations primarily measure impact on the scholarly community and do not reflect a larger societal impact of published research (Bornmann 2015).

- Influential papers published in journals with low impact factors or journals with a small circulation might remain uncited (Martin 2014).

- Not every publication that is cited has been read (Haustein 2014).

- Not every publication that is used has been cited, especially when a large number of publications exists on a topic (Camacho-Miñano and Núñez-Nickel 2009; MacRoberts and MacRoberts 2010).

- Incorrect citing is not uncommon (Broadus 1983; Eichorn and Yankauer 1987; Evans, Nadjari, and Burchell 1990).

- Scholars cite publications for reasons that are not always related to acknowledging intellectual influence of another author (Bornmann 2015; Bornmann and Daniel 2008; Simkin and Roychowdhury 2003).

Moreover, citation-based metrics can vary depending on the bibliographic database that was used to calculate them. Finally, publications that are available only in subscription-based databases and therefore difficult to obtain by nonsubscribers might receive fewer citations.

Overstressing the importance of citation indicators in research impact assessment has resulted in such problems as excessive self-citation to boost one's reputation, especially when evaluations affect research funding, tenure, and promotion (Van Noorden and Chawla 2019), and extraneous citation of important authors to increase the value of one's own papers (Bornmann 2015). Citation-based metrics have also been criticized for being based on "hidden data" and thus incorrectly evaluating the impact of individual articles or their authors (Eysenbach 2011; *PLoS Medicine* Editors 2006; Rossner, Van Epps, and Hill 2007).[13]

Although the need for more immediate, inclusive, and transparent metrics has been discussed in the literature since the 1980s,[14] the idea of altmetrics (short for alternative metrics)[15] as a new approach to measuring scholarly impact was introduced only in late 2010. The coining of the term "altmetrics" is attributed to Jason Priem, a cofounder of ImpactStory and a coauthor of the Altmetrics Manifesto (Priem et al. 2010). Priem used the word "altmetrics" for the first time in his 2010 tweet to differentiate these new metrics from other citation-based indicators. He wrote: "I like the term #articlelevelmetrics, but it fails to imply *diversity* of measures. Lately, I'm liking #altmetrics" (Priem @jasonpriem 2010). A specific definition of altmetrics, however, is still missing due to high heterogeneity in altmetrics and their lack of a conceptual foundation (Haustein 2016). At present, the word is used as an umbrella term for alternative ways of tracing, recording, and measuring how the diverse forms of scholarship are shared, discussed, and used across the social web. Even though this term suggests that altmetrics provide an *alternative* to the established citation-based metrics, in practice, altmetrics serve as a *complementary* indicator of impact, not the replacement of citation-based metrics.[16]

The goal of altmetrics is threefold: 1) to serve as an information-seeking aid to help scholars filter and navigate the increasingly overwhelming volume of scholarly works published each year; 2) to draw scholars' attention to works that have attracted the most mentions and comments on the social web; and 3) to provide insight into how these works impact the scholarly community and the public. To accomplish this goal, altmetrics trace, count, and analyze in near real time (typically with the help of public application programming interfaces [APIs]) the "digital traces" left by users of scholarly works. Examples of such "digital traces" include tweets; readership counts; mentions in blog posts; discussions in wikis; and likes, shares, ratings, and recommendations on social networking sites. "Digital traces" may also include full-text views and downloads of scholarly works, although these indicators of impact had been available long before the idea of altmetrics was introduced.

The social media platforms used by altmetrics for collecting data include social networking sites (e.g., ResearchGate and Academia.edu), blogging (e.g., ResearchBlogging and WordPress), microblogging (e.g., Twitter), social data sharing (e.g., GitHub and figshare), wikis (e.g., Wikipedia), reviewing and rating platforms (e.g., F1000Prime), and reference management sites (e.g., Mendeley). In addition to tracing the impact of scholarly works, altmetrics track teaching and service activities, such as the impact of reading lists and course packs or attendance at massive online open courses (MOOCs) (Rodgers and Barbrow 2013; Taylor 2013a). Altmetrics have also found applications in practical fields by providing insights that aid in the interpretation of data. For example, the analysis of H1N1 pandemic–related tweets on Twitter helped health authorities become aware of and respond to concerns raised by the public (Chew and Eysenbach 2010). As the Altmetrics Manifesto maintains, "Altmetrics expand our view of what impact looks like, but also of what's making the impact. This matters because expressions of scholarship are becoming more diverse" (Priem et al. 2010).

In recent years, altmetrics have grown significantly in their use and recognition within the scholarly community (Konkiel 2020). Some scholars have already been embedding altmetrics data in their curriculum vitae (Piwowar and Priem 2013) and research proposals (Piwowar 2013).[17] The rise of altmetrics can be attributed to the following key factors: 1) the diversification of scholarly products beyond publications; 2) the need for a more comprehensive picture of the reach and impact of scholarly work in the online environment; 3) the growth of social media and its uptake by scholars as a platform for sharing ideas and communicating information; and 4) the introduction of new criteria for evaluating grant proposals requiring applicants to demonstrate a broader impact of proposed research beyond the scholarly community (Martin 2017).

The most obvious benefits of altmetrics for scholars include:

- Timeliness (altmetrics are collected at a much faster speed than citation-based metrics and allow researchers to see the impact of the most recent work)
- Diversity (altmetrics track and count a great variety of research outputs, not just publications)
- Openness (the majority of altmetrics data is transparent and openly available to anyone)
- Breadth (altmetrics measure impact of research on academic and nonacademic audiences)
- Convenience (altmetrics can help scholars gain information about the importance and relevance of papers before actually reading them)

Even though altmetrics add a new dimension to measuring scholarly impact, scholars question the effectiveness of altmetrics indicators when used for evaluating research quality (Bornmann and Haunschild 2018;

Nuzzolese et al. 2019; Thelwall et al. 2013). Cronin (2013, 1523) writes: "Neither Twitter mentions nor Facebook 'likes' are, for now at any rate, accepted currencies in the academic marketplace; you are not going to get promoted for having been liked a lot, though it may well boost your ego." In a similar vein, Haustein (2016, 420) asserts that "social media activity does not equal social impact." Some scholars are also concerned about the credibility of altmetrics indicators, given that high altmetrics scores can be easily generated through multiple or fake accounts, automated paper downloads, or "robot tweeting" through automated Twitter accounts (Cheung 2013; Darling et al. 2013; Liu and Adie 2013; Thelwall et al. 2013).

Other concerns about altmetrics include:

- Data quality issues that can occur at the level of data providers, data aggregators, and users (Haustein 2016)
- Difficulty replicating and sustaining altmetrics data if data providers disappear, become obsolete, or change their services (Bornmann 2014; Haustein 2016; Haustein et al. 2014; Thelwall, et al. 2013)
- Accessibility issues with some APIs and heavy restrictions on the amount of data that can be collected per day (Erdt et al. 2016; Konkiel 2020)
- Difficulty contextualizing and assessing the real value of usage, as it can range from a simple click on the link to view a work to extensive discussion of that work (Bornmann 2015; Konkiel 2020)
- Commercialization of altmetrics services that are primarily in the hands of for-profit companies (Bornmann 2014; Haustein 2016)
- Ensuring that altmetrics data and data sources remain open for collection, analysis, and integration into altmetrics services (Konkiel 2020)

While altmetrics are making indelible contribution to openness in scholarship, there is still no conclusive evidence that answers the question whether altmetrics indicators properly reflect research impact of scholarly works (Bornmann and Haunschild 2018; Konkiel 2020) or whether these indicators are "just empty buzz" (Priem et al. 2010). According to Priem et al. (2010), to answer this question, scholarly "[w]ork should correlate between altmetrics and existing measures, predict citations from altmetrics, and compare altmetrics with expert evaluation." In other words, altmetrics "could be employed side-by-side with citations—one tracking formal, acknowledged influence, and [the other] tracking the unintentional and informal 'scientific street cred'" (Priem, Piwowar, and Hemminger 2012).

Online Author Identifiers[18]

Name ambiguity is a complex problem that affects all of the stakeholders involved in the creation, management, and distribution of scholarly content, including authors, research funders, publishers, libraries, universities, and scholarly societies. Name ambiguity makes it difficult to track all the publications by a specific author, determine the author of a particular document, or distinguish one author from another—all of which are crucial tasks for mining authorship data for citation-based impact analysis, obtaining research funding, evaluating faculty for promotion and tenure, and other related activities. The need for an accurate author identification mechanism ("the DOIs for authors," in the words of Harrison and Harrison [2016]) has become particularly challenging in recent decades due to a tremendous growth of research productivity across the world and, as the direct consequence of this growth, the increased volume of published scholarly works available both in print and online.

Name ambiguity occurs for several reasons, including:

- Identical names of multiple authors (e.g., John Smith)
- Inconsistent name formats that vary from one publication to another (e.g., the author's middle initial may be included or omitted)
- Author name change (e.g., through marriage)
- Variable spellings of non-Roman names (e.g., the names from the Cyrillic or Chinese alphabet)[19]
- Cultural differences in the order of first and last names
- Compound or hyphenated author names

The early efforts to develop a mechanism that can be used to distinguish a particular author from all other authors go back to the 1940s, when the American Mathematical Society attempted to identify all authors of works listed in the Mathematical Reviews Database (Fenner 2011). Since then, a number of author identification services have emerged, some of which are proprietary and some of which are open. Proprietary author identification services only function for publications indexed in the databases owned by the specific publisher, and that makes author search unavailable to nonsubscribers. Examples include Elsevier's Scopus Author Identifier, which is automatically assigned to all authors indexed in Scopus, and ResearcherID offered by Clarivate Analytics' Web of Science database. In open author identification services, the collected author data can be freely accessed, used, and reused by anyone. Examples include

Google Scholar Profiles and ORCID (Open Researcher & Contributor ID). Some open author identification services are discipline-specific, for example, RePEc Author Service for researchers in economics. Others are limited to a particular country, for example, Digital Author Identification (DAI) in the Netherlands. Most of these services are self-curated, although they might contain some automated components. Authors can register for an author identifier and either create their author profiles or verify their author profiles automated by the service provider. Although the majority of author profiles are limited to the lists of scholarly publications, some author identification services have a broader scope. For example, the International Standard Name Identifier (ISNI) provides a tool for disambiguating the "public identities" of creators of all kinds of works, including the works of researchers, writers, artists, musicians, performers, publishers, and producers (ISNI, n.d.).

Online author identifiers provide a number of practical benefits to all involved stakeholders. They enable authors to group together comprehensive lists of their publications and other scholarly contributions and simplify the submission of grant proposals to research-funding organizations and manuscripts to journal publishers. They also help improve attribution of their works and find potential collaborators with similar research interests. For publishers and librarians, online author identifiers help distinguish a particular author from any other author, regardless of any similarities, variant formats, or spellings of that author's name. For academic institutions, online author identifiers allow the use of quantitative measures for defining and showcasing the scholarly productivity of their faculty. For scholarly societies, they aid in tracking the accomplishments of their members.

Online author identifiers are still relatively new and not yet widely accepted in academia. One of the challenges encountered by online author identification systems includes the need to establish rigorous procedures for verification of self-claims made by scholars in their author profiles. As has been remarked in an editorial in *Nature*, "No one wants to see the system abused by individuals seeking to pad their academic credentials" (Nature 2009). Other challenges include the problems with retrospective assignment of author identifiers, time and commitment required for maintaining online scholarly identity, and the lack of universal identifier systems that are not limited to a specific discipline or country but can also be applied to interdisciplinary and multinational publications (Fenner 2011).

Presently, the most recognized system for assigning unique author identifiers is ORCID,[20] developed by an international nonprofit organization ORCID, Inc., in 2012. ORCID creates and maintains a registry of unique author identifiers (ORCID iDs) and enables automatic linkages between authors, their scholarly activities, and other author identifier systems such as ResearcherID. In addition to publications, ORCID iDs can be assigned to other types of scholarly materials such as datasets, unpublished papers, blog posts, and Wikipedia entries. Beginning in 2016, a number of scholarly publishers, including PLoS, Science, The Royal Society, Wiley, and eLife, require authors to submit their ORCID iDs during the manuscript submission process.

Transdisciplinarity

A fundamental shift toward a more democratic governance of knowledge production and distribution, which is occurring within the scholarly community, has been primarily driven by the need to address urgent, complex problems of the "real world" that have intensified in recent decades. Examples of such problems, which, if not addressed, could result in "potential self-destruction of our species" (Nicolescu 2002, 7), include climate change, biodiversity loss, resource depletion, and global health challenges, among other issues. Scholars argue that traditional science, still largely composed of individual academic disciplines, can neither properly understand these problems nor address them effectively. Concerns about the limitations of discipline-based knowledge production have resulted in the emergence of a new research approach, namely transdisciplinarity, which aims to synthesize academic and nonacademic knowledge in order to address urgent, complex real-world problems.

The term "transdisciplinarity" is a compound of two parts, both of which are of Latin origin: the prefix "trans," which means "across, beyond, on or to the other side, through, into a different state or place" (Fowler, Fowler, and Crystal 2011, 938), and the word "discipline," which refers to an organized field of knowledge, as well as to a set of rules imposed on people under control (Martin 2017). The term "transdisciplinarity" itself is rather recent. Nicolescu (2002) attributes the origins of this term to a Swiss scientist, Jean Piaget, who used it at the First International Seminar on Interdisciplinarity held in France in 1970 to distinguish transdisciplinarity from multi- and interdisciplinarity. In his post-seminar essay, Piaget described transdisciplinarity as a "higher stage succeeding interdisciplinary relationships . . . which would not only cover interactions or reciprocities between specialized research projects, but would place these relationships within a total system without any firm boundaries between disciplines" (1972, 138). Other sources credit an American astrophysicist and systems scientist, Erich Jantsch, for coining this term at the same seminar (Leavy 2011; Newell 2000; Weingart 2010). In his post-seminar paper, Jantsch (1972, 114) described transdisciplinarity as "the coordination of activities at all levels of the education/innovation system towards a common purpose."

Although the term "transdisciplinarity" has been around for over five decades, its precise meaning is still debated. Definitions vary from one author to the other and can even vary among members of the same research team (Martin 2017). Many still use the terms "transdisciplinarity," "multidisciplinarity," and "interdisciplinarity" interchangeably. The lack of agreement on a definition has led many researchers to believe that transdisciplinarity is "a rather elusive concept" (Jahn, Bergmann, and Keil 2012) and that it can only be described metaphorically. Two metaphors are invoked most frequently with regard to transdisciplinarity: the metaphor of a web and the metaphor of a rhizome, both of which convey the idea of multiplicity, interconnectedness, and complexity (Martin 2017).

Simply put, transdisciplinarity refers to a new approach to knowledge production, in which multiple participants from within and outside academia work together as equally valuable team members on researching a specific real-world problem and on jointly crafting solutions to that problem (Figure 8.1). Pohl and Hirsch Hadorn (2007, 20) describe transdisciplinarity as "public-good research" that can "(a) grasp the complexity of problems, (b) take into account the diversity of scientific and life-world perceptions of problems, (c) link abstract and case-specific knowledge, and (d) develop knowledge and practices that promote what is perceived to be the common good."

One of the most unique characteristics of transdisciplinarity is that it often involves the subjects of research as active participants throughout the research process so that the research is being carried out *with* them rather than *on* them (Martin 2017). For example, a transdisciplinary team studying the problem of addiction may include not only academics who have researched this issue from a scientific viewpoint, health professionals who have treated patients with the addiction problem, and law enforcement officers who have witnessed the effects of this problem in real-life situations but also recovering addicts themselves who can provide firsthand information on their condition and experience. The rationale of involving the subjects of research in the research process is not new. In the early 1900s, John Dewey argued that the public could not only help scholars identify societal problems

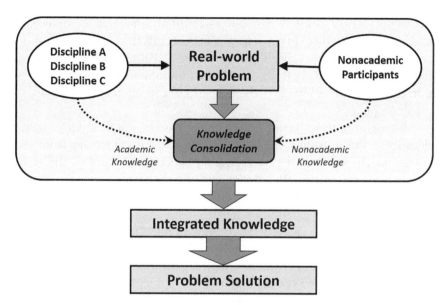

Figure 8.1 The problem-oriented transdisciplinary research model, in which academic and nonacademic participants consolidate their expertise, skills, and perspectives to create a new integrated knowledge with the goal of addressing a specific real-world problem. Adapted from Martin, Victoria. *Transdisciplinarity Revealed: What Librarians Need to Know.* Santa Barbara: Libraries Unlimited, 2017.

but could also generate the knowledge that is more useful. To clarify his point, Dewey used shoemaking as an example. He wrote: "The man who wears the shoe knows best that it pinches and where it pinches, even if the expert shoemaker is the best judge of how the trouble is to be remedied" (1927/2012, 154).

Currently, there are two major schools of transdisciplinary thought: Nicolescuian transdisciplinarity and the Zurich School's transdisciplinarity. Nicolescuian transdisciplinarity is named after a Romanian-born French quantum physicist, Basarab Nicolescu, the author of the influential book *Manifesto of Transdisciplinarity* and other writings on the topic. In his *Manifesto*, Nicolescu (2002, 44) describes the trend toward extreme disciplinary specialization as "the process of Babilization" (referring to the ancient Tower of Babel), the process in which "a theoretical particle physicist [cannot] truly hold a dialogue with a neurophysiologist, a mathematician with a poet, a biologist with an economist, a politician with a computer programmer, beyond mouthing more or less banal generalities [while] a true decision maker must be able to have a dialogue with all of them at once." According to Nicolescu, the goal of transdisciplinarity is "the understanding of the present world, of which one of the imperatives is the unity of knowledge" (Ibid.). He stresses, however, that transdisciplinarity does not intend to replace disciplinary methodologies, but rather aims to enrich them with "new and indispensable insights" (Ibid., 122).[21] Nicolescu also argues that transdisciplinarity is not simply a new research approach, but a new methodology in its own right. For Nicolescu, this methodology is based on three axioms: 1) multiple levels of reality and the Hidden Third (ontological axiom), 2) the logic of the included middle (a logical axiom), and 3) complexity (epistemological axiom). According to Nicolescu, these axioms constitute the three "pillars" of transdisciplinarity because they reveal the interdependence and interconnectedness of the universe and enable a more comprehensive understanding of the complexity of the world that "penetrate[s] each and every field of knowledge" (Ibid., 60).

The Zurich School's transdisciplinarity emerged from the International Transdisciplinary Conference held in Zurich, Switzerland, in 2000. The Zurich School offers a more pragmatic view on transdisciplinarity than Nicolescu. It views transdisciplinarity as a new way of joint problem-solving and joint decision-making rather than a new methodology. It emphasizes a paramount importance of collaborations between academic and nonacademic participants, where "the knowledge of multiple participants is enhanced" and where "[t]he sum of this knowledge [is] greater than the knowledge of any single partner" (Klein et al. 2012, 7). This view is largely based upon the Mode 2 approach to knowledge production introduced by Michael Gibbons and colleagues in their book, *The New Production of Knowledge: The Dynamics of Science and Research in Contemporary Societies* (Gibbons et al. 1994). In this book, the authors argued that besides the traditional discipline-based production of knowledge that has little need for collaboration with nonacademic participants (which they named Mode 1), there was another approach to knowledge production (which they named Mode 2) that transcended the boundaries between academic and nonacademic knowledge and produced research that was highly relevant to societal needs. Although the Zurich School has not produced a truly original concept and lacks the "bold visionary insights" of Nicolescuian transdisciplinarity (Bernstein, Hillel 2015), it has made an important contribution to scholarship by disseminating the ideas of transdisciplinarity around the world. Key proponents of the Zurich School are Gertrude Hirsch Hadorn, a professor at the Swiss Federal Institute of Technology, and Christian Pohl, a scientist at the Swiss Federal Institute of

Technology and a co-founder of td-net, a Swiss-based network for trans-disciplinary researchers and educators. Hadorn and Pohl were among the editors of the *Handbook of Transdisciplinary Research* (2008), which is considered one of the key works on the topic.

While transdisciplinary projects vary in their objectives, scope, and complexity, they share a number of key characteristics. All transdisciplinary projects are:

- *Problem-driven* (initiated by a specific real-world problem versus an abstract or laboratory version of a problem)
- *Action-oriented* (aim to translate research findings into specific actions to address the problem under investigation)
- *Highly collaborative* (involve researchers from different disciplinary fields, as well as multiple stakeholders from outside of academia, such as policy makers, educators, practitioners, and community members)
- *Integrative* (integrate academic and nonacademic knowledge)
- *Heterogenic* (involve participants with diverse disciplinary, ethnic, and cultural backgrounds)

An example of a transdisciplinary project is the SRIREP (Sustainable Regional Innovation for Reduction of Environmental Pollutions) project,[22] conducted under the auspices of the Research Institute for Humanity and Nature (Japan). This project involves a team of scientists and public and private stakeholders, including mining communities and local residents, to address the problem of mercury pollution in artisanal and small-scale gold mining areas in Indonesia, a problem that indirectly affects millions of people worldwide. Another example of a transdisciplinary project is a series of the Tissue Chip for Drug Screening projects[23] led by the National Center for Advancing Translational Sciences (NCATS) in the United States. These projects are conducted by scientists, community organizations, and patient groups who develop three-dimensional chips, mimicking human physiology, in order to understand and address the problem of drug failure in clinical trials.

Transdisciplinary research takes place across all disciplinary fields, although, by far, the greatest number of large-scale transdisciplinary projects has been undertaken in the health, environmental, and biological sciences. This situation is primarily due to the growing financial support for transdisciplinary projects directed toward the solution of problems related to the improvement of human health, environmental protection, renewable energy, nature conservation, and sustainable food production.

In the United States, major research funding agencies such as the National Institutes of Health, the National Science Foundation, the Food and Drug Administration, and the Department of Energy have allocated substantial resources for the development of complex transdisciplinary projects involving hundreds of participants from a wide range of fields, across multiple organizations, and over long time spans. For example, such large-scale transdisciplinary initiatives as the Transdisciplinary Tobacco Use Research Centers and Transdisciplinary Research on Energetics and Cancer Centers, both funded by the National Institutes of Health, have been operational for over a decade. Recently, a growing number of agencies began to require that research grants include transdisciplinary teams. For example, all proposals submitted for a new National Science Foundation program "Growing Convergence Research" must include a Convergence Management Plan describing specific activities that will enable cross-disciplinary and cross-sectorial integration of research teams.[24] Transdisciplinary research has also been supported by national research organizations such as the Social Science Research Council and the National Academies of Sciences, Engineering, and Medicine, as well as by private research institutions and foundations such as the MacArthur Foundation, the Kavli Foundation, and the NIH Common Fund. More recently, transdisciplinary research approaches have gained attention in the social sciences and the humanities, especially in those research areas that overlap with biomedical sciences. An example of such approaches includes the research conducted by the Long-Term Ecological Research (LTER) Network,[25] which integrates social sciences to provide insights into the human factors of long-term ecological change. Another example is the programs at the Health Humanities initiative at the Institute of Humanities Research (IHR),[26] which bring together researchers, educators, and practitioners from the fields of medical ethics, medical humanities, and spiritual care, with the goal to enhance the understanding of human healing, health, and well-being.

The growing recognition of transdisciplinarity as a promising approach to research has resulted in the pursuit of a large number of transdisciplinary projects in many parts of the world. There are also global transdisciplinary networks; international conferences on transdisciplinarity; and peer-reviewed transdisciplinary journals, such as *International Journal of Transdisciplinary Research*, *Epiphany: Journal of Transdisciplinary Studies*, and *Futures*.

Yet transdisciplinarity is not considered mainstream in academia, where transdisciplinary collaborations are still met with skepticism

(Martin 2017). Recent research suggests that transdisciplinary projects face more significant challenges than traditional research collaborations due to the size, diversity, and complexity of transdisciplinary teams, as well as their disciplinary, cultural, and geographical variables (Ibid.). Additional barriers to successful transdisciplinary collaborations include the absence of clearly defined methodologies for conducting transdisciplinary research and the lack of an established peer review culture for transdisciplinary projects. Transdisciplinary collaborations also make tough demands on individual researchers' time and mental energy, including the need to learn new disciplinary languages and concepts, familiarize oneself with more diffused bodies of research literature, find highly scattered relevant information, and become proficient in an ongoing "translation" of specialized disciplinary jargon into a common language understandable by nonacademic participants (Ibid.).

Transdisciplinarity is a more open way of looking at the relationship between knowledge production and society. From this perspective, transdisciplinarity shares some characteristics with citizen science,[27] although citizen science does not necessarily make the entire research process open to researchers without a scientific background. A key commonality between transdisciplinarity and citizen science is the involvement of academic and nonacademic stakeholders in a collaborative research process with the common goal—to advance science and/or generate solutions to real-world problems. By integrating academic and nonacademic knowledge, transdisciplinarity and citizen science transcend not only disciplinary boundaries but also the boundaries between science and society and thus generate knowledge that is more unified and socially relevant than that produced by any single discipline or by a combination of disciplines.

Notes

1. BioMed Central (https://www.biomedcentral.com).
2. Public Library of Science (PLoS) (https://plos.org).
3. Frontiers (https://www.frontiersin.org).
4. PeerJ (https://peerj.com).
5. F1000Research (https://f1000research.com).
6. Boyd and Ellison (2007, 211) define "social network sites" as "web based services that allow individuals to (1) construct a public or semi-public profile within a bounded system, (2) articulate a list of other users with whom they

share a connection, and (3) view and traverse their list of connections and those made by others within the system."

7. Twitter (https://twitter.com).

8. ResearchGate (https://www.researchgate.net).

9. Academia.edu (https://www.academia.edu).

10. Mendeley (https://www.mendeley.com).

11 LinkedIn (https://www.linkedin.com).

12. See, for example, Jaring and Bäck 2017; Veletsianos and Kimmons 2013; Wouters et al. 2013.

13. For additional information about the use of scholarly impact metrics, see the Declaration on Research Assessment (DORA) (https://sfdora.org/read) and The Leiden Manifesto for Research Metrics (https://www.nature.com/articles /520429a).

14. See, for example, Almind and Ingwersen 1997; Cronin 1981, 2001; Cronin et al. 1998.

15. Altmetrics should not be confused with article-level metrics, which refer to metrics aggregated for articles.

16. To address the ambiguity of the term "altmetrics," other terms have been suggested in the literature, including the terms "hidden impact" (Taylor 2013b) and "social media metrics" (Haustein et al. 2014).

17. Beginning January 2013, the National Science Foundation introduced a policy according to which principal investigators of research funding applications should list their research products, rather than just their publications, in a biography section of their research proposal. Research products "must be citable and accessible including but not limited to publications, data sets, software, patents, and copyrights" (National Science Foundation 2020).

18. The term "author" is used here in the broad sense as a creator of scholarly works, although, in most instances, this term could be replaced with the terms "researcher" or "scholar."

19. This problem is particularly pronounced for publications by authors from China, Korea, and Japan (Qiu 2008).

20. ORCID (https://orcid.org).

21. A similar conviction is expressed in *The Charter of Transdisciplinarity*, which states that "[t]ransdisciplinarity does not strive for mastery of several disciplines but aims to open all disciplines to that which they share and to that which lies beyond them" (Freitas, Nicolescu, and Morin 1994).

22. SRIREP (https://srirep.org/).

23. The Tissue Chip for Drug Screening projects (https://ncats.nih.gov /tissuechip/projects).

24. See "Growing Convergence Research (GCR)" at: https://www.nsf.gov /pubs/2019/nsf19551/nsf19551.htm.

25. LTER (https://lternet.edu).

26. Health Humanities (https://ihr.asu.edu/health-humanities).

27. Citizen science is discussed in Chapter 7.

Suggested Resources

Altmetric
https://www.altmetric.com
A commercial company that aggregates and provides altmetrics data for scholarly publications. Generates "The Attention Score" (a number of all of the online mentions that Altmetric has found for an individual scholarly output) and displays that score in its colorful "doughnut" logo, which appears on many publishers' websites and in some library catalogs. Requires a subscription but provides a free bookmarklet for viewing a quick summary of online activity on a particular journal article.

ImpactStory
https://profiles.impactstory.org
A free tool that aggregates altmetrics on scholarly output from a variety of online sources and enables researchers to create a profile for showcasing the impact of their scholarship. Free with a Twitter account.

ORCID (Open Researcher and Contributor ID)
https://orcid.org
A nonprofit, community-based organization that creates and maintains a central registry of unique 16-digit online author identifiers (ORCID iDs) that help distinguish one author from any other author.

td-net: Network for Transdisciplinary Research
http://transdisciplinarity.ch/en/td-net/Aktuell.html
A Swiss-based network for transdisciplinary researchers, educators, and other stakeholders. Provides a communication and collaboration platform for anyone involved in transdisciplinary research and teaching. Contributes to the growth and conceptualization of transdisciplinarity through the organization of conferences, publication of works on transdisciplinarity, and the upkeep of "the toolbox for co-producing knowledge," which includes specific tools for addressing the challenges of coproducing transdisciplinary knowledge.

Conclusion

The discourse on openness in scholarship is broad and ever expanding. It is increasingly incorporating diverse stakeholders—both from within and outside the knowledge industry—who are directly affected by the evolving research environment. These stakeholders include scholars from all disciplinary fields, educators, librarians, practitioners, policy makers, government representatives, and members of the public. A common thread in this discourse is that knowledge is always built upon previous knowledge, and, therefore, it should be treated as a public good rather than a commercial commodity.

While the future will likely see a continuing shift toward greater openness at every stage of knowledge production and knowledge distribution, the long-term success of openness in scholarship is "a long-term project," according to Suber (2016, 71). Open scholarship and its proponents still face unresolved issues, including the lack of a unifying conceptual framework for various, and often fractious, open initiatives. Furthermore, many scholars believe that openness should have some limits. What these limits are exactly and how to best enforce them without impeding openness is where opinions often diverge among those who advocate for openness, those who are uncertain about it, and those who are opposed to it. As Boyle (2008, 2) maintains, "it is not that openness is always right. It is not. [. . .] Rather, it is that we need a balance between open and closed, owned and free, and we are systematically likely to get the balance wrong."

One of the issues that is often cited as an underlying inhibitor for greater adoption of open practices in academia is the inadequate institutional reward system for scholars who engage in open scholarship. Although many researchers engage in open scholarship for altruistic reasons, the fact that open practices still carry little weight in the promotion and tenure process can make some faculty members reluctant to get involved in open scholarship projects. At present, open research practices are not yet a prerequisite for a scholar's role in academia. While the following aspect has not yet been systematically analyzed in the literature, one could hypothesize that a more comprehensive integration of openness into the current model of scholarly research depends upon such factors as the establishment of rigorous institutional policies supporting and rewarding open practices, development of robust platforms and tools facilitating openness in scholarship, and, not the least, an active participation of the scholars themselves in open research practices. With regard to the latter, Weller (2014, 150) posits, the transition to openness for many scholars is "less a battle with external forces usurping practice, but more an internal one, between existing practice and opportunities available."

Academic and research librarians are in a strong position to support and promote open scholarship practices in their home institutions. Their motivation for supporting and promoting these practices can be attributed to at least two reasons: 1) a close alignment of core library values of free and equal access to recorded knowledge with the values of open scholarship and 2) a potential to lower libraries' journal subscription expenses through promoting the open access publishing model. Open scholarship also provides librarians with an opportunity to continue demonstrating the importance of libraries as "fortresses of knowledge" (Boorstin 1979, 1980) in the fast-paced, rapidly evolving, and increasingly technologized research environment, but requires a mental and practical shift to ensure that library services truly reflect the needs and aspirations of current and future scholars.

Some of the ways in which librarians are already becoming effective supporters of open scholarship in their institutions include:

- Actively engaging in discussions with faculty, staff, and students on current and emerging trends and technologies in open scholarship
- Providing sustained outreach and support for open access publishing and issues related to OER creation and adoption
- Advocating and supporting the creation and adoption of OER that are reflective of the broad diversity of instructional methods, learning styles, and cultural perspectives represented in their teaching and learning communities
- Developing and implementing educational programs on current and emerging trends and technologies in open scholarship that are inclusive of the needs of all persons in the community the library serves
- Providing advice about open access options to ensure broader dissemination and impact of scholarly works, with a particular focus on authors from traditionally underrepresented groups

- Educating scholars on predatory publishing and other unethical practices associated with openness in scholarship

- Offering guidance on managing copyrights, negotiating publishing contracts, and applying open licenses to scholarly works, thereby empowering all creators and users of scholarly content through copyright and author rights tools that give everyone an opportunity to successfully participate in the increasingly open scholarly communications environment

- Actively promoting institutional repositories as a way to maximize the visibility and impact of scholarly works and as a means to comply with public access mandates of research funders, thereby ensuring the diversity of types of archived materials and the inclusive representation of contributors, particularly those whose voices as scholars have often been marginalized

- Establishing open access publishing funds to encourage and support open access publishing activities

- Partnering with university presses and other academic publishers to increase access to scholarly content through open publishing platforms

- Becoming open access publishers themselves to contribute to the creation and distribution of freely accessible knowledge

While many of these roles represent a continuation of librarians' traditional practice as knowledge managers, other roles manifest the widening scope of what librarians do and require the acquisition of new skills and, in some cases, additional investments, such as the creation of new positions for scholarly communications experts. These new roles also require a continuous cultivation of habits of mind that are similar to those expected of open scholars themselves and that challenge librarians' traditional understanding of how scholarly knowledge should be produced and disseminated. In turn, these new roles can provide librarians with a rich array of opportunities for collaboration and engagement that can lead to truly collegiate relationships between scholars and librarians that can only be achieved if they work together as equal partners in the increasingly open research environment.

Glossary

altmetrics
Alternative ways of measuring how the diverse forms of scholarship are shared, discussed, and used across the social web that are complementary to traditional citation-based metrics.

article-level metrics
Metrics aggregated for individual scholarly articles, including statistics on citations, downloads, and usage.

article processing charge (APC)
A fee charged to authors to publish an article in an *open access journal* or a journal utilizing the *hybrid open access* model.

author addendum
A legal document that modifies a publisher's standard *copyright transfer* agreement. Also known as the Addendum to Publication Agreement.

born digital content
Content created originally in digital form rather than having been created through the digitization of analog materials.

citizen science
An active, voluntary involvement of nonscientists in scientific research.

copyleft
A form of licensing for *free software* and *open source software* that grants software users the freedom to run, study, modify, and improve the program on condition that the same freedoms are preserved in any modified versions of that program.

copyleft license
A license that grants software users the freedom to use, modify, and redistribute the *source code*, provided that any modified versions of that software are released under the same *copyleft* license as the original work.

copyright
A set of four exclusive rights automatically granted by law to authors of original works. These rights include reproduction of works, distribution of copies of works, public performance and display of works, and making of derivative works.

copyright transfer
A legal agreement between the creator of the work and another party (such as a publisher) wherein the copyright of the work is reassigned to the second party, for example, as a condition of publication.

data
Raw material that is collected through observations, measurements, experiments, images, and other means and that is used as a primary source for scientific research.

data availability statement
A statement required by some scholarly journal publishers indicating where the *data* that supports the original research in submitted-for-publication manuscripts can be found.

data management plan
A written supplement to a grant proposal describing how research *data* will be generated or collected and how that *data* will be stored and shared after the research project is completed.

data repository
An online archive that stores and makes research *data* available for sharing, use, and reuse.

dataset
An organized collection of *data*.

digital object identifier (DOI)
A unique code consisting of numbers, letters, and symbols used to identify a specific digital document and link to it on the Web.

embargo
A restriction placed by the publisher on the release of the full text of a journal article for a specified amount of time.

fair use
A set of conditions under which a copyrighted work, or a portion of a copyrighted work, can be copied or quoted verbatim without permission from the copyright holder.

free software
Computer software for which the full *source code* is available for anyone to use, modify, and redistribute, both commercially and noncommercially.

gold open access
A strategy for making full-text peer-reviewed journal articles available online on the journal's website immediately upon publication, free of charge, and free of most restrictions on access or use.

gratis open access
A strategy for providing access to publications free of charge but not free of some restrictions on access or use.

green open access (or self-archiving)
A strategy used by authors for making the digital versions of their scholarly works (typically in the form of *preprints* or *postprints*) openly available in an *institutional repository* or an *open access* disciplinary archive.

Hirsch index (or the h-index)
A metric created by Hirsch (2005) that attempts to measure the research productivity and cumulative impact of an individual author's scholarly output by relating the total number of the author's published papers to the number of citations these papers received.

hybrid open access
An optional model utilized by some commercial publishers for making individual articles, typically funded by *article processing charges (APCs)*, openly available within their subscription-based journals.

institutional repository (IR)
A digital archive that collects, archives, and provides access to the intellectual output of a single institution or a multi-institutional community.

invisible colleges
Informal methods of scholarly communication among scholars who belong to the same field of study or who share research interests.

journal impact factor
A metric introduced by the Institute of Scientific Information (ISI) for measuring the impact of an individual journal that indicates the average number of citations to articles published in that journal over the two previous years.

libre open access
A strategy for providing access to works that is free of charge and free of at least some *copyright* and licensing restrictions.

metadata
The description of certain attributes of *data* such as *data* origins, purpose, format, methods of creation or collection of the *data*, time period and area covered, and date of release.

online author identifier
A unique digital code that is used to distinguish one author from any other author.

open access
The practice of providing online access to full-text scholarly literature free of charge and free of most *copyright* and technological restrictions on access or use.

open access journal
A journal that publishes *open access* articles.

open access repository
An online archive and corresponding service designed to store, preserve, and provide *open access* to *preprints*, *postprints*, *data*, *source code*, and other digital works.

open content
Content that is either in the *public domain* or licensed under an *open content license*.

open content license
A license that describes terms and conditions under which a copyrighted work can be used, reused, and shared by others.

open data
Data that anyone can freely use, reuse, and redistribute, provided that the data source is properly attributed.

open educational resources (OER)
Any material designed for use in teaching and learning that can be freely and openly used and reused by anyone without the need to request permissions from copyright holders or to pay license fees or royalties.

open peer review
A process in which the names, affiliations, and credentials of both reviewers and reviewees are disclosed to one another and sometimes to the community at large.

open scholarship
An umbrella term for a variety of open approaches to knowledge creation and knowledge distribution.

open science
The movement that aims to make the entire process of conducting scientific research open to other scientists and, when appropriate, to the public at large.

open source
The software *source code* that is available to anyone for use, reuse, adaptation, modification, and further distribution.

open source license
A license that grants software users the freedom to use, modify, and redistribute the software *source code*, including its commercial use and further distribution.

open source software
Computer software for which the full *source code* is available for anyone to copy, modify, and redistribute under an *open source license*.

openwashing
Falsely marketing a commercial product or a proprietary business as open.

paywall
A method of restricting access to certain online content to paid users.

peer review
A practice in scholarly publishing in which two or more experts from the same or related field of study (referred to as "peers") apply stringent criteria in evaluating the quality of manuscripts submitted for publication in a journal or other scholarly publication. In some cases, peer review is also employed in the evaluation of grant proposals and in the review of applications for tenure, promotion, and fellowship.

platinum (or sponsored) open access
A strategy for making the content of a journal *open access* without any subscription or article processing charges, which are covered by one or more sponsoring organizations.

postprint
The version of an article that has been peer reviewed but not yet copyedited and formatted by a publisher or the final peer-reviewed version of an article after processing by a publisher, such as copyediting and formatting changes.

predatory publishing
An unethical publishing practice that exploits the "author-pays" *open access* publishing model without providing proper peer review and editorial services offered by legitimate *open access journals*.

preprint
The version of an article that has been accepted by a publisher for publication but has not yet undergone formal *peer review*.

public domain
The realm of scholarly, creative, and artistic works that are unprotected by *copyright* and that anyone may freely use, copy, share, modify, and redistribute.

scholarly communication
The process through which scholars create new knowledge, evaluate it, and share it with their peers and with the public.

source code
The computer code written by programmers that provides a computer's operating system with instructions on producing a software application.

transdisciplinarity
An approach to new knowledge production, in which multiple participants from within and outside academia work together as equally valuable team members on researching a specific "real-world" problem and on jointly crafting solutions to that problem

References

Aksnes, Dag W., Liv Langfeldt, and Paul Wouters. "Citations, Citation Indicators, and Research Quality: An Overview of Basic Concepts and Theories." *Sage Open* 9, no. 1 (2019). https://doi.org/10.1177/2158244019829575.

Albright, Paul. "Final Forum Report." UNESCO International Institute for Educational Planning, Internet Discussion Forum on Open Educational Resources. 24 October–2 December, 2005. https://docs.iiep.unesco.org/I009621.pdf.

Allen, Gregory, Alberto Guzman-Alvarez, Marco Molinaro, and Delmar Larsen. "Assessing the Impact and Efficacy of the Open-Access ChemWiki Textbook Project." January 2015. https://library.educause.edu/resources/2015/1/assessing-the-impact-and-efficacy-of-the-openaccess-chemwiki-textbook-project.

Allen, Nicole. "College Textbooks: Do You Get What You Pay For?" Last updated October 7, 2016. https://www.huffpost.com/entry/college-textbooks-do-you_b_8261086.

Almind, Tomas C., and Peter Ingwersen. "Informetric Analyses on the World Wide Web: Methodological Approaches to 'Webometrics.'" *Journal of Documentation* 53, no. 4 (1997): 404–426. https://doi.org/10.1108/EUM0000000007205.

Altbach, Philip G. "What Counts for Academic Productivity in Research Universities?" *International Higher Education* 79 (2015): 6–7.

Anderson, Kent. "In Praise of 'Double-Dipping'—Fairness, Affordability, Vitality, and Sustainability." *The Scholarly Kitchen*. January 29, 2013. https://scholarlykitchen.sspnet.org/2013/01/29/in-praise-of-double-dipping-fairness-affordability-vitality-and-sustainability.

Anderson, Rick. 2015. "Should We Retire the Term 'Predatory Publishing'?" *The Scholarly Kitchen*. May 11, 2015. https://scholarlykitchen.sspnet.org/2015/05/11/should-we-retire-the-term-predatory-publishing.

Bailey, Charles W., Jr. "The Role of Reference Librarians in Institutional Repositories." *Reference Services Review* 33, no. 3 (2005): 259–267. https://doi.org/10.1108/00907320510611294.

Bailey, Charles W., Jr. "What is Open Access?." In *Open Access: Key Strategic, Technical and Economic Aspects,* 13–26. Edited by Neil Jacobs. Oxford: Chandos Publishing, 2006.

Banzato, Monica. "Barriers to Teacher Educators Seeking, Creating and Sharing Open Educational Resources: An Empirical Study of the Use of OER in Education in Italy." *2012 15th International Conference on Interactive Collaborative Learning (ICL)* (2012): 1–6. https://doi.org/10.1109/ICL.2012.6402105.

Beall, Jeffrey. "Predatory Publishers Are Corrupting Open Access." *Nature* 489, no. 7415 (2012): 179. https://doi.org/10.1038/489179a.

Belikov, Olga, and Robert Bodily. "Incentives and Barriers to OER Adoption: A Qualitative Analysis of Faculty Perceptions." *Open Praxis* 8, no. 3 (2016): 235–246.

Beno, Martin, Kathrin Figl, Jürgen Umbrich, and Axel Polleres. "Open Data Hopes and Fears: Determining the Barriers of Open Data." In *2017 Conference for E-Democracy and Open Government (CeDEM)* (2017): 69–81. https://doi.org/10.1109/CeDEM.2017.22.

Berger, Monica, and Jill Cirasella. "Beyond Beall's List: Better Understanding Predatory Publishers." *College & Research Libraries News* 76, no. 3 (2015): 1–4. https://crln.acrl.org/index.php/crlnews/article/view/9277/10342.

Berghmans, Stephane, Helena Cousijn, Gemma Deakin, Ingeborg Meijer, Adrian Mulligan, Andrew Plume, Sarah de Rijcke, et al. "Open Data: The Researcher Perspective." Elsevier. April 4, 2017. https://www.elsevier.com/__data/assets/pdf_file/0004/281920/Open-data-report.pdf.

Bernstein, Jay Hillel. "Transdisciplinarity: A Review of Its Origins, Development, and Current Issues." *Journal of Research Practice* 11, no. 1 (2015): Article R1. http://jrp.icaap.org/index.php/jrp/article/view/510/412.

Bernstein, Rachel. "PLOS ONE Ousts Reviewer, Editor After Sexist Peer-Review Storm." *Science News.* May 1, 2015. https://www.sciencemag.org/news/2015/05/plos-one-ousts-reviewer-editor-after-sexist-peer-review-storm.

Bethard, Steven, Philipp Wetzer, Kristen Butcher, James Martin, and Tamara Sumner. "Automatically Characterizing Resource Quality for Educational Digital Libraries." In *Proceedings of the 9th ACM/IEEE-CS Joint Conference on Digital libraries* (2009): 221–230. https://doi.org/10.1145/1555400.1555436.

"Bethesda Statement on Open Access Publishing." June 20, 2003. http://legacy.earlham.edu/~peters/fos/bethesda.htm.

Bezjak, Sonja, April Clyburne-Sherin, Philipp Conzett, Pedro L. Fernandes, Edit Görögh, Kerstin Helbig, Bianca Kramer, et al. "The Open Science Training Handbook." *Foster Open Science.* 2018. https://book.fosteropenscience.eu.

Bill & Melinda Gates Foundation. "Bill & Melinda Gates Foundation Open Access Policy." https://www.gatesfoundation.org/How-We-Work/General-Information/Open-Access-Policy.

Björk, Bo-Christer. "Open Access—Are the Barriers to Change Receding?" *Publications* 1, no. 1 (2013): 5–15. https://doi.org/10.3390/publications1010005.

Björk, Bo-Christer. "Open Access to Scientific Publications—An Analysis of the Barriers to Change?" *Information Research* 9, no. 2 (2004). http://InformationR.net/ir/9-2/paper170.html.

Björk, Bo-Christer, and David Solomon. "How Research Funders Can Finance APCs in Full OA and Hybrid Journals." *Learned Publishing* 27, no. 2 (2014): 93–103. https://doi.org/10.1087/20140203.

Björk, Bo-Christer, and Timo Korkeamaki. "Adoption of the Open Access Business Model in Scientific Journal Publishing: A Cross-Disciplinary Study." *College & Research Libraries* 81, no. 7 (2020): 1080–1094. https://doi.org/10.5860/crl.81.7.1080.

Bloemsaat, Bas, and Pieter Kleve. "Creative Commons: A Business Model for Products Nobody Wants to Buy." *International Review of Law, Computers & Technology* 23, no. 3 (2009): 237–249. https://doi.org/10.1080/13600860903262404.

Boeckhout, Martin, Gerhard Zielhuis, and Annelien Bredenoord. "The FAIR Guiding Principles for Data Stewardship: Fair Enough?" *European Journal of Human Genetics* 26, no. 7 (2018): 931–936. https://doi.org/10.1038/s41431-018-0160-0.

Boldt, Axel. "Extending ArXiv.org to Achieve Open Peer Review and Publishing." *Journal of Scholarly Publishing* 42, no. 2 (2011): 238–242. https://doi.org/10.3138/jsp.42.2.238.

Bonney, Rick. "Citizen Science: A Lab Tradition." *Living Bird* 15, no. 4 (1996): 7–15.

Bonney, Rick, Heidi Ballard, Rebecca Jordan, Ellen McCallie, Tina Phillips, Jennifer Shirk, and Candie C. Wilderman. "Public Participation in Scientific Research: Defining the Field and Assessing Its Potential for Informal Science Education." A CAISE Inquiry Group Report. 2009. https://files.eric.ed.gov/fulltext/ED519688.pdf.

Bonney, Rick, Jennifer L. Shirk, Tina B. Phillips, Andrea Wiggins, Heidi L. Ballard, Abraham J. Miller-Rushing, and Julia K. Parrish. "Next Steps for Citizen Science." *Science* 343, no. 6178 (2014): 1436–1437. https://doi.org/10.1126/science.1251554.

Bonney, Rick, Tina B. Phillips, Heidi L. Ballard, and Jody W. Enck. "Can Citizen Science Enhance Public Understanding of Science?" *Public Understanding of Science* 25, no. 1 (2016): 2–16. https://doi.org/10.1177/0963662515607406.

Boorstin, Daniel J. "Gresham's Law: Knowledge or Information? Remarks at the White House Conference on Library and Information Services." Washington, D.C., November 19, 1979.

Boorstin, Daniel J. "Remarks by Daniel J. Boorstin, The Librarian of Congress at White House Conference on Library and Information Sciences." *Journal of Information Science* 2, no. 2 (1980): 111–113. https://10.1177/016555158000200207.

Bornmann, Lutz. "Do Altmetrics Point to the Broader Impact of Research? An Overview of Benefits and Disadvantages of Altmetrics." *Journal of Informetrics* 8, no. 4 (2014): 895–903. https://doi.org/10.1016/j.joi.2014.09.005.

Bornmann, Lutz. "Letter to the Editor: On the Conceptualisation and Theorisation of the Impact Caused by Publications." *Scientometrics* 103 (2015): 1145–1148. https://doi.org/10.1007/s11192-015-1588-4.

Bornmann, Lutz, and Hans-Dieter Daniel. "What Do Citation Counts Measure? A Review of Studies on Citing Behavior." *Journal of Documentation* 64, no. 1 (2008): 45–80. https://doi.org/10.1108/00220410810844150.

Bornmann, Lutz, Hermann Schier, Werner Marx, and Hans-Dieter Daniel. "Is Interactive Open Access Publishing Able to Identify High-Impact Submissions? A Study on the Predictive Validity of Atmospheric Chemistry and Physics by Using Percentile Rank Classes." *Journal of the American Society for Information Science and Technology* 62, no. 1 (2011): 61–71. https://doi.org/10.1002/asi.21418.

Bornmann, Lutz, and Robin Haunschild. "Do Altmetrics Correlate with the Quality of Papers? A Large-Scale Empirical Study Based on F1000Prime Data." *PLoS ONE* 13, no. 5 (2018): e0197133. https://doi.org/10.1371/journal.pone.0197133.

Bosch, Stephen, Barbara Albee, and Sion Romaine. "Costs Outstrip Library Budgets. Periodicals Price Survey 2020." *Library Journal.* April 14, 2020. https://www.libraryjournal.com/?detailStory=Costs-Outstrip-Library-Budgets-Periodicals-Price-Survey-2020.

Bosch, Stephen, Barbara Albee, and Sion Romaine. "Deal or No Deal. Periodicals Price Survey 2019." *Library Journal.* April 4, 2019. https://www.libraryjournal.com/?detailStory=Deal-or-No-Deal-Periodicals-Price-Survey-2019.

Bowser, Anne, Caren Cooper, Alex de Sherbinin, Andrea Wiggins, Peter Brenton, Tyng-Ruey Chuang, Elaine Faustman, et al. "Still in Need of Norms: The State of the Data in Citizen Science." *Citizen Science: Theory and Practice* 5, no. 1 (2020): 1–16. https://doi.org/10.5334/cstp.303.

Bowser-Livermore, Anne, and Andrea Wiggins. "Privacy in Participatory Research: Advancing Policy to Support Human Computation." *Human Computation* 2, no. 1 (2015): 19–44. https://doi.org/10.15346/hc.v2i1.3.

Boyd, Danah M., and Nicole B. Ellison. "Social Network Sites: Definition, History, and Scholarship." *Journal of Computer-Mediated Communication* 13, no. 1 (2007): 210–230. https://doi.org/10.1111/j.1083-6101.2007.00393.x.

Boyle, James. "Obama's Team Must Fight 'Cultural Agoraphobia.'" *Financial Times.* December 17, 2008. https://www.ft.com/content/b506caa4-cb93-11dd-ba02-000077b07658.

Broadus, Robert N. "An Investigation of the Validity of Bibliographic Citations." *Journal of the American Society for Information Science* 34 (1983): 132–135. https://doi.org/10.1002/asi.4630340206.

Buckheit, Jonathan B., and David L. Donoho. "WaveLab and Reproducible Research." In *Wavelets and Statistics. Lecture Notes in Statistics* Vol. 103, 55–81. Edited by Anestis Antoniadis and Georges Oppenheim. New York: Springer, 1995. https://doi.org/10.1007/978-1-4612-2544-7_5.

"Budapest Open Access Initiative (BOAI)." February 14, 2002. https://www.budapestopenaccessinitiative.org/read.

Bureau of Labor Statistics, U.S. Department of Labor. "College Tuition and Fees Increase 63 Percent Since January 2006." *The Economics Daily.* August 30, 2016. https://www.bls.gov/opub/ted/2016/college-tuition-and-fees-increase-63-percent-since-january-2006.htm.

Bureau of Labor Statistics, U.S. Department of Labor. "Cost of College Tuition Has Remained Stable Since September 2019." *The Economics Daily* (August 31, 2021). https://www.bls.gov/opub/ted/2021/cost-of-college-tuition-has-remained-stable-since-september-2019.htm.

Burton, Gideon. "The Open Scholar." *Academic Evolution.* August 11, 2009. http://www.academicevolution.com/2009/08/the-open-scholar.html.

Cabezas-Clavijo, Alvaro, Nicolás Robinson-García, Manuel Escabias, and Evaristo Jiménez-Contreras. "Reviewers' Ratings and Bibliometric Indicators: Hand in Hand When Assessing Over Research Proposals?" *PLoS ONE* 8, no. 6 (2013): e68258. https://doi.org/10.1371/journal.pone.0068258.

Cadez, Simon, Vlado Dimovski, and Maja Zaman Groff. "Research, Teaching and Performance Evaluation in Academia: The Salience of Quality." *Studies in Higher Education* 42, no. 8 (2017): 1455–1473. https://doi.org/10.1080/03075079.2015.1104659.

Camacho-Miñano, María-del-Mar, and Manuel Núñez-Nickel. "The Multilayered Nature of Reference Selection." *Journal of the American Society for Information Science and Technology* 60 (2009): 754–777. https://doi.org/10.1002/asi.21018.

"Cape Town Open Education Declaration: Unlocking the Promise of Open Educational Resources." 2007. http://www.capetowndeclaration.org/read-the-declaration.

Chan, Teresa M., David Stukus, Jimmie Leppink, Lina Duque, Blair L. Bigham, Neil Mehta, and Brent Thoma. "Social Media and the 21st-Century Scholar: How You Can Harness Social Media to Amplify Your Career." *Journal of the American College of Radiology* 15, no. 1 (2018): 142–148. https://doi.org/10.1016/j.jacr.2017.09.025.

Cheung, Man Kit. "Altmetrics: Too Soon for Use in Assessment." *Nature* 494, no. 7436 (2013): 176. https://doi.org/10.1038/494176d.

Chew, Cynthia, and Gunther Eysenbach. "Pandemics in the Age of Twitter: Content Analysis of Tweets During the 2009 H1N1 Outbreak." *PLoS ONE* 5, no. 11 (2010): e14118. https://doi.org/10.1371/journal.pone.0014118.

Chignard, Simon. "A Brief History of Open Data." *Paris Innovation Review.* March 29, 2013. http://parisinnovationreview.com/articles-en/a-brief-history-of-open-data.

Clements, Kati, Jan Pawlowski, and Nikos Manouselis. "Open Educational Resources Repositories Literature Review—Towards a Comprehensive Quality Approaches Framework." *Computers in Human Behavior* 51, Part B (2015): 1098–1106. https://doi.org/10.1016/j.chb.2015.03.026.

Clinton, Virginia, and Shafiq Khan. "Efficacy of Open Textbook Adoption on Learning Performance and Course Withdrawal Rates: A Meta-Analysis." *AERA Open* 5, no. 3 (2019): 1–20. https://doi.org/10.1177/2332858419872212.

Clobridge, Abby. "Open Peer Review: The Next Wave in Open Knowledge?" *Online Searcher: Information Discovery, Technology, Strategies,* 40, no. 4 (2016): 60–62.

cOAlition S. "cOAlition S Statement on Open Access for Academic Books." https://www.coalition-s.org/coalition-s-statement-on-open-access-for-academic-books.

cOAlition S. "Plan S. Making Full and Immediate Open Access a Reality." https://www.coalition-s.org.

Cobo, Cristobal. "Exploration of Open Educational Resources in Non-English Speaking Communities." *International Review of Research in Open and Distance Learning* 14, no. 2 (2013): 106–128. https://doi.org/10.19173/irrodl.v14i2.1493.

Cohen, Laura. "Social Scholarship on the Rise." *The Stoa: A Review for Digital Classics.* May 1, 2007. https://blog.stoa.org/archives/628.

Cohn, Jeffrey P. "Citizen Science: Can Volunteers Do Real Research?" *BioScience* 58, no. 3 (2008): 192–197. https://doi.org/10.1641/B580303.

Cooper, Caren B., Janis Dickinson, Tina Phillips, and Rick Bonney. "Citizen Science as a Tool for Conservation in Residential Ecosystems." *Ecology and Society* 12, no. 2 (2007). http://www.jstor.org/stable/26267884.

Copyleft Attitude. "Free Art License (1.3.)." 2007. https://artlibre.org/licence/lal/en.

Corbett, Susan. "Creative Commons Licences, the Copyright Regime and the Online Community: Is There a Fatal Disconnect?" *The Modern Law Review* 74, no. 4 (2011): 503–531. https://doi.org/10.1111/j.1468-2230.2011.00858.x.

Cornwell, Myriah L., and Lisa M. Campbell. "Co-Producing Conservation and Knowledge: Citizen-Based Sea Turtle Monitoring in North Carolina, USA." *Social Studies of Science* 42, no. 1 (2012): 101–120. https://doi.org/10.1177/0306312711430440.

Craig, Carys J. *Copyright, Communication and Culture: Towards a Relational Theory of Copyright Law.* Northampton: Edward Elgar Publishing, 2011.

Cramer, Florian. "The Creative Common Misunderstanding." *FLOSS + Art* (2006): 128–137.

Crane, Diana. *Invisible Colleges: Diffusion of Knowledge in Scientific Communities.* Chicago: University of Chicago Press, 1972.

Crawford, Walt. Gold Open Access 2014-2019 (GOA5) Dataset. Figshare, 2020. https://doi.org/10.6084/m9.figshare.12543080.v1.

Crawford, Walt. *Open Access: What You Need to Know Now.* Chicago: American Library Association, 2011.

"Creative Commons." http://creativecommons.org.

Creative Commons. *Creative Commons for Educators and Librarians.* Chicago: American Library Association, 2020.

Cronin, Blaise. "Bibliometrics and Beyond: Some Thoughts on Web-Based Citation Analysis." *Journal of Information Science* 27, no. 1 (2001): 1–7. https://doi.org/10.1177/016555150102700101.

Cronin, Blaise. "The Evolving Indicator Space (iSpace)." *Journal of the American Society for Information Science and Technology* 64, no. 8 (2013): 1523–1525. https://doi.org/10.1002/asi.23041.

Cronin, Blaise. "The Need For a Theory of Citing." *Journal of Documentation* 37, no. 1 (1981): 16–24. https://doi.org/10.1108/eb026703.

Cronin, Catherine. "Openness and Praxis: Exploring the Use of Open Educational Practices in Higher Education." *International Review of Research in Open and Distributed Learning* 18, no. 5 (2017): 15–34. https://doi.org/10.19173/irrodl.v18i5.3096.

Cukier, Samantha, Lucas Helal, Danielle B. Rice, Justina Pupkaite, Nadera Ahmadzai, Mitchell Wilson, Becky Skidmore, et al. "Checklists to Detect Potential Predatory Biomedical Journals: A Systematic Review." *BMC Medicine* 18, no. 104 (2020a). https://doi.org/10.1186/s12916-020-01566-1.

Cukier, Samantha, Manoj Lalu, Gregory L. Bryson, Kelly D. Cobey, Agnes Grudniewicz, and David Moher. "Defining Predatory Journals and Responding to the Threat They Pose: A Modified Delphi Consensus Process." *BMJ Open* 10, no. 2 (2020b). http://dx.doi.org/10.1136/bmjopen-2019-035561.

Daniels, Jessie, and Polly Thistlethwaite. *Being a Scholar in the Digital Era: Transforming Scholarly Practice for the Public Good.* Chicago: Policy Press, 2016.

Danielsen, Finn, Neil David Burgess, Indiana Coronado, Martin Enghoff, Sune Holt, Per Moestrup Jensen, Michael K. Poulsen, et al. "The Value of Indigenous and Local Knowledge as Citizen Science." In *Citizen Science: Innovation in Open Science, Society and Policy,* 110–123. Edited by Susanne Hecker, Muki Haklay, Anne Bowser, Zen Makuch, Johannes Vogel, and Aletta Bonn. London: UCL Press, 2018.

D'Antoni, Susan, and Catriona Savage (eds.). *Open Educational Resources: Conversations in Cyberspace.* Paris: UNESCO Publishing, 2009. https://unesdoc.unesco.org/ark:/48223/pf0000181682.

Darling, Emily S., David Shiffman, Isabelle M. Côté, and Joshua A. Drew. "The Role of Twitter in the Life Cycle of a Scientific Publication." *Ideas in Ecology and Evolution* 6, no. 1 (2013): 32–43. http://dx.doi.org/10.4033/iee.2013.6.6.f.

Davidson, Keay. "Bay Area Leads Revolt Against Scientific Journals. Scientists Call for Boycott, Launch Open-Access Project." *The San Francisco*

Chronicle. October 27, 2003. https://www.sfgate.com/science/article/Bay -Area-leads-revolt-against-scientific-journals-2551886.php.

"Definition of Free Cultural Works." Last updated February 17, 2015. https:// freedomdefined.org/Definition.

Deimann, Markus. "Open Education and *Bildung* as Kindred Spirits." *E-Learning and Digital Media* 10, no. 2 (2013): 190–199. https://doi.org/10.2304 /elea.2013.10.2.190.

de Langen, Frank. "Strategies for Sustainable Business Models for Open Educational Resources." *International Review of Research in Open and Distance Learning* 14, no. 2 (2013): 53–66. https://doi.org/10.19173/irrodl .v14i2.1533.

DeMartini, Becky, Justin Marshall, and Marynelle Chew. "Putting Textbooks in Students' Hands." *Technical Services Quarterly* 35, no. 3 (2018): 233–245. https://doi.org/10.1080/07317131.2018.1456842.

Dennen, Vanessa, and Lauren Bagdy. "From Proprietary Textbook to Custom OER Solution: Using Learner Feedback to Guide Design and Development." *Online Learning* 23, no. 3 (2019): 4–20. https://doi.org/10.24059 /olj.v23i3.2068.

Dewey, John. *The Public and Its Problems: An Essay in Political Inquiry.* Edited and with introduction by Melvin L. Rogers. University Park: Pennsylvania State University Press, 1927/2012.

Dholakia, Utpal, W. Joseph King, and Richard Baraniuk. "What Makes an Open Education Program Sustainable? The Case of Connexions." May 2006. http://www.oecd.org/education/ceri/36781781.pdf.

Dickinson, Janis L., Jennifer Shirk, David Bonter, Rick Bonney, Rhiannon L. Crain, Jason Martin, Tina Phillips, et al. "The Current State of Citizen Science as a Tool for Ecological Research and Public Engagement." *Frontiers in Ecology and the Environment* 10, no. 6 (2012): 291–297. https://doi .org/10.1890/110236.

Dinevski, Dejan. "Open Educational Resources and Lifelong Learning." *ITI 2008 – 30th International Conference on Information Technology Interfaces* (2008): 117–122. https://doi.org/10.1109/ITI.2008.4588393.

Downes, Stephen. "Models for Sustainable Open Educational Resources." *Interdisciplinary Journal of E-Learning and Learning Objects* 3, no. 1 (2007): 29–44. https://www.learntechlib.org/p/44796/.

Dryad. "Joint Data Archiving Policy (JDAP)." Last updated in 2020. http:// datadryad.org/pages/jdap.

Durham, Erin, and Sherri Braxton. "Advancing an Open Educational Resource Initiative Through Collaborative Leadership." *International Journal of Open Educational Resources* 2, no. 1 (2019). https://ijoer.org/advancing -an-open-educational-resource-initiative-through-collaborative -leadership.

Dusollier, Séverine. "Open Source and Copyleft: Authorship Reconsidered?" *Columbia Journal of Law and the Arts* 26 (2003): 281–296.

Dusollier, Séverine. "Sharing Access to Intellectual Property Through Private Ordering." *Chicago-Kent Law Review* 82 (2007): 1391–1435.

Eamon, William. "From the Secrets of Nature to Public Knowledge: The Origins of the Concept of Openness in Science." *Minerva* 23, no. 3 (1985): 321–347. https://www.jstor.org/stable/41827233.

Eichorn, Philip, and Alfred Yankauer. "Do Authors Check Their References? A Survey of Accuracy of References in Three Public Health Journals." *American Journal of Public Health* 77 (1987): 1011–1012. https://doi.org/10.2105/AJPH.77.8.1011.

Eisen, Michael. "Publish and Be Praised: Why It's High Time the Results of Scientific Research Were Freely Available to Everyone." *The Guardian*. October 9, 2003. https://www.theguardian.com/education/2003/oct/09/research.highereducation.

Eitzel, Melissa V., Jessica L. Cappadonna, Chris Santos-Lang, Ruth Ellen Duerr, Arika Virapongse, Sarah Elizabeth West, Christopher Kyba, et al. "Citizen Science Terminology Matters: Exploring Key Terms." *Citizen Science: Theory and Practice* 2, no. 1 (2017). http://doi.org/10.5334/cstp.96.

Elkin-Koren, Niva. "What Contracts Cannot Do: The Limits of Private Ordering in Facilitating a Creative Commons." *Fordham Law Review* 74 (2005): 375–422.

Ellis, Aytoun. *The Penny Universities: A History of the Coffee Houses.* London: Secker and Warburg, 1956.

Engler, Jennifer, and Randi Shedlosky-Shoemaker. "Facilitating Student Success: The Role of Open Educational Resources in Introductory Psychology Courses." *Psychology Learning & Teaching* 18, no. 1 (2019): 36–47. https://doi.org/10.1177/1475725718810241.

English, P. B., M. J. Richardson, and Catalina Garzón-Galvis. "From Crowdsourcing to Extreme Citizen Science: Participatory Research for Environmental Health." *Annual Review of Public Health* 39 (2018): 335–350. https://doi.org/10.1146/annurev-publhealth-040617-013702.

Erdt, Mojisola, Nagarajan Aarthy, Joanna Sin Sei-Ching, and Yin-Leng Theng. "Altmetrics: An Analysis of the State-of-the-Art in Measuring Research Impact on Social Media." *Scientometrics* 109, no. 2 (2016): 1117–1166. https://doi.org/10.1007/s11192-016-2077-0.

European Commission. "Horizon 2020." https://ec.europa.eu/programmes/horizon2020/en.

European Commission. "Horizon Europe." https://ec.europa.eu/info/horizon-europe-next-research-and-innovation-framework-programme_en.

European Commission. "Recommendation on Access to and Preservation of Scientific Information." *Official Journal of the European Union.* April 25, 2018. https://eur-lex.europa.eu/eli/reco/2018/790/oj.

Evans, James T., Howard I. Nadjari, and Sherry A. Burchell. "Quotational and Reference Accuracy in Surgical Journals: A Continuing Peer Review Problem." *Journal of the American Medical Association* 263 (1990): 1353–1354. https://doi.org/10.1001/jama.1990.03440100059009.

Eve, Martin Paul. *Open Access and the Humanities: Contexts, Controversies and the Future.* Cambridge: Cambridge University Press, 2014. https://doi.org /10.1017/CBO9781316161012.

Eve, Martin Paul. "Open Access Publishing Models and How OA Can Work in the Humanities." *Bulletin of the Association for Information Science and Technology* 43, no. 5 (2017): 16–20. https://doi.org/10.1002/bul2.2017.1720430505.

Eysenbach, Gunther. 2011. "Can Tweets Predict Citations? Metrics of Social Impact Based on Twitter and Correlation with Traditional Metrics of Scientific Impact." *Journal of Medical Internet Research* 13, no. 4 (2011): e123. https://doi.org/10.2196/jmir.2012.

Fals-Borda, Orlando, and Muhammad Anisur Rahman (eds.). *Action and Knowledge: Breaking the Monopoly with Participatory Action Research.* New York: Apex Press, 1991.

Fecher, Benedikt, and Sascha Friesike. "Open Science: One Term, Five Schools of Thought." In *Opening Science: The Evolving Guide on How the Internet is Changing Research, Collaboration and Scholarly Publishing,* 17–47. Edited by Sönke Bartling and Sascha Friesike. Berlin: Springer Open, 2014.

Fenner, Martin. "Author Identifier Overview." *LIBREAS. Library Ideas* 18 (2011). https://libreas.eu/ausgabe18/texte/03fenner.htm.

Fernández, Gabriel E. Abad. "OpenCourseWare." In *The SAGE Encyclopedia of Online Education,* 886–888. Edited by Steven L. Danver. Thousand Oaks: SAGE Publications, 2016.

Ford, Emily. "Defining and Characterizing Open Peer Review: A Review of the Literature." *Journal of Scholarly Publishing* 44, no. 4 (2013): 311–326. https://doi.org/10.3138/jsp.44-4-001.

Fowler, Henry Watson, Francis George Fowler, and David Crystal. *The Concise Oxford Dictionary: The Classic First Edition.* Oxford: Oxford University Press, 2011.

Frandsen, Tove Faber. "Are Predatory Journals Undermining the Credibility of Science? A Bibliometric Analysis of Citers." *Scientometrics* 113, no. 3 (2017): 1513–1528. https://doi.org/10.1007/s11192-017-2520-x.

Free Software Foundation of India. "FSF India: A Q & A Session with Richard M. Stallman." January 23, 2004. https://web.archive.org/web /20061015205039/http://www.gnu.org.in/node/68.

Freitas, Lima, Basarab Nicolescu, and Edgar Morin. "The Charter of Transdisciplinarity." 1994. http://inters.org/Freitas-Morin-Nicolescu-Transdisciplinarity.

Garaizar, Pablo, Miguel A. Vadillo, Diego López-de-Ipiña, and Helena Matute. "The Web as a Platform for e-Research in the Social and Behavioral Sciences." In *Collaborative and Distributed E-Research: Innovations in Technologies, Strategies and Applications,* 34–61. Edited by Angel A. Juan, Thanasis Daradoumis, Meritxell Roca, Scott E. Grasman, and Javier Faulin. Hershey: IGI Global, 2012.

Gentleman, Robert, and Duncan Temple Lang. "Statistical Analyses and Reproducible Research." *Journal of Computational and Graphical Statistics* 16, no. 1 (2007): 1–23. https://doi.org/10.1198/106186007X178663.

Gibbons, Michael, Camille Limoges, Helga Nowotny, Simon Schwartzman, Peter Scott, and Martin Trow. *The New Production of Knowledge: The Dynamics of Science and Research in Contemporary Societies.* Los Angeles: SAGE Publications, 1994.

Giofrè, David, Geoff Cumming, Luca Fresc, Ingrid Boedker, and Patrizio Tressoldi. "The Influence of Journal Submission Guidelines on Authors' Reporting of Statistics and Use of Open Research Practices." *PLoS ONE* 12, no. 4 (2017): e0175583. https://doi.org/10.1371/journal.pone .0175583.

"GNU General Public License, Version 3." June 29, 2007. https://www.gnu.org /licenses/gpl-3.0.html.

"GNU Operating System." Last updated February 15, 2021. https://www.gnu .org.

GNU Operating System. "FOSS and FLOSS." Updated September 11, 2021. https://www.gnu.org/philosophy/floss-and-foss.html.

GNU Operating System. "What Is Free Software?" Updated October 11, 2021. https://www.gnu.org/philosophy/free-sw.en.html.

GNU Operating System. "Why Open Source Misses the Point of Free Software." Updated October 2, 2021. https://www.gnu.org/philosophy/open-source -misses-the-point.html.

Goldberg, Carey. "Auditing Classes at MIT, on the Web and Free." *The New York Times.* April 4, 2001. https://www.nytimes.com/2001/04/04/us/auditing -classes-at-mit-on-the-web-and-free.html.

Graf, Chris. "Why More Journals Are Joining Our Transparent Peer Review Pilot." Wiley. September 20, 2019. https://www.wiley.com/network/researchers /latest-content/why-more-journals-are-joining-our-transparent-peer -review-pilot.

Grassmuck, Volker. "Towards a New Social Contract: Free-Licensing into the Knowledge Commons." In *Open Content Licensing: From Theory to Practice,* 21–50. Edited by Guibault Lucie and Angelopoulos Christina. Amsterdam: Amsterdam University Press, 2011.

Grégoire, Robert, and Papa Youga Dieng. *OER Trainer's Guide.* Paris: International Organisation of La Francophonie (IOF), 2016. https://unesdoc .unesco.org/ark:/48223/pf0000266161.

Grey, François. "Citizen Cyberscience: The New Age of the Amateur." *CERN Courier* 51, no. 7 (2011): 41–43.

Griffiths, Rebecca, Jessica Mislevy, Sam Wang, Alexandra Ball, Linda Shear, and Donna Desrochers. *OER at Scale: The Academic and Economic Outcomes of Achieving the Dream's OER Degree Initiative.* Menlo Park: SRI International, 2020.

Grimme, Sara, Mike Taylor, Michael A. Elliott, Cathy Holland, Peter Potter, and Charles Watkinson. 2019. "The State of Open Monographs." https:// digitalscience.gshare.com/articles/The_State_of_Open_Monographs /8197625.

Grudniewicz, Agnes, David Moher, Kelly D. Cobey, Gregory L. Bryson, Samantha Cukier, Kristiann Allen, Clare Ardern, et al. "Predatory Journals: No Definition, No Defence." *Nature* 576 (2019): 210–212. https://doi.org/10.1038/d41586-019-03759-y.

Guédon, Jean-Claude. 2001. "In Oldenburg's Long Shadow: Librarians, Research Scientists, Publishers, and the Control of Scientific Publishing." Conference paper. Creating the Digital Future: Association of Research Libraries 138th Annual Meeting, Toronto, Ontario (Canada), May 23–25. http://eprints.rclis.org/6375.

Guédon, Jean-Claude. "Open Access: A Symptom and a Promise." In *Open Access: Key Strategic, Technical and Economic* Aspects, 27–38. Edited by Neil Jacobs. Oxford: Chandos Publishing, 2006.

Gurung, Regan. "Predicting Learning: Comparing an Open Education Research and Standard Textbooks." *Scholarship of Teaching and Learning in Psychology* 3, no. 3 (2017): 233–248. https://doi.org/10.1037/stl0000092.

Hadorn, Gertrude Hirsch, Holger Hoffmann-Riem, Susette Biber-Klemm, Walter Grossenbacher-Mansuy, Dominique Joye, Christian Pohl, Urs Wiesmann, et al. (eds). *Handbook of Transdisciplinary Research*. Dordrecht, London: Springer Science + Business Media B.V., 2008.

Haklay, Muki. 2013. "Citizen Science and Volunteer Geographic Information: Overview and Typology of Participation." In *Crowdsourcing Geographic Knowledge: Volunteered Geographic Information (VGI) in Theory and Practice*, 105–122. Edited by Daniel Sui, Sarah Elwood, and Michael Goodchild. Dordrecht: Springer, 2013. https://doi.org/10.1007/978-94-007-4587-2_7.

Hall, Marie Boas. "Oldenburg and the Art of Scientific Communication." *The British Journal for the History of Science* 2, no. 4 (1965): 277–290. https://www.jstor.org/stable/4024886.

Hames, Irene. *Peer Review and Manuscript Management in Scientific Journals: Guidelines for Good Practice*. Malden: Blackwell Publishing, 2007.

Hanick, Silvia Lin, and Amy Hofer. "Opening the Framework: Connecting Open Education Practices and Information Literacy." *OpenOregon Educational Resources*. May 31, 2017. http://openoregon.org/opening-the-framework.

Harnad, Stevan, Tim Brody, François Valliéres, Les Carr, Steve Hitchcock, Yves Gingras, Charles Oppenheim, et al. "The Access/Impact Problem and the Green and Gold Roads to Open Access." *Serials Review* 30, no. 4 (2004): 310–314.

Harrison, Andrew Marc, and Anthony Mark Harrison. "Necessary But Not Sufficient: Unique Author Identifiers." *BMJ Innovations* 2, no. 4 (2016): 141–143. http://dx.doi.org/10.1136/bmjinnov-2016-000135.

Harvey, Lee, and Diana Green. "Defining Quality." *Assessment & Evaluation in Higher Education* 18, no. 1 (1993): 9–34. https://doi.org/10.1080/0260293930180102.

Hassall, Christopher, and David I. Lewis. "Institutional and Technological Barriers to the Use of Open Educational Resources (OERs) in Physiology and Medical Education." *Advances in Physiology Education* 41, no. 1 (2017): 77–81. https://doi.org/10.1152/advan.00171.2016.

Haustein, Stefanie. "Grand Challenges in Altmetrics: Heterogeneity, Data Quality and Dependencies." *Scientometrics* 108, no. 1 (2016): 413–423. https://doi.org/10.1007/s11192-016-1910-9.

Haustein, Stefanie. "Readership Metrics." In *Beyond Bibliometrics: Harnessing Multidimensional Indicators of Performance*, 327–344. Edited by Blaise Cronin and Cassidy R. Sugimoto. Cambridge: MIT Press, 2014.

Haustein, Stephanie, Vincent Larivière, Mike Thelwall, Didier Amyot, and Isabella Peters. "Tweets vs. Mendeley Readers: How Do These Two Social Media Metrics Differ?" *Information Technology* 56, no. 5 (2014): 207–215. http://doi.org/10.1515/itit-2014-1048.

Haywood, Benjamin K. "A 'Sense of Place' in Public Participation in Scientific Research." *Science Education* 98, no. 1 (2014): 64–83. https://doi.org/10.1002/sce.21087.

Herndon, Joel, and Robert O'Reilly. "Data Sharing Policies in Social Sciences Academic Journals: Evolving Expectations of Data Sharing as a Form of Scholarly Communication." In *Databrarianship: The Academic Data Librarian in Theory and Practice*, 219–242. Edited by Linda Kellam and Kristi Thompson. Chicago: American Library Association, 2016.

Hill, Benjamin Mako. "Towards a Standard of Freedom: Creative Commons and the Free Software Movement." June 29, 2005. https://mako.cc/writing/toward_a_standard_of_freedom.html.

Hilton, John, III, and Carol Laman. "One College's Use of an Open Psychology Textbook." *Open Learning* 27, no. 3 (2012): 265–272. https://doi.org/10.1080/02680513.2012.716657.

Hirsch, Jorge E. "An Index to Quantify an Individual's Scientific Research Output." *Proceedings of the National Academy of Sciences of the United States of America* 102, no. 46 (2005): 16569–16572. https://doi.org/10.1073/pnas.0507655102.

Holbrook, J. Britt. "Peer Review." In *The Oxford Handbook of Interdisciplinarity*, 321–332. Edited by Robert Frodeman. Oxford: Oxford University Press, 2010.

Holdren, John P. "Addressing Societal and Scientific Challenges Through Citizen Science and Crowdsourcing. Memorandum to the Heads of Executive Departments and Agencies." Executive Office of the President. Office of Science and Technology Policy. Washington, D.C. September 30, 2015. https://usanpn.org/files/shared/files/holdren_citizen_science_memo_092915_0.pdf.

Holdren, John P. "Increasing Access to the Results of Federally Funded Scientific Research." Executive Office of the President. Office of Science and Technology Policy. Washington, D.C. February 22, 2013. https://

obamawhitehouse.archives.gov/sites/default/files/microsites/ostp/ostp
_public_access_memo_2013.pdf.

Hrynaszkiewicz, Iain. "Publishers' Responsibilities in Promoting Data Quality and Reproducibility." In *Good Research Practice in Non-Clinical Pharmacology and Biomedicine*, 319–348. Edited by Anton Bespalov, Martin C. Michel, and Thomas Steckler. Cham: SpringerOpen, 2020.

Hrynaszkiewicz, Iain, Natasha Simons, Azhar Hussain, Rebecca Grant, and Simon Goudie. "Developing a Research Data Policy Framework for All Journals and Publishers." *Data Science Journal* 19, no. 1 (2020): 5. http://doi.org/10.5334/dsj-2020-005.

Hug, Theo. "Defining Openness in Education." In *Encyclopedia of Educational Philosophy and Theory*, 387–392 Edited by Michael A. Peters. Springer, Singapore, 2017. https://doi.org/10.1007/978-981-287-588-4_214.

Humboldt, Wilhelm von, Herausgegeben von Andreas Flitner, and Klaus Giel. *Werke in Fünf Bänden*. Darmstadt: Wissenschaftliche Buchgesellschaft, 1960.

Ince, Darrel C., Leslie Hatton, and John Graham-Cumming. "The Case for Open Computer Programs." *Nature* 482, no. 7386 (2012): 485–488. https://doi.org/10/hqg.

Irwin, Alan. *Citizen Science: A Study of People, Expertise and Sustainable Development*. London: Routledge, 1995.

Irwin, Alan. "Constructing the Scientific Citizen: Science and Democracy in the Biosciences." *Public Understanding of Science* 10, no. 1 (2001): 1–18. https://doi.org/10.3109/a036852.

ISNI. "FAQs." https://isni.org/page/faqs.

Jacoby, William G., Sophia Lafferty-Hess, and Thu-Mai Christian. "Should Journals Be Responsible for Reproducibility?" *Inside Higher Ed.* July 17, 2017. https://www.insidehighered.com/blogs/rethinking-research/should-journals-be-responsible-reproducibility.

Jahn, Thomas, Matthias Bergmann, and Florian Keil. "Transdisciplinarity: Between Mainstreaming and Marginalization." *Ecological Economics* 79 (2012): 1–10. http://dx.doi.org/10.1016/j.ecolecon.2012.04.017.

Jamali, Hamid R. "Copyright Compliance and Infringement in ResearchGate Full-Text Journal Articles." *Scientometrics* 112, no. 1 (2017): 241–254. https://doi.org/10.1007/s11192-017-2291-4.

Jantsch, Erich. "Towards Interdisciplinarity and Transdisciplinarity in Education and Innovation." In *Interdisciplinarity: Problems of Teaching and Research in Universities*, 97–121. Edited by Leo Apostel, Guy Berger, Asa Briggs, and Guy Michaud. Paris: OECD, Centre for Educational Research and Innovation, 1972.

Jaring, Päivi, and Asta Bäck. "How Researchers Use Social Media to Promote Their Research and Network with Industry." *Technology Innovation Management Review* 7, no. 8 (2017): 32–39. http://doi.org/10.22215/timreview/1098.

Jennett, Charlene, Laure Kloetzer, Daniel Schneider, Ioanna Iacovides, Anna Cox, Margaret Gold, Brian Fuchs, et al. "Motivations, Learning and Creativity in Online Citizen Science." *Journal of Science Communication* 15, no. 3 (2016): 1–23. https://doi.org/10.22323/2.15030205.

Jhangiani, Rajiv S., and Arthur G. Green. 2018. "An Open Athenaeum: Creating an Institutional Home for Open Pedagogy." In *OER: A Field Guide for Academic Librarians*, 141–162. Edited by Andrew Wesolek, Jonathan Lashley, and Anne Langley. Forest Grove: Pacific University Press.

Jhangiani, Rajiv, Rebecca Pitt, Christina Hendricks, Jessie Key, and Clint Lalonde. "Exploring Faculty Use of Open Educational Resources at British Columbia Post-Secondary Institutions." BCcampus Research Report. Victoria, BC: BCcampus, 2016. https://eduq.info/xmlui/bitstream /handle/11515/35344/exploring-faculty-use-of-oer-british-columbia -post-secondary-institutions-bccampus-2016.pdf?sequence=2.

Jordan, Rebecca, Alycia Crall, Steven Gray, Tina Phillips, and David Mellor. "Citizen Science as a Distinct Field of Inquiry." *Bioscience* 65, no. 2 (2015): 208–211. https://doi.org/10.1093/biosci/biu217.

Jordan, Rebecca C., Steven A. Gray, David V. Howe, Wesley R. Brooks, and Joan G. Ehrenfeld. "Knowledge Gain and Behavioral Change in Citizen-Science Programs." *Conservation Biology* 25, no. 6 (2011): 1148–1154. https://doi.org/10.1111/j.1523-1739.2011.01745.x.

Jung, Insung, Sasaki Teruyoshi, and Colin Latchem. "A Framework for Assessing Fitness for Purpose in Open Educational Resources." *International Journal of Educational Technology in Higher Education* 13, no. 1 (2016): 3. https:// doi.org/10.1186/s41239-016-0002-5.

Kasperowski, Dick, and Christopher Kullenberg. "The Many Modes of Citizen Science." *Science & Technology Studies* 32, no. 2 (2019): 2–7. https://doi .org/10.23987/sts.74404.

Kasperowski, Dick, and Thomas Hillman. "The Epistemic Culture in an Online Citizen Science Project: Programs, Antiprograms and Epistemic Subjects." *Social Studies of Science* 48, no. 4 (2018): 564–588. https://doi .org/10.1177/0306312718778806.

Kawachi, Paul. "The TIPS Quality Assurance Framework for Creating Open Educational Resources: Validation." *Open University Malaysia*. May 21, 2014. https://www.open-ed.net/oer-quality/validation.pdf.

Kieslinger, Barbara, Teresa Schäfer, Florian Heigl, Daniel Dörler, Anett Richter, and Aletta Bonn. "Evaluating Citizen Science. Towards an Open Framework." In *Citizen Science: Innovation in Open Science, Society and Policy*, 81–95. Edited by Susanne Hecker, Muki Haklay, Anne Bowser, Zen Makuch, Johannes Vogel, and Aletta Bonn. London: UCL Press, 2018.

Klein, Julie Thompson. *Crossing Boundaries: Knowledge, Disciplinarities, and Interdisciplinarities*. Charlottesville: University of Virginia Press, 1996.

Klein, Julie Thompson, Walter Grossenbacher-Mansuy, Rudolf Häberli, Alain Bill, Roland W. Scholz, and Myrtha Welti (eds.). *Transdisciplinarity: Joint*

Problem Solving Among Science, Technology, and Society: An Effective Way for Managing Complexity. Basel: Springer, 2012.

Konkiel, Stacy (ed.). *The State of Altmetrics: A Tenth Anniversary Celebration.* London: Altmetric, 2020.

Kortemeyer, Gerd. "Ten Years Later: Why Open Educational Resources Have Not Noticeably Affected Higher Education, and Why We Should Care." *EDUCAUSE Review* 48, no. 2 (2013). https://er.educause.edu/articles/2013/2/ten-years-later-why-open-educational-resources-have-not-noticeably-affected-higher-education-and-why-we-should-care.

Kreutzer, Till. "User-Related Assets and Drawbacks of Open Content Licensing." In *Open Content Licensing: From Theory to Practice*, 107–136. Edited by Lucie Guibault and Christina Angelopoulos. Amsterdam: Amsterdam University Press, 2011.

Kullenberg, Christopher. "Citizen Science as Resistance: Crossing the Boundary Between Reference and Representation." *Journal of Resistance Studies* 1, no. 1 (2015): 50–76.

Kullenberg, Christopher, and Dick Kasperowski. "What Is Citizen Science? A Scientometric Meta-Analysis." *PLoS ONE* 11, no. 1 (2016): e0147152. https://doi.org/10.1371/journal.pone.0147152.

Lawrence, Christopher, and Julie Lester. "Evaluating the Effectiveness of Adopting Open Educational Resources in an Introductory American Government Course." *Journal of Political Science Education* 14, no. 4 (2018): 1–12. https://doi.org/10.1080/15512169.2017.1422739.

Leavy, Patricia. *Essentials of Transdisciplinary Research: Using Problem-Centered Methodologies.* Walnut Creek: Left Coast Press, 2011.

Lessig, Lawrence. "CC in Review: Lawrence Lessig on Supporting the Commons." *Creative Commons.* October 2, 2005. https://creativecommons.org/2005/10/06/ccinreviewlawrencelessigonsupportingthecommons.

Lessig, Lawrence. "May the Source Be with You." *Wired.* December 1, 2001. https://www.wired.com/2001/12/lessig.

Lessig, Lawrence. *Remix: Making Art and Commerce Thrive in the Hybrid Economy.* New York: The Penguin Press, 2008.

Lessig, Lawrence. *The Future of Ideas: The Fate of the Commons in a Connected World.* New York: Vintage Books, 2002.

Levy, Steven. *Hackers: Heroes of the Computer Revolution.* London: Penguin, 1984.

Liang, Lawrence. *A Guide to Open Content Licences.* Rotterdam: Piet Zwart Institute, 2004. http://pzwart.wdka.hro.nl/mdr/pubsfolder/opencontentpdf.

Liu, Jean, and Euan Adie. "Five Challenges in Altmetrics: A Toolmaker's Perspective." *Bulletin of the American Society for Information Science and Technology* 39, no. 4 (2013): 31–34. https://doi.org/10.1002/bult.2013.1720390410.

Liu, Weishu, and Yanchao Li. "Open Access Publications in Sciences and Social Sciences: A Comparative Analysis." *Learned Publishing* 31, no. 2 (2018): 107–119. https://doi.org/10.1002/leap.1114.

Ma, Jennifer, Sandy Baum, Matea Pender, and C. J. Libassi. *Trends in College Pricing.* New York: College Board, 2019.

MacRoberts, Michael H., and Barbara R. MacRoberts. "Problems of Citation Analysis: A Study of Uncited and Seldom-Cited Influences." *Journal of the American Society for Information Science and Technology* 61, no. 1 (2010). https://doi.org/10.1002/asi.21228.

Maharg, Paul, and Duncan Nigel. "Black Box, Pandora's Box or Virtual Toolbox? An Experiment in a Journal's Transparent Peer Review on the Web." *International Review of Law Computers & Technology* 21, no. 2 (2007): 109–128. https://doi.org/10.1080/13600860701492104.

Manca, Stefania. "ResearchGate and Academia.edu as Networked Socio-Technical Systems for Scholarly Communication: A Literature Review." *Research in Learning Technology* 26 (2018). https://dx.doi.org/10.25304/rlt.v26.2008.

Maron, Nancy, Rebecca Kennison, Paul Bracke, Nathan Hall, Isaac Gilman, Kara Malenfant, Charlotte Roh, et al. *Open and Equitable Scholarly Communications: Creating a More Inclusive Future.* Chicago: Association of College and Research Libraries, 2019.

Maron, Nancy, Kimberly Schmelzinger, Christine Mulhern, and Daniel Rossman. "The Costs of Publishing Monographs: Toward a Transparent Methodology." *Journal of Electronic Publishing* 19, no. 1 (2016). https://doi.org/10.3998/3336451.0019.103.

Marshall, Eliot. "Bermuda Rules: Community Spirit, with Teeth." *Science* 291, no. 5507 (2001):1192. https://doi.org/10.1126/science.291.5507.1192.

Martin, Michael, Olga Belikov, John Hilton, David Wiley, and Lane Fischer. "Analysis of Student and Faculty Perceptions of Textbook Costs in Higher Education." *Open Praxis* 9, no. 1 (2017): 79–91. https://www.learntechlib.org/p/180267.

Martin, Victoria. *Demystifying eResearch: A Primer for Librarians.* Santa Barbara: Libraries Unlimited, 2014.

Martin, Victoria. "The Concept of Openness in Scholarship." In *Open Praxis, Open Access: Digital Scholarship in Action,* 3–18. Edited by Darren Chase and Dana Haugh. Chicago: ALA Editions, 2020.

Martin, Victoria. *Transdisciplinarity Revealed: What Librarians Need to Know.* Santa Barbara: Libraries Unlimited, 2017.

Max-Plank Society. "Berlin 3, Southampton 2005. Progress in Implementing the Berlin Declaration on Open Access to Knowledge in the Sciences and Humanities." 2005. https://openaccess.mpg.de/319838/Berlin_3.

Max-Plank Society. "Berlin Declaration on Open Access to Knowledge in the Sciences and Humanities." 2003. https://openaccess.mpg.de/Berlin-Declaration.

McCormack, Nancy. "Peer Review and Legal Publishing: What Law Librarians Need to Know About Open, Single-Blind, and Double-Blind Reviewing." *Law Library Journal* 101 (2009): 59–70.

McGiffert, Michael. "Is Justice Blind? An Inquiry into Peer Review." *Scholarly Publishing* 20, no. 1 (1988): 43–48.

Medley-Rath, Stephanie. "Does the Type of Textbook Matter? Results of a Study of Free Electronic Reading Materials at a Community College." *Community College Journal of Research and Practice* 42, no. 12 (2018): 908–918. https://doi.org/10.1080/10668926.2017.1389316.

Meho, Lokman I. "The Rise and Rise of Citation Analysis." *Physics World* 20, no. 1 (2007): 32. https://doi.org/10.1088/2058-7058/20/1/33.

Merton, Robert K. *The Sociology of Science: Theoretical and Empirical Investigations.* Chicago: University of Chicago Press, 1973.

Miao, Fengchun, Sanjaya Mishra, and Rory McGreal (eds.). *Open Educational Resources: Policy, Costs, Transformation.* Paris: UNESCO Publishing, 2016. https://unesdoc.unesco.org/ark:/48223/pf0000244365.

Miller-Rushing, Abraham, Richard Primack, and Rick Bonney. "The History of Public Participation in Ecological Research." *Frontiers in Ecology and the Environment* 10, no. 6 (2012): 285–290. https://doi.org/10.1890/110278.

Moed, Henk F. "Altmetrics as Traces of the Computerization of the Research Process." In *Theories of Informetrics and Scholarly Communication. A Festschrift in Honor of Blaise Cronin*, 360–371. Edited by Cassidy R. Sugimoto. Berlin: De Gruyter, 2016.

Mons, Barend, Cameron Neylon, Jan Velterop, Michel Dumontier, Luiz Olavo Bonino da Silva Santos, and Mark D. Wilkinson. "Cloudy, Increasingly FAIR. Revisiting the FAIR Data Guiding Principles for the European Open Science Cloud." *Information Services & Use* 37, no. 1 (2017): 49–56. https://doi.org/10.3233/ISU-170824.

Morozov, Evgeny. "The Meme Hustler." *The Baffler.* April 2013. https://thebaffler.com/salvos/the-meme-hustler.

Morris, Shaneka, and Gary Roebuck. *ARL Statistics 2014–2015.* Washington, D.C: Association of Research Libraries, 2017.

Murray-Rust, Peter (@petermurrayrust). "Open Access Saves Lives." *Twitter.* January 27, 2020. https://twitter.com/petermurrayrust/status/1221808071720296449.

Murray-Rust, Peter, Cameron Neylon, Rufus Pollock, and John Wilbanks. "Panton Principles: Principles for Open Data in Science." February 19, 2010. https://pantonprinciples.org/.

Nascimento, Susana, A. Guimaraes Pereira, and Alessia Ghezzi. *From Citizen Science to Do It Yourself Science.* Luxembourg: Publications Office of the European Union, 2014. https://www.vbio.de/fileadmin/user_upload/wissenschaft/pdf/ldna27095enn.pdf.

Nascimento, Susana, Jose Miguel Rubio Iglesias, Roger Owen, Sven Schade, and Lea Shanley. "Citizen Science for Policy Formulation and Implementation." In *Citizen Science: Innovation in Open Science, Society and Policy*, 219–240. Edited by Susanne Hecker, Muki Haklay, Anne Bowser, Zen Makuch, Johannes Vogel, and Aletta Bonn. London: UCL Press, 2018.

National Academies of Sciences, Engineering, and Medicine. *Learning Through Citizen Science: Enhancing Opportunities by Design.* Washington, D.C.: The National Academies Press, 2018.

National Advisory Council for Environmental Policy and Technology (NACEPT). "Environmental Protection Belongs to the Public. A Vision for Citizen Science at EPA." Washington, D.C.: U.S. EPA, 2016. https://www.epa.gov /sites/production/files/2016-12/documents/nacept_cs_report_final _508_0.pdf.

National Human Genome Research Institute (NHGRI). "NHGRI Policy Regarding Intellectual Property of Human Genomic Sequence: Policy on Availability and Patenting of Human Genome DNA Sequence Produced by NHGRI Pilot Projects (Funded Under RFA HG-95-005)." Policy Document. Bethesda, MD. April 9, 1996. https://www.genome.gov /10000926.

National Institutes of Health (NIH). "Changes to Public Access Policy Compliance Efforts Apply to All Awards with Anticipated Start Dates on or after July 1, 2013." February 14, 2013. https://grants.nih.gov/grants/guide /notice-files/NOT-OD-13-042.html.

National Institutes of Health (NIH). "Final NIH Policy for Data Management and Sharing." October 29, 2020. https://grants.nih.gov/grants/guide/notice -files/NOT-OD-21-013.html.

National Institutes of Health (NIH). "Final NIH Statement on Sharing Research Data." 2003. https://grants.nih.gov/grants/guide/notice-files/NOT-OD-03 -032.html.

National Institutes of Health (NIH). "NIH Data Sharing Policy and Implementation Guidance." Last updated November 3, 2020. https://grants.nih.gov /grants/policy/data_sharing/data_sharing_guidance.htm

National Institutes of Health (NIH). "Revised Policy on Enhancing Public Access to Archived Publications Resulting from NIH-Funded Research." January 11, 2008. http://grants.nih.gov/grants/guide/notice-files/NOT -OD-08-033.html.

National Research Council. *Sharing Research Data.* Washington, D.C.: The National Academies Press, 1985. https://doi.org/10.17226/2033.

National Science Foundation. "Dissemination and Sharing of Research Results. NSF Data Sharing Policy." https://www.nsf.gov/bfa/dias/policy/dmp.jsp.

National Science Foundation. "Proposal & Award Policies & Procedures Guide." 2020. https://www.nsf.gov/pubs/policydocs/pappg20_1/index.jsp.

Nature. "Credit Where Credit Is Due." *Nature* 462, no. 825 (2009). https://doi .org/10.1038/462825a.

Nature. "Data Availability Statements and Data Citations Policy: Guidance for Authors." September 2016. https://www.nature.com/documents/nr-data -availability-statements-data-citations.pdf.

Nature. "Rise of the Citizen Scientist." *Nature* 524, no. 7565 (2015): 265–265. https://www.nature.com/news/rise-of-the-citizen-scientist-1.18192.

Naughton, Linda, and David Kernohan. "Making Sense of Journal Research Data Policies." *Insights* 29, no. 1 (2016): 84–89. htttp://doi.org/10.1629/uksg .284.

Nesbit, John, Karen Belfer, and Tracey Leacock. "Learning Object Review Instrument (LORI). User Manual. Version 2.0." September 1, 2009. https://www .academia.edu/7927907/Learning_Object_Review_Instrument_LORI_.

Newell, William H. "Transdisciplinarity Reconsidered." In *Transdisciplinarity: Recreating Integrated Knowledge*, 42–48. Edited by Margaret A. Somerville and David J. Rapport. Montréal: McGill-Queen's Press, 2000.

Newman, Greg, Andrea Wiggins, Alycia Crall, Eric Graham, Sarah Newman, and Kevin Crowston. "Citizen Science Futures: Emerging Technologies and Shifting Paradigms." *Frontiers in Ecology and the Environment* 10, no. 6 (2012): 298–304. https://doi.org/10.1890/110236.

Nicolaisen, Jeppe. "Citation Analysis." *Annual Review of Information Science and Technology* 41, no. 1 (2007): 609–641. https://doi.org/10.1002/aris.2007 .1440410120.

Nicolescu, Basarab. *Manifesto of Transdisciplinarity*. Albany: SUNY Press, 2002.

Nosek, Brian A., George Alter, George C. Banks, Denny Borsboom, Sara D. Bowman, Steven J. Breckler, Stuart Buck, et al. "Promoting an Open Research Culture." *Science* 348, no. 6242 (2015): 1422–1425. https://doi.org /10.1126/science.aab2374.

Novak, Jasminko, Mathias Becker, François Grey, and Rosy Mondardini. "Citizen Engagement and Collective Intelligence for Participatory Digital Social Innovation." In *Citizen Science: Innovation in Open Science, Society and Policy*, 124–145. Edited by Susanne Hecker, Muki Haklay, Anne Bowser, Zen Makuch, Johannes Vogel, and Aletta Bonn. London: UCL Press, 2018.

Nuijten, Michèle B., Jeroen Borghuis, Coosje L.S. Veldkamp, Linda Dominguez-Alvarez, Marcel A.L.M. Van Assen, and Jelte M. Wicherts. 2017. "Journal Data Sharing Policies and Statistical Reporting Inconsistencies in Psychology." *Collabra: Psychology* 3, no. 1 (2017): 31. https://doi.org/10.1525 /collabra.102.

Nuzzolese, Andrea Giovanni, Paolo Ciancarini, Aldo Gangemi, Silvio Peroni, Francesco Poggi, and Valentina Presutti. "Do Altmetrics Work for Assessing Research Quality?" *Scientometrics* 118, no. 2 (2019): 539–562. https:// doi.org/10.1007/s11192-018-2988-z.

Nyamweya, Mo. "A New Method for Estimating OER Savings." *SPARC*. November 20, 2018. https://sparcopen.org/news/2018/estimating-oer-student -savings.

Open Access Scholarly Publishers Association (OASPA). "Membership Applications, Complaints and Investigations." https://oaspa.org/membership /membership-applications/.

Open Education Consortium. "About The Open Education Consortium." https:// www.oeconsortium.org/about-oec.

Open Government Working Group. "The 8 Principles of Open Government Data." December 7–8, 2007. https://opengovdata.org.

Open Knowledge Foundation. "Open Data Handbook." http://opendatahandbook .org.

Open Knowledge Foundation. "Open Definition: Defining Open in Open Data, Open Content and Open Knowledge. Version 2.0." https://opendefinition .org/od/2.0/en.

OpenMusic. "Free Music for a Free World." http://openmusic.linuxtag.org.

Open Publication License (v1.0, 8, June 1999). https://opencontent.org /openpub.

Open Source Initiative. Last updated February 9, 2021. https://opensource.org.

Organization for Economic Co-operation and Development (OECD). *Giving Knowledge for Free: The Emergence of Open Educational Resources*. Paris: OECD Publishing, 2007. http://www.oecd.org/education/ceri/38654317.pdf.

Ortega, José Luis. "Disciplinary Differences in the Use of Academic Social Networking Sites." *Online Information Review* 39, no. 4 (2015): 520–536. https://doi.org/10.1108/OIR-03-2015-0093.

Ottinger, Gwen. "Buckets of Resistance: Standards and the Effectiveness of Citizen Science." *Science, Technology, & Human Values* 35, no. 2 (2009): 244–270. https://doi.org/10.1177/0162243909337121.

Oxford English Dictionary (OED). Oxford: Oxford University Press, 2021.

Pawlyshyn, Nancy, Braddlee Braddlee, Linda Casper, and Howard Miller. "Adopting OER: A Case Study of Crossinstitutional Collaboration and Innovation." *EDUCAUSE Review*. November 4, 2013. https://er.educause .edu/articles/2013/11/adopting-oer-a-case-study-of-crossinstitutional -collaboration-and-innovation.

Peoples, Brandon K., Stephen R. Midway, Dana Sackett, Abigail Lynch, and Patrick B. Cooney. "Twitter Predicts Citation Rates of Ecological Research." *PLoS ONE* 11, no. 11 (2016): e0166570. https://doi.org/10.1371/journal. pone.0166570.

Perakakis, Pandelis, Michael Taylor, Marco Mazza, and Varvara Trachana. "Natural Selection of Academic Papers." *Scientometrics* 85, no. 2 (2010): 553–559. https://doi.org/10.1007/s11192-010-0253-1.

Perens, Bruce. "The Open Source Definition." In *Open Sources: Voices From the Open Source Revolution*, 171–188. Edited by Chris DiBona and Sam Ockman. Sebastopol: O'Reilly Media, 1999.

Perkel, Jeffrey M. "A Toolkit for Data Transparency Takes Shape." *Nature* 560, no. 7718 (2018): 513–516. https://doi.org/10.1038/d41586-018-05990-5.

Peters, Michael A. "Open Education and Education for Openness." In *Encyclopedia of Educational Philosophy and Theory*. Edited by Michael Peters. Springer, Singapore, 2017. https://doi.org/10.1007/978-981-287-588-4.

Peters, Michael A., and Rodrigo G. Britez. "Introduction." In *Open Education and Education for Openness*, xvii–xxii. Edited by Michael A. Peters and Rodrigo G. Britez. Rotterdam: Sense Publishers, 2006.

Peters, Michael, and Peter Roberts. *The Virtues of Openness: Education, Science, and Scholarship in the Digital Age*. Oxford: Routledge, 2011.

Peterson, Christine. "How I Coined the Term 'Open Source'." *Opensource.com*. February 1, 2018. https://opensource.com/article/18/2/coining-term -open-source-software.

Piaget, Jean. "The Epistemology of Interdisciplinary Relationships." In *Interdisciplinarity: Problems of Teaching and Research in Universities*, 127–139. Edited by Leo Apostel, Guy Berger, Asa Briggs, and Guy Michaud. Paris: OECD, Centre for Educational Research and Innovation, 1972.

Pinfield, Stephen, Jennifer Salter, and Peter A. Bath. "The 'Total Cost of Publication' in a Hybrid Open-Access Environment: Institutional Approaches to Funding Journal Article-Processing Charges in Combination with Subscriptions." *Journal of the Association for Information Science and Technology (JASIST)* 67, no. 7 (2016): 1751–1766. https://doi.org/10.1002/asi.23446.

Piwowar, Heather. "Value All Research Products." *Nature* 493, no. 7431 (2013): 159. https://doi.org/10.1038/493159a.

Piwowar, Heather, and Jason Priem. "The Power of Altmetrics on a CV." *Bulletin of the American Society for Information Science and Technology* 39, no. 4 (2013): 10–13. https://doi.org/10.1002/bult.2013.1720390405.

Piwowar, Heather A., Roger S. Day, and Douglas B. Fridsma. "Sharing Detailed Research Data Is Associated with Increased Citation Rate." *PLoS ONE* 2, no. 3 (2007): e308. https://doi.org/10.1371/journal.pone.0000308.

Piwowar, Heather, and Todd Vision. "Data Reuse and the Open Data Citation Advantage." *PeerJ* 1 (2013): e175. https://doi.org/10.7717/peerj.175.

PLoS Medicine Editors. "The Impact Factor Game." *PLoS Medicine* 3, no. 6 (2006): e291. https://doi.org/10.1371/journal.pmed.0030291.

PLoS ONE. "Licenses and Copyright." https://journals.plos.org/plosone/s /licenses-and-copyright.

Pohl, Christian, and Gertrude Hirsch Hadorn. *Principles for Designing Transdisciplinary Research*. Munich: Oekom, 2007.

Pölönen, Janne, and Mikael Laakso. "Open Access and Research Assessment in Social Sciences" (Accepted/In press). In *Handbook on Research Assessment in the Social Sciences*. Edited by Tim C. E. Engels and Emanuel Kulczycki. Cheltenham: Edward Elgar, 2022. Postprint available at: https://haris .hanken.fi/ws/portalfiles/portal/28192356/Po_lo_nen_Laakso_RASS _final_.pdf.

Ponti, Marisa, Thomas Hillman, Christopher Kullenberg, and Dick Kasperowski. 2018. "Getting It Right or Being Top Rank: Games in Citizen Science." *Citizen Science: Theory and Practice* 3, no. 1 (2018). http://doi.org/10.5334 /cstp.101.

Pöschl, Ulrich, and Thomas Koop. "Interactive Open Access Publishing and Collaborative Peer Review for Improved Scientific Communication and Quality Assurance." *Information Services & Use* 28, no. 2 (2008): 105–107. https://doi.org/10.3233/ISU-2008-0567.

Powell, Maria C., and Mathilde Colin. "Participatory Paradoxes: Facilitating Citizen Engagement in Science and Technology From the Top-Down?" *Bulletin of Science, Technology & Society* 29, no. 4 (2009): 325–342. https://doi.org/10.1177/0270467609336308.

Poynder, Richard. "Interview with Lawrence Lessig." *Open and Shut?*. April 7, 2006. https://poynder.blogspot.com/2006/04/interview-with-lawrence-lessig.html.

Priem, Jason. "Beyond the Paper." *Nature* 495, no. 7442 (2013): 437–440. https://doi.org/10.1038/495437a.

Priem, Jason. (@jasonpriem). "I like the term #articlelevelmetrics, but it fails to imply *diversity* of measures. Lately, I'm liking #altmetrics." *Twitter.* September 28, 2010. https://twitter.com/jasonpriem/status/25844968813.

Priem, Jason, Dario Taraborelli, Paul Groth, and Cameron Neylon. "Altmetrics: A Manifesto." October 26, 2010. http://altmetrics.org/manifesto.

Priem, Jason, Heather A. Piwowar, and Bradley M. Hemminger. "Altmetrics in the Wild: Using Social Media to Explore Scholarly Impact." ArXiv.org. March 20, 2012. http://arxiv.org/abs/1203.4745.

Project Gutenberg. "No Cost, or Freedom?" https://www.gutenberg.org/about/background/free_ebook.html.

Prug, Toni. "Open-Process Academic Publishing." *Ephemera: Theory & Politics in Organization* 10, no. 1 (2010): 40–63.

Pyne, Ros, Christina Emery, Mithu Lucraft, and Anna Sophia Pinck. "The Future of Open Access Books: Findings From a Global Survey of Academic Book Authors." London: SpringerNature, 2019. https://doi.org/10.6084/m9.figshare.8166599.

Qiu, Jane. "Scientific Publishing: Identity Crisis." *Nature* 451, no. 7180 (2008): 766–767. https://doi.org/10.1038/451766a.

Raymond, Eric S. "Shut Up and Show Them the Code." *Linux Today.* June 28, 1999. https://www.linuxtoday.com/developer/1999062802310NWSM.

Raymond, Eric S. *The Cathedral and the Bazaar: Musings on Linux and Open Source by an Accidental Revolutionary.* Sebastopol: O'Reilly Media, 2001.

Regazzi, John J. *Scholarly Communications: A History from Content as King to Content as Kingmaker.* Lanham: Rowman & Littlefield, 2015.

Resnik, David B., Kevin C. Elliott, and Aubrey K. Miller. "A Framework for Addressing Ethical Issues in Citizen Science." *Environmental Science & Policy* 54 (2015): 475–481. https://doi.org/10.1016/j.envsci.2015.05.008.

Rets, Irina, Tim Coughlan, Ursula Stickler, and Lluisa Astruc. "Accessibility of Open Educational Resources: How Well Are They Suited for English Learners?" *Open Learning: The Journal of Open, Distance and e-Learning* (2020): 1–20. https://doi.org/10.1080/02680513.2020.1769585.

Riesch, Hauke, and Clive Potter. 2014. "Citizen Science as Seen by Scientists: Methodological, Epistemological and Ethical Dimensions." *Public Understanding of Science* 1 (2014): 107–120. https://doi.org/10.1177/0963662513497324.

Robinson, Lucy Danielle, J. D. Cawthray, Sarah Elizabeth West, Aletta Bonn, and Janice Ansine. "Ten Principles of Citizen Science." In *Citizen Science: Innovation in Open Science, Society and Policy*, 27–40. Edited by Susanne Hecker, Muki Haklay, Anne Bowser, Zen Makuch, Johannes Vogel, and Aletta Bonn. London: UCL Press, 2018.

Rodgers, Emily, and Sarah Barbrow. *A Look at Altmetrics and Its Growing Significance to Research Libraries*. Ann Arbor: The University of Michigan University Library, 2013.

Rosevelt, Carolyn, Marc Los Huertos, Corey Garza, and Hannahrose Nevins. "Marine Debris in Central California: Quantifying Type and Abundance of Beach Litter in Monterey Bay, CA." *Marine Pollution Bulletin* 71, no. 1–2 (2013): 299–306. https://doi.org/10.1016/j.marpolbul.2013.01.015.

Rossini, Carolina Almeida Antunes. "Green-Paper: The State and Challenges of OER in Brazil: From Readers to Writers?" Berkman Center Research Publication No. 2010-0. February 8, 2010. https://ssrn.com/abstract=1549922.

Rossner, Mike, Heather Van Epps, and Emma Hill. "Show Me the Data." *The Journal of Cell Biology* 179, no. 6 (2007): 1091–1092. https://doi.org/10.1083/jcb.200711140.

Rotman, Dana, Jenny Preece, Jen Hammock, Kezee Procita, Derek Hansen, Cynthia Parr, Darcy Lewis, and David Jacobs. "Dynamic Changes in Motivation in Collaborative Citizen-Science Projects." In *Proceedings of the ACM 2012 Conference on Computer Supported Cooperative Work*, 217–226. 2012. https://doi.org/10.1145/2145204.2145238.

Rowland, Fytton. "The Peer-Review Process." *Learned Publishing* 15, no. 4 (2002): 247–258.

Rowland, Katherine. "Citizen Science Goes 'Extreme.'" *Nature News*. February 17, 2012. https://www.nature.com/news/citizen-science-goes-extreme-1.10054.

Ruth, David. "More Than Half of All Colleges and 2.94 Million Students Using Free OpenStax Textbooks This Year." *OpenStax*. September 11, 2019. https://openstax.org/press/more-half-all-colleges-and-294-million-students-using-free-openstax-textbooks-year.

Sandman, John. "Ridiculously Expensive Text Books: Legislation Introduced to Drop Cost." *The Street*. November 19, 2013. https://www.thestreet.com/personal-finance/ridiculously-expensive-text-books-legislation-introduced-d-12784254.

Sandve, Geir Kjetil, Anton Nekrutenko, James Taylor, and Eivind Hovig. "Ten Simple Rules for Reproducible Computational Research." *PLoS Computational Biology* 9, no. 10 (2013): e1003285. https://doi.org/10.1371/journal.pcbi.1003285.

Sauermann, Henry, and Chiara Franzoni. "Crowd Science User Contribution Patterns and Their Implications." *Proceedings of the National Academy of Sciences* 112, no. 3 (2015): 679–684. https://doi.org/10.1073/pnas.1408907112.

Schlimgen, Joan B., and Michael R Kronenfeld. "Update on Inflation of Journal Prices: Brandon/Hill List Journals and the Scientific, Technical, and Medical Publishing Market." *Journal of the Medical Library Association* 92, no. 3 (2004): 307–314.

Science. "Science Journals: Editorial Policies." https://www.sciencemag.org /authors/science-journals-editorial-policies.

Seaman, Julia E., and Jeff Seaman. *Freeing the Textbook: Educational Resources in U.S. Higher Education, 2018.* Babson Park: Babson Survey Research Group, 2018. https://www.onlinelearningsurvey.com/reports/freeingthetextbook2018 .pdf.

Seaman, Julia E., and Jeff Seaman. *Inflection Point: Educational Resources in U.S. Higher Education, 2019.* Oakland: Bay View Analytics, 2020. https://www .onlinelearningsurvey.com/reports/2019inflectionpoint.pdf.

Seaman, Julia E., and Jeff Seaman. *Opening the Textbook: Educational Resources in US Higher Education, 2017.* Babson Park: Babson Survey Research Group, 2017. https://www.onlinelearningsurvey.com/reports/openingthetextbook2017 .pdf.

Severin, Anna, Matthias Egger, Martin Paul Eve, and Daniel Hürlimann. "Discipline-Specific Open Access Publishing Practices and Barriers to Change: An Evidence-Based Review." *F1000Research* 7 (2020). https:// f1000research.com/articles/7-1925/v2.

Shamir, Lior J., John F. Wallin, Alice Allen, Bruce Berriman, Peter Teuben, Robert Nemiroff, Jessica Mink, et al. "Practices in Source Code Sharing in Astrophysics." *Astronomy and Computing* 1 (2013): 54–58.

Shamoo, Adil E., and David B. Resnik. *Responsible Conduct of Research.* New York: Oxford University Press, 2009.

Shavers, Vickie L., Charles F. Lynch, and Leon F. Burmeister. "Racial Differences in Factors that Influence the Willingness to Participate in Medical Research Studies." *Annals of Epidemiology* 12, no. 4 (2002): 248–256. https://doi.org/10.1016/S1047-2797(01)00265-4.

Shen, Cenyu, and Bo-Christer Björk. "'Predatory' Open Access: A Longitudinal Study of Article Volumes and Market Characteristics." *BMC Medicine* 13, no. 1 (2015): 230. https://doi.org/10.1186/s12916-015-0469-2.

Sherbino, Jonathan, Vineet M. Arora, Elaine Van Melle, Robert Rogers, Jason R. Frank, and Eric S. Holmboe. "Criteria for Social Media-Based Scholarship in Health Professions Education." *Postgraduate Medical Journal* 91, no. 1080 (2015): 551–555. http://dx.doi.org/10.1136/postgradmedj-2015-133300.

Shiva, Vandana. *Biopiracy: The Plunder of Nature and Knowledge.* Berkeley: North Atlantic Books, 2016.

Siemens, George. "Connectivism: Learning as Network-Creation." *ASTD Learning News* 10, no. 1 (2005): 1–28.

Silvertown, Jonathan. 2009. "A New Dawn for Citizen Science." *Trends in Ecology & Evolution* 24, no. 9 (2009): 467–471. https://doi.org/10.1016 /j.tree.2009.03.017.

Simkin, Mikhail V., and Vwani P. Roychowdhury. "Read Before You Cite!" *Complex Systems* 14 (2003): 269–274.

Smith, Linda C. "Citation Analysis." *Library Trends* 30 (1981): 83–106.

Smith, Marshall S., and Catherine M. Casserly. "The Promise of Open Educational Resources." *Change: The Magazine of Higher Learning* 38, no. 5 (2006): 8–17. https://doi.org/10.3200/CHNG.38.5.8-17.

Smith, Richard. "Opening Up BMJ Peer Review: A Beginning that Should Lead to Complete Transparency." *BMJ* 318 (1999): 4. https://doi.org/10.1136/bmj.318.7175.4.

Soderberg, C. K., T. M. Errington, and B. A. Nosek. "Credibility of Preprints: An Interdisciplinary Survey of Researchers." *Royal Society Open Science* 7, no. 10 (2020). https://doi.org/10.1098/rsos.201520.

Soergel, David A. W. "Rampant Software Errors May Undermine Scientific Results [version 2; peer review: 2 approved]." *F1000Research* 3 (2015): 303. https://doi.org/10/gc5sjg.

SPARC. "Open Education." https://sparcopen.org/open-education.

SPARC (@SPARC_NA). https://twitter.com/SPARC_NA.

Spier, Ray. "The History of the Peer Review Process." *Trends in Biotechnology* 20, no. 8 (2002): 357–358. https://doi.org/10.1016/S0167-7799(02)01985-6.

Springer Nature. "Data Availability Statements. Guidance for Authors and Editors." https://www.springernature.com/gp/authors/research-data-policy/data-availability-statements/12330880.

SpringerOpen. "What Is SpringerOpen?" https://www.springeropen.com/about/what-is-springeropen.

Srivastava, Manoj. "Draft Debian Position Statement About the GNU Free Documentation License (GFDL)." 2006. https://people.debian.org/~srivasta/Position_Statement.xhtml.

Stallman, Richard. "Free/Libre Scientific Publishing." 2013. https://stallman.org/articles/free-scientific-publishing.html.

Stallman, Richard. *Free Software, Free Society: Selected Essays of Richard M. Stallman*. Boston: GNU Press, 2006.

Stallman, Richard. "The GNU Manifesto." 1985. https://www.gnu.org/gnu/manifesto.en.html.

Stallman, Richard. "Why 'Free Software' Is Better Than 'Open Source'." In *Free Software, Free Society: Selected Essays of Richard M. Stallman*, 55–60. Edited by Joshua Gay. Boston: Free Software Foundation, 2002.

Stanford University. "Research Policy Handbook." https://doresearch.stanford.edu/policies/research-policy-handbook.

Stevens, Matthias, Michalis Vitos, Julia Altenbuchner, Gillian Conquest, Jerome Lewis, and Muki Haklay. "Taking Participatory Citizen Science to Extremes." *IEEE Pervasive Computing* 13, no. 2 (2014): 20–29. https://doi.org/10.1109/MPRV.2014.37.

Stieglitz, Stefan, Konstantin Wilms, Milad Mirbabaie, Lennart Hofeditz, Bela Brenger, Ania López, and Stephanie Rehwald. "When Are Researchers

Willing to Share Their Data? Impacts of Values and Uncertainty on Open Data in Academia." *PLoS ONE* 15, no. 7 (2020): e0234172. https://doi .org/10.1371/journal.pone.0234172.

Stilgoe, Jack. *Citizen Scientists: Reconnecting Science with Civil Society*. London: Demos, 2009.

Stodden, Victoria. "Beyond Open Data: A Model for Linking Digital Artifacts to Enable Reproducibility of Scientific Claims." In *P-RECS '20: Proceedings of the 3rd International Workshop on Practical Reproducible Evaluation of Computer Systems, June 2020* (2020): 9–14. https://doi.org/10.1145 /3391800.3398172.

Stodden, Victoria. "Intellectual Property and Computational Science." In *Opening Science: The Evolving Guide on How the Internet Is Changing Research, Collaboration and Scholarly Publishing*, 225–235. Edited by Sönke Bartling and Sascha Friesike. Berlin: Springer Open, 2014.

Stodden, Victoria, Peixuan Guo, and Zhaokun Ma. "Toward Reproducible Computational Research: An Empirical Analysis of Data and Code Policy Adoption by Journals." *PLoS ONE* 8, no. 6 (2013): e67111. https://doi .org/10.1371/journal.pone.0067111.

Storksdieck, Martin, Jennifer Lynn Shirk, Jessica L. Cappadonna, Meg Domroese, Claudia Göbel, Muki Haklay, Abraham J. Miller-Rushing, et al. "Associations for Citizen Science: Regional Knowledge, Global Collaboration." *Citizen Science: Theory and Practice* 1, no. 2 (2016). http://doi .org/10.5334/cstp.55.

Strasser, Bruno, Jérôme Baudry, Dana Mahr, Gabriela Sanchez, and Elise Tancoigne. "'Citizen Science'? Rethinking Science and Public Participation." *Science & Technology Studies* 32, no. 2 (2019): 52–76. https://doi .org/10.23987/sts.60425.

Strinzel, Michaela, Anna Severin, Katrin Milzow, and Matthias Egger. "Blacklists and Whitelists to Tackle Predatory Publishing: A Cross-Sectional Comparison and Thematic Analysis." *mBio* 10, no. 3 (2019): e00411–19. https://doi.org/10.1128/mBio.00411-19.

Suber, Peter. "A Field Guide to Misunderstandings about Open Access." *SPARC Open Access Newsletter* 132 (April 2, 2009). http://nrs.harvard.edu/urn -3:HUL.InstRepos:4322571.

Suber, Peter. "Creating an Intellectual Commons through Open Access." In *Understanding Knowledge as a Commons. From Theory to Practice*, 171–208. Edited by Charlotte Hess and Elinor Ostrom. Cambridge: MIT Press, 2011.

Suber, Peter. *Knowledge Unbound: Selected Writings on Open Access, 2002–2011*. Cambridge: MIT Press, 2016.

Suber, Peter. *Open Access*. Cambridge: MIT Press, 2012.

Suber, Peter. Preface. In *Open Access and the Humanities: Contexts, Controversies and the Future* by Martin Paul Eve, ix–xi. Cambridge: Cambridge University Press, 2014. https://doi.org/10.1017/CBO9781316161012.

Suber, Peter. "Removing the Barriers to Research: An Introduction to Open Access for Librarians." *College & Research Libraries News* 64 (2003): 92–94, 113.

Taichman, Darren B., Peush Sahni, Anja Pinborg, Larry Peiperl, Christine Laine, Astrid James, Sung-Tae Hong, et al. "Data Sharing Statements for Clinical Trials: A Requirement of the International Committee of Medical Journal Editors." *Annals of Internal Medicine* 167, no. 1 (2017): 63–65. https://doi .org/10.7326/M17-1028.

Tarantino, Giuseppe Roberto. "If You Love Something, Set It Free? Open Content Copyright Licensing and Creative Cultural Expression." PhD dissertation, York University, 2019.

Tauginienė, Loreta, Eglė Butkevičienė, Katrin Vohland, Barbara Heinisch, Maria Daskolia, Monika Suškevičs, Manuel Portela, et al. "Citizen Science in the Social Sciences and Humanities: The Power of Interdisciplinarity." *Palgrave Communications* 6, no. 1 (2020): 1–11. https://doi.org/10.1057 /s41599-020-0471-y.

Taylor, Mike. "Exploring the Boundaries: How Altmetrics Can Expand Our Vision of Scholarly Communication and Social Impact." *Information Standards Quarterly* 25, no. 2 (2013a): 27–32. https://doi.org/10.3789 /isqv25no2.2013.05.

Taylor, Mike. "Towards a Common Model of Citation: Some Thoughts on Merging Altmetrics and Bibliometrics." *Research Trends* 35 (2013b): 19–22.

Tennant, Jonathan, Ritwik Agarwal, Ksenija Baždarić, David Brassard, Tom Crick, Daniel J. Dunleavy, Thomas R. Evans, et al. "A Tale of Two 'Opens': Intersections Between Free and Open Source Software and Open Scholarship." *SocArXiv Papers*. (2020). https://doi.org/10.31235/osf.io/2kxq8.

Tenopir, Carol, Natalie M. Rice, Suzie Allard, Lynn Baird, Josh Borycz, Lisa Christian, Bruce Grant, et al. "Data Sharing, Management, Use, and Reuse: Practices and Perceptions of Scientists Worldwide." *PLoS ONE* 15, no. 3 (2020): e0229003. https://doi.org/10.1371/journal.pone.0229003.

Thelwall, Mike, and Kayvan Kousha. "Academia.edu: Social Network or Academic Network?" *Journal of the Association for Information Science and Technology* 65, no. 4 (2014): 721–731. https://doi.org/10.1002/asi.23038.

Thelwall, Mike, and Kayvan Kousha. "ResearchGate Articles: Age, Discipline, Audience Size, and Impact." *Journal of the Association for Information Science and Technology* 68, no. 2 (2017): 468–479. https://doi.org/10.1002 /asi.23675.

Thelwall, Mike, Stefanie Haustein, Vincent Larivière, and Cassidy R. Sugimoto. "Do Altmetrics Work? Twitter and Ten Other Social Web Services." *PLoS ONE* 8, no. 5 (2013). https://doi.org/10.1371/journal.pone.0064841.

Tovar, Edmundo, Nelson Piedra, Jorge López, and Janneth Chizaiza. "Open Education Practices as Answer to New Demands of Training in Entrepreneurship Competences: The Role of Recommender Systems." In *Computer Supported Education*, 3–18. Edited by Susan Zvacek, Maria Teresa Restivo,

James Uhomoibhi, and Markus Helfert. Cham: Springer, 2015. https://doi.org/10.1007/978-3-319-29585-5_1.

Tuomi, Ilkka. "Open Educational Resources and the Transformation of Education." *European Journal of Education* 48, no. 1 (2013): 58–78. https://doi.org/10.1111/ejed.12019.

UK Research and Innovation. "Guidance on Best Practice in the Management of Research Data." July 2018. https://www.ukri.org/wp-content/uploads/2020/10/UKRI-020920-GuidanceBestPracticeManagementResearchData.pdf.

Uljens, Michael, and Rose M. Ylimaki. "Non-Affirmative Theory of Education as a Foundation for Curriculum Studies, Didaktik and Educational Leadership." In *Bridging Educational Leadership, Curriculum Theory and Didaktik*, 3–145. Edited by Michael Uljens and Rose M. Ylimaki. Cham: Springer, 2017.

UNESCO. "Ljubljana OER Action Plan." Second World Open Educational Resources (OER) Congress, UNESCO, Ljubljana, Slovenia, September 18–20, 2017. https://en.unesco.org/sites/default/files/ljubljana_oer_action_plan_2017.pdf.

UNESCO. "Recommendation on Open Educational Resources (OER)." November 25, 2019. http://portal.unesco.org/en/ev.php-URL_ID=49556&URL_DO=DO_TOPIC&URL_SECTION=201.html.

UNESCO. "The Paris OER Declaration 2012." World Open Educational Resources (OER) Congress, UNESCO, Paris, June 20–22, 2012. https://en.unesco.org/oer/paris-declaration.

UNESCO. "UNESCO Promotes New Initiative for Free Educational Resources on the Internet." July 10, 2002. http://www.unesco.org/education/news_en/080702_free_edu_ress.shtml.

United Nations General Assembly. "Universal Declaration of Human Rights." Paris: UN General Assembly, 1948. https://www.ohchr.org/EN/UDHR/Documents/UDHR_Translations/eng.pdf.

U.S. Congress. "America COMPETES Reauthorization Act of 2010." 2011. https://www.congress.gov/111/plaws/publ358/PLAW-111publ358.pdf.

U.S. Congress. "Crowdsourcing and Citizen Science Act of 2016." 2017a. https://www.congress.gov/114/bills/hr6414/BILLS-114hr6414ih.pdf.

U.S. Congress. "Grant Reporting Efficiency and Agreements Transparency (GREAT) Act of 2019." 2019. https://www.congress.gov/116/plaws/publ103/PLAW-116publ103.pdf .

U.S. Congress. "Open, Public, Electronic and Necessary (OPEN) Government Data Act." 2017b. https://www.congress.gov/115/bills/hr1770/BILLS-115hr1770ih.pdf.

U.S. Congress. "Public Access to Science Act." 2003. https://www.congress.gov/108/bills/hr2613/BILLS-108hr2613ih.pdf.

U.S. Copyright Office. *Copyright Law of the United States and Related Laws Contained in Title 17 of the United States Code*. Washington, D.C.: Library of Congress, 2020.

Uvalić-Trumbić, Stamenka, and John Daniel (eds.) *A Guide to Quality in Post-Traditional Online Higher Education.* Dallas: Academic Partnerships, 2015. https://idea-phd.net/images/doc-pdf/Guide_to_online_post_traditional_highered.pdf.

Vainio, Niklas, and Tere Vadén. "Free Software Philosophy and Open Source." *International Journal of Open Source Software and Processes (IJOSSP)* 4, no. 4 (2012): 56–66. https://doi.org/10.4018/ijossp.2012100105.

Van Allen, Jennifer, and Stacy Katz. "Developing Open Practices in Teacher Education: An Example of Integrating OER and Developing Renewable Assignments." *Open Praxis* 11, no. 3 (2019): 311–319.

Van Noorden, Richard. "Online Collaboration: Scientists and the Social Network." *Nature News* 512, no. 7513 (2014): 126–129. https://doi.org/10.1038/512126a.

Van Noorden, Richard, and Dalmeet Singh Chawla. "Hundreds of Extreme Self-Citing Scientists Revealed in New Database." *Nature* 572, no. 7771 (2019): 578–580. https://doi.org/10.1038/d41586-019-02479-7.

Van Raan, Anthony F. J. "Measuring Science." In *Handbook of Quantitative Science and Technology Research*, 9–50. Edited by Henk F. Moed, Wolfgang Glänzel, and Ulrich Schmoch. Dordrecht: Kluwer, 2004. https://doi.org/10.1007/1-4020-2755-9_2.

Vasilevsky, Nicole A., Jessica Minnier, Melissa A. Haendel, and Robin E. Champieux. "Reproducible and Reusable Research: Are Journal Data Sharing Policies Meeting the Mark?" *PeerJ* 5 (2017): e3208. https://doi.org/10.7717/peerj.3208.

Vayena, Effy, and John Tasioulas. "Adapting Standards: Ethical Oversight of Participant-Led Health Research." *PLoS Medicine* 10, no. 3 (2013): e1001402. https://doi.org/10.1371/journal.pmed.1001402.

Veletsianos, George, and Royce Kimmons. "Assumptions and Challenges of Open Scholarship." *International Review of Research in Open and Distributed Learning* 13, no. 4 (2012): 166–189, https://doi.org/10.19173/irrodl.v13i4.1313.

Veletsianos, George, and Royce Kimmons. "Scholars and Faculty Members' Lived Experiences in Online Social Networks." *Internet and Higher Education* 16 (2013): 43–50. https://doi.org/10.1016/j.iheduc.2012.01.004.

Vence, Tracy. "Identifying Predatory Publishers: How to Tell Reputable Journals From Shady Ones." *The Scientist.* July 16, 2017. https://www.the-scientist.com/careers/identifying-predatory-publishers-31225.

Vest, Charles. "Why MIT Decided to Give Away All Its Course Materials via the Internet." *The Chronicle of Higher Education* 50, no. 21 (January 30, 2004): B20. http://www.chronicle.com/article/Why-MIT-Decided-to-Give-Away/9043.

Vetter, Jeremy. "Introduction: Lay Participation in the History of Scientific Observation." *Science in Context* 24, no. 2 (2011): 127–141. https://doi.org/10.1017/S0269889711000032.

Vines, Timothy H., Rose L. Andrew, Dan G. Bock, Michelle T. Franklin, Kimberly J. Gilbert, Nolan C. Kane, Jean-Sébastien Moore, et al. 2013. "Mandated Data Archiving Greatly Improves Access to Research Data." *The FASEB Journal* 27, no. 4 (2013): 1304–1308. https://doi.org/10.1096/fj.12-218164.

Waldrop, M. Mitchell. "Science 2.0: Great New Tool, or Great Risk? Wikis, Blogs and Other Collaborative Web Technologies Could Usher in a New Era of Science. Or Not." *Scientific American* 298, no. 5 (2008): 68–73. https://doi.org/10.1038/scientificamerican0508-68.

Watters, Audrey. "From 'Open' to Justice." *Hack Education. The History of the Future of Education Technology.* November 16, 2014. http://hackeducation.com/2014/11/16/from-open-to-justice.

Weingart, Peter. "A Short History of Knowledge Formations." In *The Oxford Handbook of Interdisciplinarity*, 3–14. Edited by Robert Frodeman, Julie Thompson Klein, and Carl Mitcham. Oxford: Oxford University Press, 2010.

Weller, Martin. *The Battle for Open: How Openness Won and Why It Doesn't Feel Like Victory.* London: Ubiquity Press, 2014.

Weller, Martin. *The Digital Scholar: How Technology Is Transforming Scholarly Practice.* London: Bloomsbury Academic, 2011.

Wen-Hao, David Huang, Grace Lin Meng-Fen, and Wendi Shen. "Understanding Chinese-Speaking Open Courseware Users: A Case Study on User Engagement in an Open Courseware Portal in Taiwan." *Open Learning: The Journal of Open, Distance and E-Learning* 27, no. 2 (2012): 169–182. https://doi.org/10.1080/02680513.2012.678614.

White House. "The President's Management Agenda." *Office of Management and Budget.* 2018. https://www.whitehouse.gov/omb/management/pma/.

Wiggins, Andrea, and Kevin Crowston. "From Conservation to Crowdsourcing: A Typology of Citizen Science." In *2011 44th Hawaii International Conference on System Sciences*, 1–10 (2011). https://doi.org/10.1109/HICSS.2011.207.

Wiley, David. "Defining the 'Open' in Open Content and Open Educational Resources." http://opencontent.org/definition.

Wiley, David. "No, Really—Stop Saying 'High Quality.'" *Improving Learning.* April 1, 2015. https://opencontent.org/blog/archives/3830.

Wiley, David. "On the Sustainability of Open Educational Resource Initiatives in Higher Education. Paper Commissioned by the OECD's Centre for Educational Research and Innovation (CERI) For the Project on Open Educational Resources." 2007. https://www.oecd.org/education/ceri/38645447.pdf.

Wiley, David. "OpenContent." Last updated June 30, 2003. http://web.archive.org/web/20030802222546/http://opencontent.org/.

Wiley, David. "Stop Saying 'High Quality.'" *Improving Learning.* March 27, 2015. https://opencontent.org/blog/archives/3821.

Wiley, David. "The Access Compromise and the 5th R." *Improving Learning.* March 5, 2014. https://opencontent.org/blog/archives/3221.

Wiley, David. "What Is Open Pedagogy?" *Improving Learning.* October 21, 2013. https://opencontent.org/blog/archives/2975.

Wiley, David. "Where I've Been; Where I'm Going." *Improving Learning.* March 1, 2013. https://opencontent.org/blog/archives/2723.

Wiley, David, and Seth Gurrell. "A Decade of Development. . . ." *Open Learning: The Journal of Open, Distance and E-Learning* 24, no. 1 (2009): 11–21. https://doi.org/10.1080/02680510802627746.

Wilkinson, Mark D., Michel Dumontier, I. Jan Aalbersberg, Gabrielle Appleton, Myles Axton, Arie Baak, Niklas Blomberg, et al. "The FAIR Guiding Principles for Scientific Data Management and Stewardship." *Scientific Data* 3 (2016):160018. https://doi.org/10.1038/sdata.2016.18.

Willems, Julie, and Carina Bossu. "Equity Considerations for Open Educational Resources in the Glocalization of Education." *Distance Education* 33, no. 2 (2012): 185–199. https://doi.org/10.1080/01587919.2012.692051.

Williams, Sam. *Free as in Freedom: Richard Stallman's Crusade for Free Software.* Sebastopol: O'Reilly Media, 2011.

Willinsky, John. *The Access Principle: The Case for Open Access to Research and Scholarship.* Cambridge: MIT Press, 2006.

Wing, Steve, Rachel Avery Horton, Naeema Muhammad, Gary R. Grant, Mansoureh Tajik, and Kendall Thu. "Integrating Epidemiology, Education, and Organizing for Environmental Justice: Community Health Effects of Industrial Hog Operations." *American Journal of Public Health* 98, no. 8 (2008): 1390–1397. https://doi.org/10.2105/AJPH.2007.110486.

Wolfram, Dietmar, Peiling Wang, Adam Hembree, and Hyoungjoo Park. "Open Peer Review: Promoting Transparency in Open Science." *Scientometrics* 125 (2020): 1033–1051. https://doi.org/10.1007/s11192-020-03488-4.

Woolley, J. Patrick, Michelle L. McGowan, Harriet J.A. Teare, Victoria Coathup, Jennifer R. Fishman, Richard A. Settersten, Sigrid Sterckx, et al. "Citizen Science or Scientific Citizenship? Disentangling the Uses of Public Engagement Rhetoric in National Research Initiatives." *BMC Medical Ethics* 17, no. 33 (2016). https://doi.org/10.1186/s12910-016-0117-1.

Wynne, Brian. "May the Sheep Safely Graze? A Reflexive View of the Expert-Lay Knowledge Divide." In *Risk, Environment and Modernity: Towards a New Ecology,* 44–83. Edited by Scott Lash, Bronislaw Szerszynski, and Brian Wynne. London: Sage Publications, 1996.

Xia, Jingfeng, Jennifer L. Harmon, Kevin G. Connolly, Ryan M. Donnelly, Mary R. Anderson, and Heather A. Howard. "Who Publishes in 'Predatory' Journals?" *Journal of the Association for Information Science and Technology* 66, no. 7 (2015): 1406–1417. https://doi.org/10.1002/asi.23265.

Yu, Harlan, and David G. Robinson. "The New Ambiguity of Open Government." *UCLA Law Review Discourse* 59 (2011): 178–208.

Index